INTERNATIONAL POLITICAL ECONOMY

International Political Economy: Contrasting world views is a major new introductory textbook for students of International Political Economy that combines theoretical perspectives, real-world examples, and comparative policy analysis. Written by an experienced teacher and scholar, the text is intended to give students an in-depth understanding of the core perspectives in International Political Economy, which will allow them to critically evaluate and independently analyze major political and economic events.

Features and benefits of the text:

- It is organized around the three major perspectives in the field: free market, institutionalist, and historical materialist.
- Each perspective is developed thoroughly via the presentation of its unique thought model, its world view, and its application to real-world problems.
- It compares and contrasts different analytical and policy approaches to a wide range of core issues such as trade, finance, transnational corporations, development, and environmental sustainability.
- It explains the role of key thinkers in the field, from Adam Smith, Karl Marx, David Ricardo, and Thorstein Veblen to John Kenneth Galbraith, John Maynard Keynes, Milton Friedman, and Susan Strange.
- It contains boxed biographies, graphics, review questions, suggestions for further reading, and a detailed glossary to enhance student learning.

Raymond C. Miller has been national president of two professional associations: the Association for Integrative Studies and the Society for International Development. He was founding editor of *Issues in Integrative Studies.* Professor Miller served as a member of the faculty at San Francisco State University for 43 years, where he is now Professor Emeritus of International Relations and Social Science.

INTERNATIONAL POLITICAL ECONOMY

Contrasting world views

Raymond C. Miller

Routledge
Taylor & Francis Group

LONDON AND NEW YORK

First published 2008
by Routledge
2 Park Square, Milton Park, Abingdon, Oxon OX14 4RN

Simultaneously published in the USA and Canada
by Routledge
270 Madison Avenue, New York, NY 10016

Routledge is an imprint of the Taylor & Francis Group, an informa business
© 2008 Raymond C. Miller

Typeset in Garamond by Prepress Projects Ltd, Perth, UK
Printed and bound in Great Britain by TJ International Ltd,
Padstow, Cornwall

British Library Cataloguing in Publication Data
A catalogue record for this book is available from the British Library

Library of Congress Cataloging in Publication Data
Miller, Raymond C.
International political economy: contrasting world views/Raymond C.
Miller.
p. cm.
Includes bibliographical references and index.
[etc.]
1. International economic relations. I. Title.
HF1359.M557 2008
337—dc22
2007050656

ISBN 10: 0-415-38408-7 (hbk)
ISBN 10: 0-415-38409-5 (pbk)
ISBN 10: 0-203-92723-0 (ebk)

ISBN 13: 978-0-415-38408-7 (hbk)
ISBN 13: 978-0-415-38409-4 (pbk)
ISBN 13: 978-0-203-92723-6 (ebk)

CONTENTS

ILLUSTRATIONS

FIGURES

TABLES

PREFACE FOR STUDENTS

For 43 years I have been teaching political economy, first American and then international. I chose political economy as my field of study and teaching because I wanted to make a contribution to the improvement of the human condition. I came to the realization that without a solid foundation in political economy, improvement programs are not likely to succeed. Not only do I still believe that is true, but I also believe that persons cannot consider themselves truly educated unless they understand the basics of political economy. After all, we are really talking about how the human world works.

Based on feedback from students during my teaching career, I have tried to continuously improve the effectiveness of my presentation. My goal has always been to give students usable knowledge: after completing my classes, students should be able to read or listen to statements made about political-economic issues with a deeper level of understanding that enables them to make independent and critical judgments. In other words, educated people need more than a "gut feeling" about whether or not they agree with statements being made or an argument being put forth.

The development of your critical faculties in the realm of political economy requires deepening your skills in several areas. First, you need an understanding of how important institutions work. For instance, understanding how money works requires an understanding of how monetary policy is supposed to work. Monetary policy is closely related to movements in price levels, which in turn affect ratios of exchange between currencies. These relationships are complicated, but without an understanding of them you could not make an independent judgment on questions such as: "What is the correct value of the Chinese currency in relationship to the U.S. dollar?" Or for that matter: "Why is such a question important in the first place?" In 2007 many American officials and politicians were contending that the Chinese currency was "undervalued." What does that mean? Why do the Chinese disagree? Understanding this type of issue requires both political and economic information. Information of this sort should definitely be covered in a political economy course, but it should be explained in a way that does not require the use of the language of mathematics. In my experience some students are comfortable with the language of mathematics, but others are very uncomfortable. Therefore, my classes and this text take a rigorous but non-mathematical approach.

Second, you need to develop a whole new vocabulary. Words do count. Careful analysis requires careful definition of terms. A great deal of misunderstanding can come unnecessarily from the sloppy use of terms. I have identified, defined, and consistently used key terms, and a glossary is provided near the end of this book for quick reference. The semantics of political economy can be tricky, because different people may be using the same terms but with quite different meanings in mind. For instance, a term such as "capital" has multiple meanings, dependent on the context. Unfortunately, the language used in financial discourse (such as stock market reports) is often different than the language and the explanations used by economists. Until the differences are cleared up, confusion can occur. A related concern is the plethora of acronyms. Remembering what they all stand for can be a challenge. Yet it is necessary to use them because there are many instances when only the acronym is used in the literature. Who, for instance, uses the full name of UNESCO when discussing that organization? Not many people know the exact terms for which the initials stand. Actually, the correct identification may not be all that important. It is what the organization does that is important. But it can be frustrating when a reader comes across an acronym that "doesn't ring a bell." I have tried to avoid that problem, either by spelling out the name or by using it frequently. A list of acronyms is provided near the front of this book.

Third, it is important to understand "where people are coming from." When people comment on political-economic issues, they are understanding those issues from some perspective. Undoubtedly that perspective is embedded in a comprehensive **world view**, whether they know it or not. My strategy in organizing the material for this text is to organize everything explicitly around three dominant world views. In my opinion, once a person has a good grasp of these different world views, it is possible not only to know where a speaker is coming from, but also to know what he or she is likely to think about any political-economic issue. For example, at the global level the dominant political-economic world view for the last several decades has been the "free market." Following logically from the free market approach are policies promoting "free trade" and the "free transfer" of funds between countries. Supporting and embedded within the free market world view is an intellectual model of how a free market works. That market model is the centerpiece of the academic discipline of Economics. Therefore, in order to understand the rationale for the market world view, one needs to understand the underlying conceptual model of Economics. World view, however, goes beyond what one is likely to encounter in an Economics class. Articulating an underlying world view brings out the assumptions that view comprises about human nature, the nature of society, the morally most desirable behavior, preferred future outcomes, and so on. For instance, advocates of the free market approach, such as the late Nobel laureate in Economics, Milton Friedman, believe strongly that not only is the market the best analytical device, but it is also the morally preferred decision-making system.

This text presents three major and rather different political-economic world views. Initially they can be identified as free market, institutional, and Marxist views on capitalism. This threefold division is not new in the field, but the way in which the world views are presented is my own construction. The pedagogical principles that I have tried to follow are clarity, sufficient depth, and logical consistency. Each world view has its own simple **model** of how things work, which are presented in the text. The world out there is much too complex—"messy" if you will—to be accurately and completely described by any model. Models, therefore, are necessarily simplified "idealizations." The intent of models is to provide insight into how things work, not to capture every aspect of reality. For instance, the market model assumes that the decisions of all actors are determined by maximizing material interests. This assumption gives the model logical consistency, but not descriptive reality.

For models to be helpful to your understanding, you need to put them on a level of abstraction above everyday experience. On occasion that elevation might prove difficult to achieve, but, based on my experience, once you get there you will have a much clearer conception of how different world views perceive the political-economic landscape. To assist you in obtaining that clearer conception, I have included visual depictions of the internal relationships of each of the three major models.

Good luck! I hope that my efforts reap intellectual benefits for you, and that you will feel more confident making critical and independent judgments about a variety of crucial political-economic issues.

Raymond C. Miller
Professor Emeritus of International Relations and Social Science
San Francisco State University

PREFACE FOR INSTRUCTORS

I thought that it might be helpful to lay out for instructors as well as for students the pedagogical strategy that informs the preparation of this text. While doing that I will take the opportunity to identify the known intellectual ancestors of my approach as well as to explicate some of my pedagogical devices that might not be immediately evident.

As a graduate student at the University of Chicago, I learned that all academic disciplines are creations of communities of scholars. Each develops a theoretical consensus that changes over time, sometimes quite dramatically. In my teaching, therefore, I wanted to make sure that my students understood that what one thinks about anything depends upon the perspective from which one approaches it. To me, the only way to teach that insight was to show how every discipline has a perspective embedded within it. But to effectively show how a perspective influences the way a person sees the world, it's necessary to show how contrasting perspectives interpret the same events. That means teaching comparative perspectives. That endeavor cannot be effectively accomplished without a schema of common categories within which the perspectives are compared.

World view is the organizing concept that provides for me the schema of common categories, the common questions to ask. My presumption is that everybody perceives and acts under the influence of some world view. It's a very anthropological concept, in which my first mentor was Robert Redfield. In the 1950s he argued that world view is the shared philosophy of life of a people that includes assumptions about the nature of life and moral norms. He contended that all cultures construct their own world views. In the 1960s Thomas Kuhn applied the world view idea to scientific communities, though he initially called disciplinary world views "paradigms." Kuhn did not think that the social science disciplines were sufficiently coalesced around agreed-upon research strategies for them to be studied in the same way as disciplines like Physics. But despite Kuhn's

Table 0.1 Political Science and Economics compared

Dimensions	Political Science	Economics
Core subject matter	Forms, qualities, and processes of governments	Production and distribution
Central concepts	Power, governance, and policy	Supply and demand, exchange, and choice
Explanatory strategies	Organization and systems theories and ideologies	Market model and rational choice
Normative orientation	Superiority of democratic pluralism	Superiority of competitive market
Data collection	Voting surveys, case studies, and "great texts"	Quantitative indices
Data analysis	Statistics, comparative analysis, and interpretation	Statistics and mathematical modeling

advice, other scholars went ahead anyway and applied his ideas to the social sciences. I did that myself in the early 1980s, creating a world view schema for comparing disciplinary modalities of the seven conventional social science disciplines. I filled in the boxes with my impressions of the dominant themes in American social science practice. My comparison of Political Science and Economics is relevant background here, as they are the constituent disciplines of Political Economy.

These impressionistic contrasts helped my students understand how disciplines differed on many dimensions and even where their disciplinary instructors were coming from. Kuhn and some disciplinarians would probably have been skeptical about the exercise, but my purpose was a pedagogical one, not the rigorous stipulation of research strategies. After all, academic disciplines are specialized communities with their own subcultures. Some observers have even compared them to tribes. Therefore, I have found that the anthropological concept of world view is a useful device for understanding each discipline's "outlook on life."

When I was first asked to teach International Political Economy, I was delighted to discover that IPE had a multiple-perspective approach built in to the field. Three major and presumably incommensurate schools of thought provided competing perspectives on how the global political economy does and should function. From the beginning I organized my class around comparing the three approaches. However, the major textbooks were not primarily organized that way. They were more likely to organize their presentations around history and/or themes, such as trade and development, and to discuss the three perspectives within the context of a particular theme. I felt that students would get a more coherent sense of the differing perspectives if each one was presented as a complete package.

Furthermore, I was not comfortable with the way that the schools of thought were sometimes labeled. One popular text identified them as "liberalism, mercantilism and radicalism" (Lairson and Skidmore, *International Political Economy*), but all of these three labels have misleading qualities. In the current American political discourse, liberalism has almost the opposite meaning of its classic, nineteenth-century free market meaning. I agree with Susan Strange that mercantilism privileges the nation-state and gives insufficient attention to the role that transnational corporations play in the global political economy. Radicalism seems more of a Cold War political label than an accurate designation. After all, in many respects the tenets of the market society are actually more radical than Marx's critique of capitalism, presuming that radical means a sharp break with the past.

Additionally, I felt that the presentations of the three schools should have a solid foundation in their economic content. My guidance in that respect comes from Ken Cole, John Cameron, and Chris Edwards. Their book, *Why Economists Disagree*, lays out three schools of thought, significantly differentiated by their contrasting theories of value. Chris Edwards then carried this framework into the international arena with his book *The Fragmented World*. Their approach is signaled by the subtitle of the first book, *The Political Economy of Economics*. They provide sophisticated presentations of each intellectual framework, note which political interest group is likely to prefer which school of thought, and illustrate the policy consequences of adopting one theoretical approach over another.

These works have provided the rationale for the approach taken in this text. My approach to explicating world views leans heavily on the economic component. Each of the three world views covered is presented as a model, using an overall framework that sets up specific aspects of each world view for comparison: assumptions or premises, internal interactions, and outcomes. Two of the three models, the market model and Marx's model of the capitalist mode of production, are my versions of relatively well-known mental constructs. The third model, to which I've given the name *multi-centric organizational*, or MCO, is my composite of several intellectual strands, in particular the institutionalists and the neo-Ricardians. The major institutionalist upon whom I rely is John Kenneth Galbraith, and the work of Piero Sraffa is the foundation for the neo-Ricardian contribution. Cole, Cameron, and Edwards call this school of thought the "cost of production" approach. In my classes for many years I presented the ideas of institutionalists such as Veblen, Galbraith, Polanyi, Strange, Korten, and others, but not as a coherent model-like package, till one day a very bright student said, "How come you don't present these views in the same kind of logical structure as you do the other two major points of view?" She was right; the presentations were not comparable. In my subsequent classes and in this text I've tried to remedy that imbalance. I hope you find my construct helpful in presenting this perspective.

In the process of discussing the three models/world views, I tend to use some of the terms associated with the originating scholars so that students will recognize them when they see them in other literature. However, there are a few important exceptions. In order to keep key term usage fairly consistent over all three models and reduce confusion for students, I made some modifications in the usage of terminology. The two terms for which this is especially true are *capital* and *surplus*. As you know, *capital* is a term used in many different ways. I use it throughout as it is defined by neoclassical economists, making the distinction between the actual production-enhancing goods and services investment on the one hand and the financial facilitation of the saving process on the other hand (simplistically characterized as physical vs. financial capital). This usage has the most problematic implications for Marxism, but I think it works. For Marx, the use of the term *surplus* is privileged, as in *surplus value*. Consequently, I have to find other words for what Sraffa called surplus, as his meaning is different than Marx's. This semantic consistency approach is a pedagogical strategy that I have found helpful for students. I hope it works for you.

I have tried to give all three points of view a fair presentation. In my classes I know that I have succeeded in that effort when students ask me at the end of the semester, "So what world view do you prefer?" I can give enthusiastic lectures on all three models. After all, each has an important contribution to make. Each perspective illuminates the others. That's why I disagree with those authors who try to conflate the three perspectives into one. I believe that students need to understand that it does make an important difference for policy, and even for scholarship, which world view decision-makers or scientists hold, especially if they are committed to one point of view.

Because of the world view emphasis of this text, I have not given complete historical accounts of the major conventional topics in the field such as, for example, trade policy. There are many books that already accomplish that task quite well. This text does give historical, institutional, and policy examples in order to help students make sense of abstract ideas; but if you want to include in your course comprehensive historical coverage of all the major topics in IPE, in addition to presenting contrasting world view perspectives, then this text is probably best used as a complement to history-oriented materials.

Finally, my use of *international* rather than *global* as the primary modifier of political economy does not imply a strong intellectual preference. It actually arises from my sense that the designating phrase *International Political Economy* has a more natural, historical fit with the field. Besides, the acronym "IPE" just sounds right.

Raymond C. Miller
Professor Emeritus of International Relations and Social Science
San Francisco State University

ACKNOWLEDGMENTS

The process of preparing for and writing this book has covered many decades. Consequently, there are many people to whom I owe my gratitude. My professorial mentors at the universities of Denver, Chicago, and Syracuse started me on the path of political economy. Since I taught Political Economy for 43 years, I am thankful to many generations of students for their patient attention and reaffirmation of our mutual learning process.

The culmination of this long gestation process started several years ago with a contract with Routledge. Craig Fowlie, Publisher and Editor, has been supportive and flexible throughout. We agreed on four professional reviewers who have read, commented, and made suggestions on the entire manuscript. They are Professors Eric Helleiner of Waterloo University, Joanna Moss of San Francisco State University, William Newell of Miami University (Ohio), and Rick Szostak of Alberta University. Another one of my colleagues at San Francisco State, Dr. Glenn Fieldman, has provided me with extensive recommendations for textual improvement. I have had the additional good fortune of recent teaching assistants (Beate Antonich, Robin Chang, and Justine Miley) giving me the benefit of their feedback. All three of the world views covered in the text are represented among the reviewers. Asking for critical reviews from such a talented group is indeed humbling. Thanks to their insightful suggestions, the text has been through many revisions. Whatever I still have not managed to get right certainly can not be laid at their feet. They did their best to straighten me out. The same can be said of the excellent copy editor assigned to me, Suzanne Peake.

My deepest and special thanks go to my "production team." That would be my wife Anja and daughter Elna. Not only have they been personally supportive throughout the entire process, but they have also been intimately involved in the production process itself. They both have read and commented on the entire manuscript. In addition, my wife has helped with the logistics, and my daughter has done the graphics. No one could have a better team.

Raymond C. Miller

Bibliography

Cole, Ken, John Cameron, and Chris Edwards, *Why Economists Disagree: The Political Economy of Economics* (Longman: London) 1983.

Edwards, Chris, *The Fragmented World: Competing Perspectives on Trade, Money and Crisis* (Methuen: London) 1985.

Kuhn, Thomas S. *The Structure of Scientific Revolutions* (University of Chicago Press: Chicago) 1962.

Lairson, Thomas and David Skidmore, *International Political Economy: The Struggle for Power and Wealth* (Harcourt Brace: Fort Worth, Texas) 1993.

Redfield, Robert *The Little Community* (University of Chicago Press: Chicago) 1956.

Strange, Susan, *States and Markets* (Pinter: London) 1988; 2nd edition, 1994.

ABBREVIATIONS AND ACRONYMS

BRIC	Brazil, Russia, India, and China
CEO	chief executive officer
ECB	European Central Bank
ECOSOC	United Nations Economic and Social Council
EU	European Union
FDI	foreign direct investment
Fed	Federal Reserve System (U.S. central bank)
FOMC	Federal Open Market Committee
GATS	General Agreement on Trade in Services
GATT	General Agreement on Tariffs and Trade
GDP	Gross Domestic Product
GEF	Global Environmental Facility
GM	genetically modified (e.g., crops)
GNP	Gross National Product
IBRD	International Bank for Reconstruction and Development
ICONE	Institute for the Study of Trade and International Negotiations
IMF	International Monetary Fund
IPE	International Political Economy
ISEW	Index of Sustainable Economic Welfare
LIBOR	London Inter-Bank Offer Rate
MCO	multi-centric organizational (model)
MEA	multilateral environmental agreement

MFN	most favored nation
MTBE	methyl tertiary butyl ether (gasoline additive)
NAFTA	North American Free Trade Agreement
NGO	non-governmental organization
NIEO	New International Economic Order
OECD	Organisation for Economic Co-operation and Development
OPEC	Organization of the Petrolem Exporting Countries
PPP	purchasing power parity
SAPs	structural adjustment programs
SDRs	Special Drawing Rights
TNC	transnational corporation
TNI	Trans-National Index
TRIMs	Trade Related Investment Measures
TRIP	Trade Related Intellectual Property
U.K./UK	United Kingdom
UNCTAD	United Nations Conference on Trade and Development
UNEP	United Nations Environmental Programme
UNESCO	United Nations Educational, Scientific and Cultural Organization
WIPO	World Intellectual Property Organization
WTO	World Trade Organization

CHAPTER 1

The Field of Study Known as "IPE"

International Political Economy (IPE) is a central component of the interdisciplinary field of International Studies. Its current version is only about three decades old. IPE combines primarily the relevant parts of the disciplines of Political Science and Economics. It also draws on relevant facets of other disciplines such as Sociology, Geography, and Women's Studies to deepen and broaden the analysis. Contemporary IPE is a reconstitution of a field of study that existed throughout the nineteenth century. The generally recognized founder of the older and classical version of IPE is Adam Smith, a Scottish moral philosopher, whose 1776 book *The Wealth of Nations* is considered the originating treatise.

During the nineteenth century the European scholars who followed in Adam Smith's footsteps created the field of study that is now known as classical political economy. Together they created a field that provided comprehensive social analysis. However, near the end of the nineteenth century, as an integral part of the evolution of the Industrial Revolution, greater and greater specialization permeated all aspects of life. The university was no exception. Consequently, classical political economy was divided into the modern academic disciplines of Economics, Political Science, and Sociology. Thus for most of the twentieth century these subject matters were studied separately. However, by the 1980s the increasing evidence of comprehensive global interdependences could no longer be ignored. The issues that were being studied in disciplinary isolation required a more integrative analysis. Therefore, the field of International Political Economy was recreated (Wolf, *Europe and the People without History*).

In the late twentieth century technological developments in transportation and communications brought the world together in ways that had never before been possible. Thanks to the Internet, international financial transactions could now be carried on instantaneously 24 hours a day, seven days a week. Manufacturing processes could now be located in multiple countries, with the result that it has become almost impossible to tell what the home-production country of any complex product such as an automobile actually is. Transnational corporations operate globally with decreasing loyalty to any particular nation-state. Nation-states, through international organizations such as the World Trade Organization, try to retain some kind of control. Countries such as China and India, which hardly counted just 20 to 30 years ago in the post–World War II world economy, are now major players. Studying a world of such complexity required a new field that could effectively encompass all of these rapidly changing circumstances (Amin et al., "Forum for heterodox international political economy").

Formally, therefore, **International Political Economy** is an interdisciplinary social science field of study that investigates, analyzes, and proposes changes in the processes of economic flows and political governance that cross over and/or transcend national boundaries. These flows include the exchange of goods and services (trade), funds (capital), technology, labor, natural resources, environmental pollution, and so on. The field attempts to provide explanations, to evaluate consequences, and to propose possible policy initiatives. Within the field there are competing perspectives that offer different analyses of the same phenomena.

To better understand the origin and development of the field, it should be helpful to briefly recount the historical evolution of the political-economic practices that it studies and the modern intellectual effort to make sense of them.

HISTORICAL BACKGROUND

The subject matter of International Political Economy has a long history. In fact, one of the main subjects, long-distance trade, goes back thousands of years. During this long period trade has served as a major means of exchanging commodities, accumulating wealth, diffusing ideas, imposing control, and spreading religion. Organized long-distance trade was engaged in by many civilizations, starting 6,000 years ago with the Assyrians, who established regular trade between Mesopotamia (Iraq) and Anatolia (Turkey) to the west and India to the east. One thousand years later the Phoenicians (in what is now Lebanon) established the first civilization based predominantly on trade. Within another thousand years the first known laws regulating trade and commerce were promulgated in Babylon, as part of the Hammurabi Code. Long-distance trade was a very lucrative but dangerous activity, and both the merchants and states who gained from the trade had a strong interest in protecting it. One of the most interesting examples of this connection was the overland trading route from China to the eastern Mediterranean that has come to be called the Silk Road. It was at its safest and most dependable when the Mongol Empire controlled its entire length. For more than a thousand years the camel caravans on the Silk Road provided the most cost-efficient method available of transporting high-value goods. Ocean-going ships did not become competitive until the thirteenth century, when significant technological developments in ship design, construction, and navigation took place in both China and the Italian city-states (Chanda, *Bound Together*).

However, largely due to the state of transportation technology, the long-distance trade carried on for several thousands of years by these pre-modern civilizations was mostly limited to high-value goods for the benefit of the elite, such as silk, spices, ivory, and precious metals. Furthermore, most people would not have had any direct contact with the traders or the commodities traded, as around 90 percent of the population lived in small villages and gained their livelihood from agriculture. However, influences from trade did diffuse out to the countryside, religion being one example. Chanda argues that traders are especially comfortable spreading religions that claim universal applicability, since they have to deal with people of many different cultures, countries, and languages. The first religion to follow this path was Buddhism, the second was Christianity, and the third was Islam. In fact, Mohammed himself was a merchant and trader (Chanda, *Bound Together*).

Besides long-distance trade, markets are another example of institutions that have been around a long time. However, when people in pre-modern, rural-based societies spoke about markets, they were not referring to the larger realm of economic activity, as would be the case today. Instead markets were once-a-week gatherings in the region's biggest village or town where people brought their chickens or turnips or wooden benches to exchange, often through bartering, for something they needed.

The pre-modern **market** was a place, and its only purpose was the trading of commodities. Sometimes, in pre-modern times, especially in the larger markets such as those in Baghdad and Rome, slaves were among the "commodities" traded, but the numbers were small. In medieval Europe trading in the marketplace was supposed to be conducted at the "just price," that is, the seller was supposed to only recover costs, nothing more. Official Church morality frowned upon merchants who made their living from trade. Morally speaking, money-lending was even worse. At that time Christianity shared with Islam the condemnation of usury, the extraction of presumably undeserved interest payments from borrowers (Heilbroner, *The Making of Economic Society*).

The extent and intensity of long-distance trade varied over time, reflecting the relative strength and objectives of the involved governments and peoples. Trading centers and routes had to be protected from bandits and arbitrary confiscation. With the collapse of the Roman Empire in the fifth century, European-wide trade contracted significantly. But by the eighth century the Vikings had established a trading network stretching from Scandinavia to Constantinople. Arab trading, centered in the Middle East, was most active in the tenth to thirteenth centuries, encompassing most of the known world including southern Europe, northern and eastern Africa, and central, southern, and southeastern Asia. The spread of Islam follows quite closely the geographic spread of this extensive trading network. In the Baltic and North Sea area the Hanseatic League of northern European cities dominated trading from the thirteenth to the sixteenth centuries. In the 1400s the Chinese had the biggest ships and the largest merchant fleets in the world, but they allowed their control of the ocean-going trade in Asia to slip away when the Emperor decided to focus the regime's economic energies inward. The trading prowess of the Italian city-states in the Mediterranean area reached its peak in the fifteenth century (Landes, *The Wealth and Poverty of Nations*).

Not until the fifteenth and sixteenth centuries did Western Europeans begin to embark on expeditions and conquests that would result in a truly global trading network. Thanks to developments in navigation, ship-building, and military technology (especially cannons), the Portuguese began exploring the world and establishing trading enclaves in Africa, Asia, and South America. Their basic technology was borrowed from the Arabs, who had occupied southern Spain and Portugal for 500 years. The Arabs in turn had acquired some of their knowledge from the ancient Greeks and Chinese. For instance, the invention of the compass, an important navigation instrument, has been attributed to the Chinese. These pre-modern connections demonstrate that there was a diffusion of information and commodities over long distances, but there was not yet an integrated global political-economic system.

The symbolic date of the beginning of the establishment of the *first global economy* is 1492, when Columbus arrived in the Caribbean. Columbus was financed by Spanish royalty, who were actually more interested in finding (and stealing) gold and silver than in finding a direct trading route to the spices, tea, porcelain, and silk in Asia. In an act of royal arrogance, the Spanish and Portuguese kings divided up the world between them. Columbus headed west across the Atlantic for Spain while the Portuguese ships sailed around Africa. The ostensible objective of these expeditions was a trading route to the luxurious commodities of the East that avoided the merchants of the Middle East and the Mediterranean, who always took a substantial cut of the trading profits. The Spanish had a special interest in gold and silver because these precious metals were the basis of wealth, the means with which to buy the consumption goods necessary for better living and war-making. Both kings experienced successful results. Portuguese ships made it to the Indian Ocean and beyond. Meanwhile the Spanish were so successful in their acquisition of gold and silver from the Americas, especially from Mexico and Peru, that by the seventeenth century the European money supply, which was based on gold and silver, had doubled. Many observers believe that this massive transfer of wealth was crucial in the ultimate rise of the European economies to global pre-eminence. An indigenous Latin American leader recently made the claim that if the Europeans were to return these precious metals in bullion form to their original home with 500 years of compound interest, the weight would be greater than that of the planet earth (Guaicaipuro Cuautemoc, in Simms, *Ecological Debt*).

Whereas the Portuguese initiated global trading in the 1500s, it was the Dutch and then the English who really developed the global trading system in the 1600s. They initiated a system of credit, built large fleets of ships, greatly expanded the colonial production of **cash crops** such as cotton, tobacco, and sugar, gave monopoly franchises to trading companies, and militarily defended their global reach. Even though private firms were involved, the key instigator of the system was the state. This state-run commercial expansion was known as **mercantilism.** State-sanctioned monopolies, or exclusive franchises, gave the trading companies the "right" to establish colonies, which at first were small port enclaves and later encompassed whole countries. The most famous of the trading companies were the English East India Trading Company, which colonized India, and the Dutch East India Trading Company, which colonized the group of islands in Southeast Asia that is known today as Indonesia. Located within the Indonesian archipelago was one of the biggest prizes of that time, the Spice Islands, which were the world's only source of nutmeg, cloves, and mace (Landes, *The Wealth and Poverty of Nations*).

Even though the initial impetus for the colonial trade system was access to the highly desired commodities of Asia—spices, tea, silk, porcelain, and so forth—the most profitable endeavor turned out to be the so-called **triangular trade** between Europe, Africa, and the Americas. Sailing south, the Europeans traded guns and other small manufactured goods for African slaves. From there, going west, slaves were brought to South America (especially Brazil), the Caribbean, and North America, where they provided labor for the cash-crop plantations of sugar, tobacco, and cotton. The cash crops were then shipped back east to Europe in exchange for small manufactured goods and food. This cash-crop juggernaut lasted for several hundred years, devastated the lives of millions of people, and destroyed the environments of many areas. For example, the land in many Caribbean islands was totally dedicated to sugar cane cultivation, which required the destruction of all forest cover and other agricultural crops. Some places, such as Haiti, have never recovered. However, the triangular trade made the successful merchants and the states that sponsored them very wealthy. In the early mercantile period annual returns of 50 percent, especially on sugar, were possible. The ultimate winners were the commercial and government elites in Western Europe, especially the English, the Dutch, and the French (Blaut, *The Colonizer's Model of the World*).

Despite their early leadership role in trade and technology, the Spanish and Portuguese lost their dominant position by the seventeenth century. Their economies and their trading practices did not keep up with those of their rivals, partly due to the intolerance of the Inquisition. Starting in the sixteenth century the Spanish king and the Catholic Church imposed a regime of strict religious requirements. All those who were deemed non-Christian or insufficiently orthodox were either deported or tried in the Inquisition courts. Merchants, money-lenders, and scholars were targeted, especially since many of them were Jews. As the business and intellectual elites fled, were jailed, or were executed, the Spanish and Portuguese economies went into a slump that was to last for several hundred years (Landes, *The Wealth and Poverty of Nations*).

Mercantilism paved the way for the really profound economic transformation that began in the eighteenth century, initially in the United Kingdom. That massive change, which was destined to sweep over the whole earth, affected all of society, not just a small elite. It was called the **Industrial Revolution**. Thanks to the adoption of new energy sources, new production methods, and many inventions, especially the steam engine, production efficiency increased enormously. In some areas, such as steel production, this increase was two-hundred-fold. It was the defining transformation that created the modern world.

Since the Industrial Revolution is still under way as part of the globalization process, it is instructive to inquire what were the circumstances that came together in eighteenth-century England to generate the world's first experience of industrialization. It's an interesting inquiry because although many of the same circumstances had been in place in China many hundreds of years earlier, the Industrial Revolution did not happen there. Scholars have therefore sought to identify the historical conditions that facilitated the emergence of the unique set of technological and societal breakthroughs known as industrialization. It might have been necessary for all of the conditions to be present simultaneously. We do not really know. Listed below are the historical circumstances that have been identified as playing a contributory role in the creation of the first Industrial Revolution in England (Bernstein, *The Birth of Plenty*; Heilbroner, *The Making of Economic Society*; Landes, *The Wealth and Poverty of Nations*):

1 *Increases in agricultural efficiency.* Because of the adoption of new technologies and new crops, and the commercial consolidation of

farming land via the enclosure process, higher yields were achieved with fewer farmers. More efficient agriculture freed up labor and capital resources for use in the building of the industrial economy. The enclosure process of the seventeenth and eighteenth centuries was a victory of private property law over customary rights to hold land in common. Lands that peasants had previously used in common for grazing and other agricultural purposes were fenced off, that is, "enclosed," as they were designated the private property of landowners.

2   *Middle-class revolution.* In 1688 England experienced the first European middle-class revolution, which gave more political power to merchants and the guarantee of the protection of private property from arbitrary government seizure. Because of this greater property security, merchants were more inclined to invest in industrial ventures. Some observers believe that the establishment of an effective legal system that protected both property and liberty was the key foundation. The more famous and comparable French Revolution did not occur until 1789, more than 100 years later.

3   *Openness to technology and science.* Already in the 1600s the English were welcoming science and honoring inventors. This trend was formalized in 1662 with the establishment of the Royal Society of London for the Promotion of Natural Knowledge. In most other countries at the time, the religious and political establishments considered scientific innovations as threats to their authority. In England, however, scientific and technical discoveries were put into print and widely distributed.

4   *Financial system.* At the initiative of a Scottish businessman, the English established the first national central bank (1694) and a relatively stable system of credit and money. The existence of flourishing capital markets in which those wishing to build manufacturing plants could borrow at reasonable rates encouraged economic development. Though the financial innovations came first from the Italians and then the Dutch, it was the English who first developed a truly national financial system. One of the innovations the English copied from the Dutch was the regular provision of financial information. Starting in 1697 traders had access to publications that followed the prices of stocks, government bills, and foreign exchange.

5   *Natural resources.* Besides being an island with plentiful rainfall and navigable rivers, Great Britain possessed the key raw materials for the beginning of the industrial system of production: coal and iron ore.

6   *Wealth transfer.* Through trade, a superior navy, piracy, and colonial extraction, the English had developed a dominant system of

obtaining the wealth and raw materials necessary to promote their industrialization. One of those raw materials was cotton, which initially came from their North American colonies and later from India and Egypt. Many Spanish galleons loaded with gold and silver were hijacked by English pirates.

7   *Nation-state*. The English were the first to effectively implement the principles established in the 1648 Treaty of Westphalia. In particular, the government exercised full territorial control within its recognized borders by eliminating internal barriers to trade and imposing standardized systems of measures, money, governance, and language. They also built a national transport system of canals and roads that facilitated commerce. By contrast, Germany did not come together as a nation-state until the nineteenth century, which delayed its industrialization.

8   *Market society*. Great Britain had the first nationally integrated market economy functioning within its borders. In order for a comprehensive market to work, all of the ingredients in the economy must be considered available for sale in the market. That especially meant making land and labor available for sale at a price determined by supply and demand. In other words, land and labor had to be transformed into commodities so that they could be bought and sold in the same way that a bushel of wheat or a bolt of cloth was bought and sold. Great Britain was well on its way to becoming a market society by the middle of the eighteenth century. As pointed out above, having a market society is very different from just having a number of localized market places.

9   *Favorable religion*. During the Middle Ages, Catholic doctrine taught that seeking material gain was immoral. This stance is antithetical to the market/capitalistic system, which is driven by individuals seeking material gain. Consequently, a moral revolution had to occur if a market society were to come into being. This moral revolution did occur thanks to the Protestant Reformation of the sixteenth century. England became and remained Protestant by a series of historical accidents, in particular King Henry VIII's break with the Pope over his wish to get approval for his divorce. Thus, over time, the United Kingdom developed a religious environment that facilitated the necessary changes in moral values, including not only the acceptability of material gain as a motive in personal and business behavior, but also the tolerance of empirical science and technological change.

CLASSICAL POLITICAL ECONOMY

Whenever a society experiences this kind of pervasive change in all of its major institutions, its intellectuals set out to make sense out of what is happening. Three new institutions that required explanation were:

1   the worldwide system of trade and investment;

2   the industrial system of production; and

3   the market system of decision-making.

In the process of writing pamphlets and treatises to explain the nature of these new institutions, a new field of study was invented. As mentioned above, one of the first and most important scholars in this endeavor was **Adam Smith** (1723–1790). Smith had no way of knowing that his creative masterpiece, *The Wealth of Nations*, would become the foundation for a whole new field of knowledge. That field would eventually be called Political Economy. In time Adam Smith and other pioneers who followed him would become known as the classic scholars of this field. The reign of classical political economy lasted from about 1770 to 1890. From its beginning, Political Economy tried to make intellectual sense of this new set of decision-making institutions—the nation-state, the all-pervasive market, complex financial systems, newly emerging forms of business organization (especially the corporation), and capitalism itself (Heilbroner, *The Worldly Philosophers*).

ADAM SMITH
1723–1790
Scottish moral philosopher. His 1776 book, *The Wealth of Nations*, is considered the originating treatise in classical and neoclassical economics. Famous for inventing the concept of the self-regulating market and for using the phrase "the invisible hand."

One of Adam Smith's great contributions was his explication of the **self-regulating market**. He argued that a competitive, demand-and-supply–driven market could make decisions for a nation's economy without the intrusions of government guidance or business control. He called this market-organized decision-making system the "invisible hand." He considered the competitive market an exceptionally positive mechanism, as it forced businesses to produce the goods and services that people really wanted and to sell them at the lowest possible prices. Furthermore, Smith thought that these desirable social outcomes solved a difficult moral dilemma. Smith believed that though the market was driven by individuals seeking the highest material gain (a morally suspect motivation), the positive outcomes of the competitive market for the whole society justified the self-interested motivations of the individual participants. Not only would members of the society get more of what they wanted at reasonable prices, but also there was a built-in proclivity for continuous economic expansion. That occurred because businesses were responding to real economic opportunity, not monopolistic price-gouging or governmental favoritism. Consequently, Adam Smith was optimistic about the future of the market society because he believed that it would raise the standard of living across the board (Heilbroner, *The Worldly Philosophers*).

It followed from his belief in competitive markets that Adam Smith was opposed to the state-franchised trading-company monopolies of mercantilism. He also opposed the state protection of local producers via taxes (tariffs) on imports of cheaper products from other countries. The most infamous example of this **protectionism** was the so-called Corn Laws, which imposed tariffs on the importation of grain into the United Kingdom. They had been in place for several hundred years during the whole period of mercantilism. They were not fully repealed until 1849, nearly 60 years after Adam Smith's death. After their repeal, England became the major promoter and supporter of a global free trade regime that involved most European countries and their current and former colonies. This British-led free trade regime lasted until the beginning of World War I in 1914. Because of the worldwide extent of trade and investment during the period 1850 to 1914, it was known as the first era of globalization.

Adam Smith also challenged another central tenet of mercantilism, namely, what constitutes the best indicator of a country's wealth. Mercantilists focused on the store of precious metals, especially gold. Gold was earned when countries sold more than they bought, because those on the short end had to make up the difference with gold. The winners had a favorable balance of trade, that is, they had more exports than imports. As a consequence they accumulated larger stores of gold. Smith argued that a country's *real wealth* is not its stockpile of gold but its capacity to produce. The more goods and services a country has the means to make, the better off its population and the greater its security. One cannot eat gold, nor fight a battle with it. Once gold is expended, it's gone. But once a country has developed its ability to produce, it turns out goods and services year after year. Of course, gold could be used to finance the development of a country's production system. And that is what the English did, in contrast to the Spanish, who did not understand Smith's insight. The Spanish frittered away their substantial gold reserves on massive military expenditures and luxurious consumption.

England had already demonstrated its superior production abilities by the time that Smith was writing, but his views were overwhelmingly confirmed by the production expansion brought about by the Industrial

Revolution. However, gold did not go away. In fact, it remained the basis of monetary systems, both within and between countries, for almost 200 years after the publication of his monumental book. London was not only the center of the most powerful production system in the world, but also the center of the world's gold-based financial system until 1914. The United States played the same role from 1945 to 1971, when the world economy weaned itself away from gold (Heilbroner, *The Worldly Philosophers*).

With the emergence of the more specialized social science disciplines in the late nineteenth century, the question became which one would claim Adam Smith as its founder. The answer was the new discipline of Economics. Economists set out to elaborate on Smith's self-regulating market, focusing on detailing the decision-making processes associated with production and distribution. The political and social dimensions were largely left to other disciplines. Of course, there were scholars who considered themselves economists, such as Thorstein Veblen (1857–1929), who resisted this narrow focus. But they lost out to the school of thought that has come to be called **neoclassical economics.** The "neo" before classical recognizes that this new disciplinary perspective significantly differs from the broader classical tradition. The neoclassical economists developed a tightly deductive model of how a market makes decisions. They relied on more mathematically precise formulations; and they went beyond the classical political economists, who identified labor as the essential source of value in the production process, by adding capital and natural resources as independent creators of value. Economists share Smith's belief in the market's superior qualities as a decision-making mechanism. As the discipline has grown and evolved over its approximately 130-year existence, its members have developed a highly articulated world view that specifies how they understand the workings of a market economy and what policies should be followed in order to maximize its inherent efficiencies. The underlying **market model** of neoclassical economics forms the basis of the first school of thought in IPE that this text will present.

Over the course of the nineteenth century Adam Smith was followed by a number of great classical thinkers. The first who is of special interest to us is **David Ricardo** (1772–1823). Ricardo was a successful trader in the financial markets and a member of the British Parliament. His family history traces the shift of technological and financial leadership in the sixteenth to eighteenth centuries in Europe. His ancestors were Portuguese Jews who had escaped the Spanish and Portuguese Inquisition by migrating to the Netherlands. When the economic leadership of the Netherlands began to fade, the family moved to the new leading country, England. In contrast to Adam Smith, who was optimistic about the equitable distribution of the growing income from the market-industrial society, Ricardo was pessimistic. He thought that those who own a scarce and limited resource—land, in his day—would reap unequal benefits while others would suffer. Ricardo was one of the authors whom an English essayist of the time had in mind when he labeled Political Economy the "dismal science." However, Ricardo agreed with Smith on the advantages of free trade, even coming up with a more sophisticated justification for it called "comparative advantage" (Heilbroner, *The Worldly Philosophers*). It will be further discussed in the next chapter.

DAVID RICARDO
1772–1823
Classical political economist whose pessimism about equity in income distribution helped Political Economy acquire a reputation as the dismal science. Also a successful London trader, who is probably best known as the inventor of the theory of comparative advantage.

Ricardo can also be considered the father of a modern, but much smaller, school of thought, the **neo-Ricardians**. It is based on his insight that the market does not necessarily create a fair and equitable distribution of income. The modern scholarly architect of this school is an Italian, Piero Sraffa (1898–1983). Sraffa spent most of his professional life in England because of intellectual oppression in his home country. Both Sraffa and Veblen rejected the narrow market approach of the neoclassical economists. The scholars who followed Veblen's lead have been called **institutionalists**. By putting the insights of the two schools together, it is possible to create a coherent world view that pays primary attention to the role of power, that is, organizational politics, whether those organizations are governments or corporations. This combined world view of the neo-Ricardians and the institutionalists becomes the second school of thought that this text presents. The members of this school have also created a model of how things work in the political economy. The scholar who has done the most to create that model is John Kenneth Galbraith (1908–2006). This text calls it the **multi-centric organizational (MCO) model**.

After Adam Smith and David Ricardo, the third great classical political economist who is of special interest to us is **Karl Marx** (1818–1883). Because he lived later than Smith and Ricardo, he observed more of the development of the Industrial Revolution and its spread around the world than either of his predecessors. Even though he was born and educated in Germany, Marx spent most of his professional life in London, at the center of the Industrial Revolution. He came to England, as did many others, to escape intellectual oppression. Marx earned some small fees as a freelance journalist; in fact, one of the newspapers that Marx wrote for was *The New York Tribune*. But his major financial support came from his close collaborator, Friedrich Engels. Marx died before neoclassical economics became the dominant point of view in England and the United States, but he was critical of what he called "vulgar economics." He saw the market as a mechanism of exploitation and not a liberator, as Smith and his followers saw it. However, Marx agreed with his fellow classical political economists that it was foolish to separate politics from economics analytically because societies can be understood only in their holistic interconnectedness and in their historical context. The historical context on which he focused was capitalism. Marx developed his own model of how capitalism works, what was wrong with it, and what was going to happen to it (Heilbroner, *The Worldly Philosophers*). This text identifies it as the **capitalist mode of production model**, and it is the centerpiece of the third world view that will be presented, classical Marxism.

KARL MARX
1818–1883
Last of the great classical political economists. Founder of the major school of thought critical of capitalism. Born and educated in Germany, but lived and wrote in London from 1849 until his death. Worked as a journalist, serving as the European correspondent for *The New York Tribune*. Famous for *The Communist Manifesto*, which he wrote with his long-time collaborator Friedrich Engels in 1847, and for his three-volume work on capitalism, simply titled *Capital* (1867, 1885, and 1894).

Therefore, three different and competing world views are descended from Smith, Ricardo, and Marx, respectively. They compose the analytical core of the field of International Political Economy. Though all three scholars were a part of classical political economy, they have spawned three quite different perspectives. Smith is associated with the market model of neoclassical economics. Ricardo is associated with the organizational power model of institutional political economy. Marx is associated with his critical model of capitalism and subsequent elaborations. The three schools of thought differ on many dimensions. For instance, on the dimension of who are the central actors in the political economy, the market school sees them as individuals; the institutional school sees them as organizations; and the Marxist school sees them as classes. Consequently, whatever issue one picks in the realm of international political economy, such as trade, or investment, or equity, or economic growth, or ecological sustainability, the three world views will have different ways of explaining how they work and how they should be addressed.

The overriding purpose of the following chapters is to explicate these three perspectives, the differences between them, and their implications. Each world view and its model will be covered in two chapters. The first chapter articulates the underlying model. The second chapter demonstrates how the model has been or could be applied in actual current global circumstances. Finally, a summation chapter will juxtapose the three world views in comparisons of their approaches to several key issues: trade, transnational corporations, development, and the environment.

REVIEW QUESTIONS

1 What are the ways in which trade connects peoples?

2 Discuss the configuration of conditions that facilitated the emergence of the first Industrial Revolution in Great Britain.

3 Explain the historical conditions that are related to the emergence of classical political economy in the nineteenth century and International Political Economy in the twentieth century.

4 Why is Adam Smith considered such an important person? Present his key ideas.

5 On what key ideas did Adam Smith agree with David Ricardo and Karl Marx? On what ideas did they disagree?

6 What is the field of study known as "IPE?"

7 Briefly describe the three contrasting perspectives in IPE that will be presented in this text.

BIBLIOGRAPHY

Amin, A., B. Gills, R. Palan, and P. Taylor. "Forum for heterodox international political economy," *Review of International Political Economy* (Vol. 1, No. 1) Spring 1994, pp. 1–12.

Bernstein, William J., *The Birth of Plenty: How the Prosperity of the Modern World Was Created* (McGraw-Hill: New York) 2004.

Blaut, J. M., *The Colonizer's Model of the World: Geographical Diffusionism and Eurocentric History* (Guilford Press: New York) 1993.

Chanda, Nayan, *Bound Together: How Traders, Preachers, Adventurers, and Warriors Shaped Globalization* (Yale University Press: New Haven, Connecticut) 2007.

Heilbroner, Robert, *The Making of Economic Society* (Prentice-Hall: Englewood Cliffs, New Jersey) 1986 (first published in 1962).

Heilbroner, Robert, *The Worldly Philosophers: The Lives, Times and Ideas of the Great Economic Thinkers,* 6th edn. (Simon and Schuster: New York) 1986.

Landes, David S., *The Wealth and Poverty of Nations: Why Some Are So Rich and Some Are So Poor* (W. W. Norton: New York) 1998.

Simms, Andrew, *Ecological Debt: The Health of the Planet and the Wealth of Nations* (Pluto Press: London) 2005.

Smith, Adam, *The Wealth of Nations* (Prometheus Books: Amherst, New York) 1991 (first published in 1776).

Wolf, Eric R., *Europe and the People without History* (University of California Press: Berkeley) 1982.

CHAPTER 2

The Market Model and World View

The first school of thought that we will address uses the self-regulating market as its underlying world view. As mentioned in the first chapter, Adam Smith was the first to conceptually develop this approach in the latter part of the eighteenth century. Over the course of the nineteenth century, in conjunction with the rise of industrial capitalism, the idea of the market as decision-maker was further refined. The scholars who developed this perspective were philosophically inspired by **liberalism**, the view that individuals should be free to make their own decisions, especially without interference from the government. The idea of a self-regulating market was highly attractive to them because it meant that the central economic decisions of production and distribution could be made in a purely non-political way. Individual choices would rule, not governments. The intellectual pursuit of this idea resulted in a fully articulated model of how the market works. This chapter presents that model through a discussion of its premises, its internal interactions, and its logical outcomes.

The **market model** provides not only insight into how a market economy ideally works but also guidelines for setting up an actual market society. The model demonstrates the superior outcomes that follow from market-based decision-making. The basic model as presented in textbooks is known as the *purely competitive market model*. It is a simplified abstraction of conditions that exist only partially in market societies—conditions that presumably flourished in Western Europe and the United States in the latter part of the nineteenth and the early twentieth centuries. The model was codified into textbook form before World War II by Cambridge University professor Alfred Marshall (Heilbroner, *The Worldly Philosophers*) and after

World War II by MIT professor Paul Samuelson. Marshall was the one who invented those ubiquitous supply-and-demand graphs that appear in all Economics textbooks.

The inventors of the market model believed that they were improving upon Adam Smith's original formulations. Since they modified a number of the elements of classical political economy, they have been called **neoclassical economists**. The pioneers in the late nineteenth century were mostly Austrian, but there were important figures in the United Kingdom, the United States, and elsewhere as well.

Some of the key ways in which the neoclassical approach differs from the approach of classical political economy include:

1   *The economic dimension is separated out from the political.* As noted in Chapter 1, neoclassical economics replaces the holistic approach of the classicists with a more specialized and focused division of intellectual analysis. The market system provides a way of achieving purely economic decision-making without the intervention of politics. Government and political decision-making can then be set aside and studied by another discipline, Political Science. Thus, the rise of neoclassical economics split political economy into two realms, each with its own academic discipline.

2   *The market is ahistorical, that is, the analysis is focused on the interactions that are happening in the present.* In neoclassical economics the broader historical context need not be referenced as it will be reflected in the decisions that are made within the market. Implicitly, the cultural context is not relevant either as the market interactions between supply and demand are universal.

3   *The role of labor is diminished.* In classical political economy labor is the basic input to the production process and the underlying source of relative value. That is, prices, or the values of specific goods and services, reflect the amount of labor involved in producing the item. In the neoclassical version, labor is only one of three inputs, the other two being land and capital. Land refers to all natural resources, and capital refers to all things, such as machines, that are used to make other things. Furthermore, and most significantly, the value of anything exchanged in the market reflects only the relative supply and demand for the item. There is no underlying or inherent value.

4   *Supply and demand determine the value of anything at the point where they meet.* This is called *determination of value at the margin*, or the last item considered in the exchange. Whatever is paid for the last item offered will become the price or the value of all other similar items. That includes inputs, such as labor, as well as outputs, such as goods

and services. The **marginal analysis** of price determination facilitates the application of mathematical reasoning to the neoclassical economic approach.

5 *The logical form of the model is deductive.* Its premises and assumptions about the attributes of the actors in the market and the conditions under which they function are not strictly empirical. The model takes observed proclivities to their fullest extent and transforms them into absolute conditions, or "totally true" statements. For instance, decisions by the actors in the model (who are not real people but "logical entities") are always based on maximizing their material interests. By assuming that the basic conditions always hold, the model necessarily produces "true" conclusions, or predictable logical consequences. Such is the nature of a *deductive model*.

Within the social sciences the use of a purely deductive model as the core of the discipline is unique to Economics. The more usual approach in the convention of science is "inductive." With an inductive approach scientists make observations of a sample of things or behaviors and try to formulate generalizations about them. Since they are studying only a sample of a much larger population, they can only guess on a probabilistic basis about whether the generalizations hold for the full population. Conclusions can never be absolutely "true," as is the case using a deductive approach.

The three aspects of the deductively structured market model that we will look at in this chapter are:

1 *Premises.* These are the conditions that are assumed about the activity in the model. They hold 100 percent of the time. They set out the underlying "truth."

2 *Internal interactions.* These are the dynamics of the relationships between the actors in the model as they make economic decisions (in accordance with the preset premises of the model).

3 *Outcomes.* These are the logically predictable consequences that inevitably flow from the actors' decisions in the market. Since the premises are absolutely true, then the outcomes that follow must be absolutely true.

THE SEVEN PREMISES OF THE MARKET MODEL

1. Free, rational individuals

The actors in the market are freely acting independent individuals whose behavior choices in the market context are influenced solely by market criteria. Neither custom (the way it has always been done) nor political dominance (orders from government officials) constrains this freedom. The word "rational" refers to the use of economic (market-defined) calculations in the decision-making process. Irrational behavior involves straying from market-maximizing calculations and actions. This use of the term "irrational" differs from the vernacular, in which it generally refers to behavior based on emotion, passion, or superstition. In the market model irrationality refers specifically and exclusively to not perfectly following market-derived objective criteria. The market is based on this "rational" exercise of free choice, especially by individual consumers. Because the market model is driven by these individual or subject preferences, the value theory of the neoclassical approach is called **subjective preference theory.**

2. Decision-making via aggregation of individual choices

Decisions in the market are reached by aggregating, or adding up, the innumerable rational choices of all the individual actors in the market. These individual decisions, when summed up into demands (what actors or buyers are willing to pay) and supplies (what price actors or sellers are willing to accept) for all the products and resources in the economy, provide the information that enables the market to answer the production and distribution questions in the society. Economic decisions are not made by some central authority, nor even a democratically elected government, but only by supply and demand. The price or value of anything exchanged is determined at the point where what demanders are willing to pay equals what suppliers are willing to accept. That point is the equilibrium price. But those points in the market model are the sums of many individual decisions.

3. Monetization

All things involved in production and distribution are exchanged through the medium of money, and thus have a monetary value established by the market. By placing a monetary value on all ingredients in the economic process, a simple calculus can be used by which to compare any item exchanged to any other item, and by which the aggregation process can be made meaningful. Money is the universal solvent by which the market assumes its impersonal form.

Money has three functions. The first function is as a universal **medium of exchange**, one that is accepted by society as a whole, such that it facilitates fluid transactions in the market. Almost anything can serve as money, as long as it is relatively scarce and easily portable. Historically, shells and even cigarettes have served as money. Precious metals, especially gold and silver, have been in widespread use as money. More recently paper notes and bills have been utilized. In modern economies, however, the most frequent form of money is deposit or checking accounts in banks and other financial institutions. Monetary amounts are offered in payment of obligations through checks, debit cards, or electronic account transfers. Credit cards are considered "near-money." In order for the exchange comparisons that the market model is based upon to be effectively implemented, all economic transactions within its purview must take place in the same unit of account.

The second function of money is as a **measure of relative value**. That is, money provides a universal measuring stick by which all items in the market can be compared with each other. For example, if a leather jacket is priced at $200 and a pair of running shoes costs $100, you could compare the relative value of one jacket as equivalent to two pairs of running shoes. The costs of production—the land, labor, and capital used in producing anything—must be measured by the same monetary measure, so that a business can compare its costs with its sales revenue and determine whether or not it is profitable.

Finally, money is a **store of value** over time—it is not by definition perishable, it can be saved, and it maintains its relative value into the future. By maintaining its value over time it provides businesses with stability and predictability for making future contracts; it enables actors to save funds that can be exchanged for anything of value in the future; and it makes possible a single measure of the price of time (the interest rate). The market values immediacy. Therefore, one should be compensated for delaying pleasure, that is, consumption. Thanks to the market's single monetary measure, time trade-offs can be priced the same as any other exchanged item.

Since rational decisions in the market depend on an all-pervasive use of stable money, threats to its stability are serious impediments to well-functioning markets. That is why neoclassical economists are very concerned about instability in the average level of prices, either inflation that would raise the average price level or deflation that would lower it.

4. Material gain

All actors in the market model seek the maximum material result from all of their decisions. Because all items transacted in the market have monetary value, it is always possible to calculate which option will provide the highest return. This is the famous "economic man" dictum pronounced by Adam Smith. All other objectives, whether altruistic, sentimental, religious, or social, are subordinate to the material maximization decision-making process. Material objectives are presumed to be insatiable, thus creating a state of relative scarcity in which all actors are trying to get as many of their wants satisfied as possible. Because wants always exceed available material means, choices must be made. The market is the vehicle for making those choices.

5. Mobility

Everything that is exchanged in the market must be free to move from one position to another without any artificial barriers. All of the resources or factors of production (land, labor, and capital) are free to move from one use to another in response to market signals. There are no geographic barriers, and no ethnic or class or gender discrimination barriers. No psychological impediments exist. Anyone is free to set up a business. The latest technology is available to anyone (no patents or copyrights). The actors can purchase anything they can afford. The basic idea is that everything in the market economy should be used where it can provide the most material value, which is only possible when no non-economic barriers exist that might interfere with that objective.

6. Competition

The accepted mode of interaction between individuals in the market model is competition. However, this mode is impersonal, as all actors—necessarily many buyers and sellers in all markets—compete for maximum gain without any noticeable effect on the market from their individual actions alone. Each individual actor is such a small part of the total realm of activity that his/her impact is minuscule and cannot noticeably affect the aggregated outcome. Consequently, individual decisions are independent of each other so that only price affects decisions. A fully competitive environment requires perfect information, open and easy access to productive activity, and no "artificial" distinctions between things exchanged in the market (brand names). Actors need access to all the correct information about the qualities and prices of all feasible options in order to make the best maximizing decisions. No institutional arrangements can exist that would impede the fullest implementation of competition. Therefore, no monopolies, whether by private producers, governments, or resource controllers (e.g., labor unions), are allowed in the perfect model.

7. Government support

Even though the market is supposed to make the production and distribution decisions for the economy and the role of government is limited, the market model presumes that government will play an essentially supportive role. Government is responsible for (1) establishing the rules—laws on contracts and protection of property, laws against monopoly and discrimination, and so on; (2) interpreting the rules—the judicial system; and (3) enforcing the rules—regulators and police. In addition, government is responsible for ensuring the provision of the essential infrastructure (e.g., energy, water, education, transportation, banking, hospitals, and communications), even though some or even all of the components of the infrastructure may be provided by the private sector. Government also has the responsibility of providing security for its citizens, both within and beyond the borders. Adam Smith recognized that defending the country against external attacks was the special responsibility of the state.

INTERNAL INTERACTIONS OF THE MARKET MODEL

Roles

Based on these premises, a continuous flow of decision-making interactions—exchanges—occurs among the actors as they play their roles in the market. There are three fundamental roles: (1) consumers, (2) controllers of resources, and (3) managers of productive organizations. Individual actors may play all three roles, but each role requires a different orientation and type of activity. Each role involves a different type of material gain objective.

When actors are thinking like *consumers*, they have to match their preferences with the available goods and services. Their decision-making is constrained by the amount they have to spend (their budget), how much satisfaction they anticipate receiving from consuming the goods and services that they prefer, and the prices of their preferred products. Consumers are then presumed to go about maximizing their satisfaction by obtaining the most preference pleasure possible from the budget available to them.

The term *product* encompasses both goods and services. *Consumer goods* can be either durable or non-durable. Durable goods are items such as computers, refrigerators, and automobiles. Examples of non-durable goods are food and clothing. *Consumer services* are things such as entertainment, medical care, appliance repairs, banking, and haircuts. Goods are physical in nature whereas services are intangible. In the most economically developed societies, services are the biggest sector in terms of both employment and value.

The market model divides *resource* inputs into three categories: land, labor, and capital. These are also called *factors of production. Land* includes all natural resources, from trees to sheep, from uranium to gold, from water to soil. *Labor* includes all varieties of labor contributions to production, from managers to custodians, from assembly-line workers to teachers, from police officers to nuclear physicists. *Capital* refers to those human-made things that are used to make or enhance the making of other products. They range from a hammer to a steel plant, from a tractor to an oil refinery, from a grocery store to an airport.

The role of **controllers of resources** involves the provision of these resources or factors to the production process. These actors provide their resources where they can obtain the best return. Each resource has a specific type of return. Land gets rent; labor gets wages; and capital gets interest. Each return is a form of income, so that one could say controllers of resources seek to maximize their incomes. The control over these resources is seldom distributed equally, so that the only resource that is widely controlled is labor.

The third role is that of the **managers of productive organizations**. The managers have the complex task of figuring out what consumers are likely to buy on the one hand while on the other hand finding the best combination of resources to make those products at a cost less than what consumers are willing to pay. Therefore, the managers' maximization objective is to obtain the largest difference possible between their productive organizations' earnings and costs, or, in other words, to maximize profit.

Market model diagram

The ways in which these roles dynamically interact with one another can be graphically portrayed in what has been called the *circular flow diagram of the market model*, or the market model diagram (see Figure 2.1).

The flows connect two locations: households and productive organizations. **Households** contain the actors who play two roles, those of consumers and controllers of resources. The provision of the controlled resource, usually labor, to the market generates the income that provides the budget that the household members use to play the role of consumer. In a basic sense, consuming allows the household to stay alive and capable, therefore, of continuously providing resources to the market.

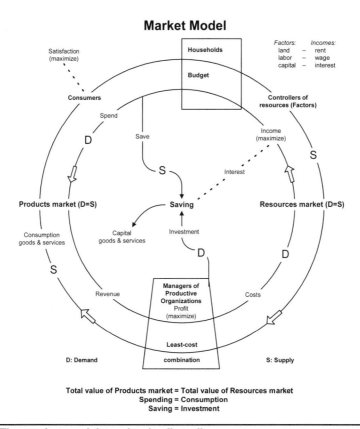

Figure 2.1 The market model—a circular flow diagram.

Productive organizations are places where resources are brought together in order to make goods and services that consumers have an interest in purchasing. The managers need to access the appropriate amounts and types of land, labor, and capital that enable their organizations to meet market demands. Since their profit-maximizing objective requires them to keep their costs as low as possible, they put together their resources in the **least-cost combination**. If labor is relatively expensive, they will use more capital in their production mix. As economies industrialize, they usually move toward less labor and more capital in their resource combinations, especially in the manufacture of goods.

As can be seen in the market model diagram, the activities of these two locations, households and productive organizations, are connected by two circular flows. One is the flow of things, which moves in a clockwise direction. Resources leave the households on their way to the productive organizations where they are transformed into goods and services, which are then made available to the consumers of the households. The counterclockwise flow is that of money. In the market, as assumed by the monetization premise, all exchanges are made through the medium of money. Thus, land, labor, and capital are exchanged for monetary incomes. Those incomes become the monetary budget that the households expend on consumer goods and services. The expenditures of the consumers become monetary revenue to the productive organizations, which enables them to pay their costs of obtaining resources. The costs of the productive organizations when paid to the controllers of resources become the controllers' monetary incomes. So in the circular flow we are back to the location where we started. It's an ongoing cycle in which things are exchanged for money. But the form and name of the flows differs, dependent on their position in the exchange process. For instance, when money comes in to the productive organization it's called revenue. When it leaves, it's called costs. If revenue exceeds costs, then profit is made. Thus, in the market, only productive organizations can receive profit. That is the only circumstance to which the term "profit" correctly applies.

Supply–demand relationships

But we have not discussed two other crucial meeting places in the market, namely, the places where the prices of the things exchanged are determined. These are the market for products and the market for resources. In the *market for products*, consumer goods and services are supplied by productive organizations in response to the demands of consumers. Consumers express their demands for specific goods and services by indicating how much they are willing to pay for them. Suppliers will respond to those demands as long as their costs do not exceed the prices that consumers are willing to pay. In the *market for resources*, the suppliers are the controllers and the demanders are the productive organizations. The prices, or **exchange values**, of resources are established by these supply–demand relationships. Therefore, in the market model, rent, wages, and interest (the prices of land, labor, and capital, respectively) are determined by their relative supply and demand. The higher the demand in relation to supply, the higher the price will be, and vice versa. The market presumes that the incomes determined by the interaction of supply and demand provide an accurate valuation of the contributions that the resources make to the production process.

The interactive flows of the market are very dynamic as any change anywhere causes multiple changes elsewhere. A change in any supply–demand relationship may have repercussions throughout the whole market economy. For instance, if consumers decide that they want to cut their meat consumption to only 10 percent of the previous level, the immediate effect will be a dramatic fall in the price of meat, as supply will be much greater than demand. All of the suppliers of meat, from the butchers, through the meat-processing plants, to the ranchers, will have their revenues and incomes reduced or eliminated. The only way to replace the lost revenues and incomes is to shift the productive capacities and resources to supplying products for which there is an effective demand. Of course, that will be easier for some than for others. This shifting around of resources will change the supply–demand relationships and therefore the prices of all other resource applications. In turn, that will induce managers of productive organizations to change their calculations of their production cost situations. In the meantime those people who have reduced or lost incomes will have their ability to demand consumer products significantly changed. That changes the production decisions of production managers as well. Although supply–demand relationships throughout the whole market are affected, it is that very interconnectedness that demonstrates the market's exceptional capacity to adjust the entire range of production and distribution decisions in response to the new prevailing prices. The prices will be accurate reflections of the changing circumstances, as all actors are assumed to be behaving in a rational, fully informed, maximizing, competitive fashion. Note also that the initiating change came from consumers. The market model privileges consumers as the dominant force in the economy. This attribute of the market is sometimes called **consumer sovereignty**.

Economic growth and capital investment

When the output of an economy increases from one year to the next, then **economic growth** has occurred. Economic growth is a highly valued objective as it provides the potential for raising the society's standard of living. The two major methods for obtaining this objective are (1) adding to the capacity of the means of production and (2) improving the efficiency of the means of production. Both of these methods involve the process of capital investment. **Capital investment** entails making things that produce other things. These producing things are known as "capital products"; and, similar to consumption products, capital products can be either goods or services. Capital goods range from a weaver's loom to a textile factory, from a windmill to a nuclear power plant. Capital services involve intangible ways in which products and production processes can be improved, such as through research and development, training, education, and so on. Enhancing human knowledge and skills is a capital service, but the benefiting humans are still considered labor. Drawing the line between consumption and capital products is not always easy. The same automobile can be used for both business (capital) and pleasure (consumption). A home computer has the same mixed-uses potential. Though some of the research and development contracted by the Defense Department is of a capital nature, most military expenditures are consumption.

If an economy is using all of its production capacity to make consumption products, then no capital products can be made until some of that capacity is diverted. The process that enables the freeing-up of that capacity starts with saving. **Saving** occurs when households (or productive organizations when they earn profit) are not using all their claims for consumption, that is, they are not expending all of their budgets. Because not immediately consuming all they could is considered a sacrifice (a reduction in possible satisfaction), the act of saving requires material compensation. The compensation that savers receive is called an *interest payment.* In effect, interest income allows savers to consume more in the future as they get back their saving plus interest. Of course, that works only if the purchasing power of the saving in the future remains essentially the same. Interest is paid by the productive organizations, as they are the ones interested in making the capital investments. Therefore, productive organizations generate the demand for capital-making production capacity while households, through their saving, provide the supply. This set of relationships is portrayed in the market model diagram (Figure 2.1).

There are productive organizations that specialize in bringing savers and investors together. They are called **banks.** Because they play this connecting role, banks are also known as intermediaries. Their revenue is derived from the difference between what they pay savers on the one hand and what they charge investors on the other hand. In the market model that difference is probably best understood as a fee for financial services. That's because the interest rate that both savers and investors face should be the same as they are on different sides of the same supply–demand relationship. There will be more discussion of the banking system in the section on monetary policy in the next chapter.

Interest is the special price of capital investment. It is over and above the other resource costs involved in making a capital product, building a factory for instance. Productive organizations are willing to pay interest as a necessary cost of expanding or improving the efficiency of their operation, which in turn will lower their production costs. If a productive organization does not take advantage of available technology, it will fall behind competitively and eventually be forced out of business. **Technology**, incidentally, is defined as knowledge or ideas about products or production processes. The capital investment process, through research and development, often plays a role in inventing technology. The potential of new technology is not realized until it is actually applied in the production process. Rational managers of productive organizations will not take that step until they have ascertained that the cost of making the capital investment, including the interest paid, will be more than covered by the revenue flows anticipated. The rate of interest, like all prices in the market, is determined by supply and demand.

Bonds and **stocks** are financial instruments that facilitate the saving/investment process. Market actors are willing to exchange their saving for bonds and/or stocks. When bonds or stocks are first issued, they serve as a means of turning saving—claims on productive capacity—over to productive organizations for their use in capital investment. Banks can be involved in bringing buyers and sellers of bonds and stocks together, but not necessarily. When companies, or governments for that matter, borrow savings on a long-term basis (a year or more), they make a contractual commitment to pay back the amount borrowed, called the *principal*, within a stipulated time period and also to pay a certain amount of interest per year for the duration of the contract. These long-term credit contracts are called **bonds**. The ownership of most bonds can be transferred from one party to another. They are, in other words, marketable instruments that are traded in the bond markets. The only way a private issuer of bonds can avoid fulfilling the credit contract is by declaring bankruptcy.

Bond markets are important to a market economy because they serve as a vehicle for determining the market price of borrowing—the **interest rate**. Since bonds are marketable, their prices go up and down according to changes in supply and demand. As the price fluctuates, yield, or the *effective interest rate*, also fluctuates. For example, a $1,000 bond with a ten-year maturity may pay $100 per year to the owner of record. The effective interest rate on the par value, $1,000, is then 10 percent. However, if the demand for bonds increases in reference to supply, the price for this bond will increase, let's say to $1,100. The effective interest rate will then drop to 9 percent, as the bond holder will still get the contractual $100 per year. The inverse is also true: If the supply were to increase more than demand, the bond price might decline to $900. The effective interest rate would then rise to 11 percent. Therefore, there is an inverse relationship between the price of the bond and its effective interest yield. The effective interest rates of different types of bonds emerge out of the daily trading in the markets.

In contrast to the credit contract that bonds represent, **stocks** are shares in property ownership. For that reason they are called *equities*. In order for a business to be able to issue stocks it must be legally organized as a corporation. Common stockholders may share in the profits of the corporation via dividends paid to them. They also expect their shares to increase in value over time as they are traded in stock markets. However, there is no guarantee that either one of these gains will materialize. Consequently, stocks are a riskier instrument than bonds. Therefore, over time stocks yield a better return than bonds, as savers need an incentive to pick them instead of bonds. In many respects the bond and stock markets resemble the process conceptualized in the market model. However, to reiterate, only when bonds or stocks are first issued are they a part of the basic saving/investment process that is central to economic growth. All other transactions in the bond and stock markets are transfers of ownership. Consequently, most transactions that occur in the bond and stock markets are speculative in nature. Traders are hoping for movements in prices that will benefit them. Ironically, in financial jargon all of these transactions are known as "investing," even though from an economist's point of view only the initial issuance of stocks or bonds has any direct connection to real capital investment. On the other hand, the markets for stocks and bonds provide the "pools of liquidity" that facilitate the connections between savers and investors. Liquidity refers to the degree of funding or credit available.

Stocks and bonds come in many variations, but an especially interesting new development is the *sukuk*, or Islamic bond. The Koran is generally interpreted as prohibiting interest (earning money on money), speculation, and earning income from immoral business activities such as those dealing with gambling, alcohol, pork, defense, and entertainment. Therefore, if a person or organization wanted to abide by this interpretation, they could buy only financial instruments that were declared by a credible cleric as consistent with these prohibitions. *Sukuk*s are structured so that their returns can be understood as profits on asset performance. As one specialist in the field stated, "Islamic finance tries to replicate the conventional market, but in a structure that uses profits rather than interest" ("Islamic Finance," *Financial Times Special Report*, p. 2). The legal structures for accomplishing this objective can be very complex. The major markets for Islamic bonds are in Malaysia, the Persian Gulf states, and London.

Since stocks and bonds, as well as other exchangeable items, are easily sold on a global basis, an intervening market is necessary, namely the *foreign exchange market*. For instance, in order to buy a bond issued by the U.S. government, the buyer must have U.S. dollars. How much of a foreign buyer's currency is required in order to acquire the necessary dollars is determined by supply and demand in the foreign currency market. Much of the activity in the foreign exchange market is also speculative. Foreign exchange will be further discussed in the next chapter.

In recent years the financial markets have become more and more complex as a new phenomenon has appeared: derivatives. **Derivatives** are financial instruments whose value is derived from some underlying asset. The underlying asset could be stocks, bonds, or currencies, but it could also be stock indexes, interest rate returns, or bundles of outstanding debt such as mortgages. Derivatives usually involve the contractual right to exercise some type of option in the future. In order to obtain an option to buy or sell or swap something in the future, the option purchaser must pay a premium. The pricing of option premiums is a tricky business, as the price has to incorporate the expected changes in the value of the underlying asset over a period of time—not only the general direction, but also the ups and downs. In 1973 two scholars won a Nobel Prize for proposing a mathematical equation that would enable traders to more accurately price options. Options are traded in public exchanges or over the counter. Over-the-counter trades are private deals that are less transparent and individually tailored to the buyer's needs. Derivatives can be used for conservative purposes, such as hedging, or they can be used for pure speculation. *Hedging* involves protecting oneself from uncertain future movements in prices. An exporter, for instance, might wish to protect future contracted sales from unfavorable changes in currency values. For a premium the exporter could buy an option that allowed for a future exchange of the involved foreign currency at the current price. The exporter would definitely exercise the option if the future decline in the currency value exceeded the cost of the premium (Levinson, *Guide to Financial Markets*).

Market totals

The market is a dynamic set of ever-changing relationships. Changing prices send signals to the actors, who are presumed to respond appropriately. Nevertheless, it is important to note that at any point in time the total monetary value circulating around the market is the same anywhere on the circular flow. Thus, a snapshot of the market will reveal that the total value of transactions in the resource market equals the total value of transactions in the product market. Since the market model is an enclosed exchange system with no leakages, other monetary totals that are measuring the same set of transactions from different perspectives at any point in time must necessarily be the same. For instance, the value spent on consumption has to equal the value of consumption products. Also, the total amount spent on capital products (capital investment) has to equal the total amount of savings. All of these equalities or identities are depicted in the circular flow diagram of the market model (Figure 2.1).

LOGICAL CONSEQUENCES OF THE MARKET MODEL

Because the market model has a deductive form, the consequences of the supply–demand interaction are fully predictable—at least logically. With the premises 100 percent in place, the internal interactions of the market will create outcomes that can be logically deduced. There are three such logically predictable consequences: (1) the full utilization of all resources and products, (2) a tendency to eliminate profits, and (3) the optimum allocation of resources.

Full utilization of all resources and products

All products (goods and services) and all resources (land, labor, and capital) that are offered in the market will be exchanged at some price. They become part of some supply that will interact with the corresponding demand, and the market will be cleared; that is, all supply will be sold, at the equilibrium price. The resulting prices may not be as high as suppliers would like or as low as demanders would like, but an exchange value that clears the market will be determined. Both suppliers and demanders change their behavior as soon as feasible if they don't like the prices in the market. Changing behavior is harder in some cases than in others. Consumers who have a strong need for a product (e.g., cigarettes or alcohol) will not readily shift their buying practices even when the price increases substantially. When farmers have made a commitment in the ground to growing a particular crop, they cannot shift to another in the same crop cycle, even when its price falls below their costs of production.

Full utilization means that full employment of all resources, including labor, occurs as a "natural" result of the market. Unemployment is logically impossible. Shortages or surpluses can only occur when there is non-market intervention by powerful players such as governments. If a government were to impose price controls in an emergency situation such as wartime, in order to prevent inflated prices from high demand and low supply, *shortages* would occur. Then instead of using the market to allocate the available supply, the government usually resorts to a rationing scheme. Rationing is intended to make the distribution of essentials, such as milk, more equitable. Otherwise, only the rich could afford to pay the inflated market prices. *Surpluses* can occur when the government guarantees a minimum price, as has been done for agricultural products in the United States, the European Union, Japan, and other countries. In such cases the government usually ends up buying the surpluses. But in the unrestricted market model, all offered supply is sold at some price; in other words, it is fully utilized. The ensuing results are not necessarily equitable or fair. Unskilled labor, for instance, could receive a wage that is below subsistence level. The market only ensures that the outcomes reflect supply and demand.

Tendency to eliminate profit

The competitive market drives the prices of all products to the lowest cost. Costs for all firms will tend to become more alike because all resources, including technology, are equally accessible to all. Competition forces firms to continue lowering prices until they have reached their lowest feasible cost point, where profit is eliminated. Beyond that production point their revenues will no longer cover all their expenses. This outcome is what Adam Smith meant when he called the competitive market "self-regulating." Competition prevents price-gouging and unseemly profits. The only way to gain a temporary profit advantage is to introduce a new product or a cost-cutting innovation, but since others will quickly copy it, the advantage will be short-lived. However, it is conceivable that profit could still be earned, even in the purely competitive market economy, by the most dynamic and efficient firms. That's why this outcome is stated as a "tendency." Those firms that earn profit either spend or save it and thereby return it to the flow of the market.

Because this proclivity to eliminate profit is such a paradoxical result of the competitive market, it is important to note that when economists talk about profit in this context, they are referring to revenue that is over and beyond all costs. It is "pure gravy." Business accountants have a more inclusive definition of profits. (These differing definitions of the same concept create confusion. In order to deal with this semantic problem, the use of a concept must be related to its context. Business and financial uses and professional economic uses of the same major concepts are sometimes at odds. There may be solid reasons for these differences, but it does make understanding these complex matters more difficult.) Economists presume that all businesses should earn a "natural rate of return," that is, what the owners would receive if they put their resources into the general market (the prevailing rate of interest) rather than into their own businesses. To an economist this is one of the legitimate costs of running a business. However, although accountants recognize the legitimacy of the return, they still classify it as profit.

Optimum allocation of resources

As market prices direct resources (land, labor, and capital) to those applications with the highest possible returns, the **optimum allocation** occurs. That means that resources are being used to make products that provide consumers with the greatest satisfaction possible. They get what they want at the best possible prices. Consumers direct the market by expressing what they want and how much they will pay for it. Producers respond to that demand by using resources in the most cost-effective way. Consequently, the total value of consumption products is the greatest that the economy is capable of producing at that point in time. This result is what economists call *economic efficiency*. The Soviet system provided an example of a non-market economy with quite different results for consumers. The planners decided what consumer products to make available and how much consumers had to pay for them. For example, snow boots were available for a pretty good price if you liked purple and could use a large size. Blue jeans were not available at all. On the other hand, airplane trips were so cheap that peasants could bring baskets of strawberries to Moscow and make enough selling them informally to cover the cost of the trip. Since consumer demand and actual supply scarcities were not being used in making production decisions, the available resources were not being used in a way that gave Russian consumers what they wanted for the best prices. This misallocation of resources was one of the causes of the eventual disintegration of the Soviet system.

Some proponents of the market system suggest other consequences that they see as connected with its actual implementation. The most significant example would be a non-economic outcome: a democratic political system. **Milton Friedman** (1912–2006) argued that the free choice and mobility required by the premises of the market model can only happen in a free, democratic society (Friedman and Friedman, *Free to Choose*). This particular tying together of economics and politics explains why some pundits and politicians discuss democracy and free markets in one phrase as if they were the same thing.

MILTON FRIEDMAN
1912–2006
Foremost advocate of the free market libertarian point of view. Professor at the University of Chicago and recipient of the Nobel Prize for his work in monetary history and theory. His best-known books expressing his economic philosophy are *Capitalism and Freedom* (1962) and *Free to Choose* (1979).

ANSWERS TO BASIC ECONOMIC QUESTIONS

Another way of comprehending the way in which the market model functions is to see how it provides answers to the basic economic questions that all societies must handle in some way or another. These questions come under the headings of production and distribution, the central subject matter of neoclassical economics. Production refers to all those activities involved in making and delivering goods and services to the ultimate consumers. Distribution refers to how the products that are made are divided among the different components of the society. The basic production and distribution questions are posed and answered below.

Production

1 *What products are going to be made?* In the market productive organizations make the products, but they will make only those goods

and services for which consumers and other productive organizations express an effective demand. *Effective demand* is represented by the number of consumers who are willing to pay a price for a product that at least covers the cost of production. Therefore, those consumers with the means to realize their preferences determine which products are actually made. That holds for consumption products as well as capital products. That's because effective demands for capital products are reliant on anticipated effective demands from consumers for the products that would be made with the capital investment. Again we see the importance of consumer sovereignty in the market model.

2   *How many of each of those products are going to be made?* Consumers may be interested in buying a product, but producers will make only as many as there are buyers who are willing to actually pay the price that at least covers the cost of making it. *Demand schedules* (which can be expressed as curves on a graph) are made up of expressed wishes to buy a product, from those people willing to pay the most to those willing to pay the least. Production stops when demand equals supply, or when willingness to buy a certain quantity equals the cost of producing that same quantity. That is the point of equilibrium. That is where price is set. Achieving equilibrium is considered a tendency because getting it exactly right in dynamic circumstances is highly unlikely.

3   *By what means are the products to be made?* Essentially, managers of productive organizations decide how to produce everything. But they are driven by the competitive necessity to seek the lowest cost of production. They look at the available technology and the relative costs of land, labor, and capital, and then they decide which combination is the least expensive. If the society has a large supply of labor (such as India or China) in relation to demand, labor will be relatively cheap. The production combination in that situation, therefore, will likely use more labor relative to other resources. In other words, the combination will be *labor-intensive*. As labor gets more expensive, it makes market sense to begin replacing it with capital, as happened, for instance, in the economic development of the United States. These least-cost combination considerations on the part of rational managers will determine how products will be produced.

Distribution

1   *How are the claims on products (incomes) divided among the resource contributors?* So how much do controllers of resources receive for contributing their land, labor, or capital to the production process?

Like everything else in the market, the answer is provided by supply and demand. The market declares that the true scarcity value of any factor of production can be known only by the free interplay of supply and demand. Laborers, for instance, should move around according to market signals, that is, wherever they can get the highest wages. Attempts to "second guess" the market by collective bargaining or government programs, such as a minimum wage, reduce economic efficiency and interfere with the incentive dynamics and true-value determination by the market. In other words, the distribution of income determined by the market provides controllers of resources with what they really deserve. Other societies have used customary status, class standing, or sheer power to determine who gets what of the production pie. According to its advocates, the market provides a much fairer system of distribution. People benefit according to the value of their contribution, which, of course, is determined impersonally by the market. The underlying assumption of the market model is that all households have at least one member with a resource to contribute.

2 *How is the production of the society divided between private and public purposes?* Or how much of the society's income should be diverted from private persons and spent by the government on public projects? Taxes are the means by which governments divert some of the private income into public budgets for spending on such things as schools, police, roads, parks, defense, and social security programs. Societies make very different decisions through their respective political processes about what proportion of the nation's income goes into the public budget. In the United States it is about one-third. Western European countries average almost 50 percent. Those who believe that private individuals in the market always make more appropriate decisions than the government strongly resist the imposition of taxes and the public programs that they pay for. This is a political struggle that should be familiar to anyone who follows current events. Even when the political process determines that there is a need for a government program, market proponents argue that market criteria should be utilized in determining expenditures. For instance, they think that public works projects should be evaluated by benefit–cost measures that are based on market prices. Only those projects with the highest projected net returns should be built, not those with the most influential politician behind them (pork barrel projects). Furthermore, production should not be carried out by government enterprises, because with the absence of the discipline of the competitive market, inefficiency and even corruption will prevail. This type of reasoning supports smaller government budgets,

privatization, and deregulation. It was the approach of the structural adjustment programs imposed on indebted developing countries by the World Bank and International Monetary Fund in the 1980s and 1990s.

3 *How is the production of the society divided between the present and the future?* Another distribution decision that societies must make involves how much of their resources to use for the present, that is, for immediate consumption, and how much for the future. In the market the present vs. the future decision is manifest in how much saving is done in relationship to spending. Saving enables capital investment that makes possible more production in the future. And the return on saving—interest—enables the recipients to enjoy more consumption in the future than they would have with immediate spending. This is delayed, but greater, satisfaction. The amount of saving, or production capacity set aside for the future, is determined by the market in the relationship between the supply of saving by households and the demand for saving by productive organizations wishing to invest. In the conventional market model the interest rate ties together the saving and investment decisions. The demand of investors for saving is limited by the relationship between expected rates of return (profit) and the prevailing interest rates. Therefore, only those investment opportunities whose expected returns exceed the interest rate will attract productive organization managers. But this relationship is subject to several changing variables. Households might change their saving behavior, affecting the supply of saving one way or the other. The availability of new technology might encourage productive organizations to increase their demand for saving. If that leads to a higher interest rate, more saving might be forthcoming. Where the interest rate settles will depend on the relative magnitudes of the supply–demand changes.

All of the foregoing should reinforce the importance of the supply-and-demand relationships in the market model. All prices, that is, the relative values of all things exchanged, are determined solely by supply and demand. In the most elemental sense the overriding answer to all questions of relative worth in the market model is supply and demand! It's the heart of value theory for the market. However, since the entire network of supply-and-demand relationships is driven ultimately by the individual preferences of consumers, the value theory has been labeled **subjective preference**. Supply and demand set prices at their intersection, that is, where the monetary amount of the last or marginal product or resource offered (supply) equals the same monetary amount of the willingness to buy that last or marginal item (effective demand). In basic textbooks in Economics this equilibrium relationship at the margins is depicted graphically as the point where the upward sloping cost or supply line crosses the downward slopping demand line. Furthermore, rational consumers will allocate their spending so that the last dollar that they spend on every product they buy will generate the same amount of satisfaction. The same principle holds for resource allocation, though there the objective is equal productivity from every last dollar spent. In this fashion the market achieves peak efficiency.

COMMENTS

The great majority of European and American economists see the world through the filter of this basic market model. It is an elegant and powerful intellectual tool. It provides coherence to Economics that is lacking in other social science disciplines such as Political Science. Even though neoclassical economists certainly recognize other patterns, the standard against which these patterns are compared is the market model. The underlying assumptions about human nature are clear. The normative implications or preferred rules of conduct are not difficult to infer from the premises. Individual decision-making in a free market is the generally preferred approach. Freely expressed supply and demand determine "true value." Government intervention is perceived as appropriate only when it is supportive of market-organized decision-making. Economic efficiency is the desired objective. Economists call non-maximizing behavior "irrational" and institutional conditions diverging from these premises "market imperfections." The moral views implicit in these labels are not very subtle.

Neoclassical economists differ on how strictly they apply the pure model to policy issues. Some see the model as only an analytical device, but others see it as an ideal, even an ideology. Libertarians (those who follow nineteenth-century free market liberalism), such as the late Nobel laureate Milton Friedman, adhere the closest to its principles when discussing public policy. In the 1980s when the free market ideas of President Reagan and Prime Minister Thatcher dominated the global public policy arena, the whole package of associated programs was known as **neoliberalism**. Because the Washington-based World Bank and International Monetary Fund also advocated the free market approach during this era, neoliberalism was also called the *Washington Consensus*. Any policy that is based on a free market approach, such as free trade, draws its intellectual rationalization—in fact, its inspiration—from the market model and the perceived benefits of its expected outcomes, especially economic efficiency.

The next chapter will look at several institutions that are organized around the conceptual framework of the market model. Most members of the public may not be aware of how deeply ingrained the market way of organizing our reality is in influencing how we perceive our choices, how we measure our success, and how we set our public policy.

REVIEW QUESTIONS

1 What are the major differences between classical political economy and neoclassical economics?

2 What is it about the deductive form of the market model that gives it a unique quality in the social sciences?

3 Define briefly each of the premises or assumptions of the market model.

4 Describe the three roles that drive the decisions within the market.

5 Discuss the interactions among households and productive organizations in the market model.

6 Explain how the markets for products and resources are central to the decision-making processes of the market.

7 Explain how the process of economic growth works in the market. Include the roles of banks, bonds, stocks, and derivatives.

8 What are the outcomes of the market model, and why do they necessarily follow?

9 Discuss how the market answers the basic economic questions.

10 Why is the value theory of the market model called "subjective preference"?

11 What are the conceptual similarities and differences between nineteenth-century liberalism and twentieth-century neoliberalism?

BIBLIOGRAPHY

Barrat Brown, Michael, *Models in Political Economy: A Guide to the Arguments* (Penguin Books: London) 1995.

Cole, Ken, John Cameron, and Chris Edwards, *Why Economists Disagree: The Political Economy of Economics* (Longman: London) 1983.

Friedman, Milton, *Capitalism and Freedom* (University of Chicago Press: Chicago) 1962.

Friedman, Milton and Rose Friedman, *Free to Choose: A Personal Statement* (Harcourt, Brace, Jovanovich: New York) 1980.

Heilbroner, Robert, *The Economic Problem* (Prentice-Hall: Englewood Cliffs, New Jersey) 1968.

Heilbroner, Robert, *The Worldly Philosophers: The Lives, Times and Ideas of the Great Economic Thinkers*, 6th edn. (Simon and Schuster: New York) 1986.

Heilbroner, Robert and William Milberg, *The Crisis of Vision in Modern Economic Thought* (Cambridge University Press: New York) 1995.

Heilbroner, Robert and Lester Thurow, *Economics Explained: Everything You Need to Know about How the Economy Works and Where It's Going* (Simon and Schuster: New York) 1994.

"Islamic finance," *Financial Times Special Report*, May 23, 2007.

Levinson, Marc, *Guide to Financial Markets* (Bloomberg Press: Princeton, New Jersey) 2003.

Rhoads, Steven E., *The Economist's View of the World: Government, Markets and Public Policy* (Cambridge University Press: New York) 1985.

Samuelson, Paul A., *Economics*, 8th edn. (McGraw-Hill: New York) 1970.

Thurow, Lester C., *Dangerous Currents: The State of Economics* (Random House: New York) 1983.

CHAPTER 3

Market Applications

As noted at the end of Chapter 2, many of the policies, institutions, and accounting practices in modern societies have their intellectual foundations in Adam Smith's conception of the self-regulating market. In some instances, the market model itself provides the intellectual framework. Probably the best example of that practice is the accounting convention known as the *national income and product accounts*. Therefore, we will start our discussion of market applications with this national record-keeping approach that is followed all over the world. Next we will look at how market thinking has affected discourse, institutions, and practices on that ancient activity discussed in Chapter 1, long-distance *trade*. The new mantra is *free trade*. The accounting convention associated with international trade is the *balance of payments*, covered in the next section. Trade and other cross-national border activities such as investment are complicated by the many different national currencies. That reality generates the next section on *foreign exchange*, which is followed by a section on the historical role of gold in settling accounts between countries. Operationally, foreign exchange markets are very close to the market model. Within countries there are efforts to manage the national money, usually via central banks. That intervention is known as *monetary policy*, which in its modern form assumes a market society. The monetary institutions discussed in the section on monetary policy are those of the United States, as they are still the most important to the global economy and the institutions in other countries are similar in nature. The chapter concludes with a discussion of one of the most famous revisions of the original neoclassical market model, the one provided by the English economist John Maynard Keynes. While the market model is at the heart of analyzing the individual units of the economy (the realm of microeconomics), Keynes's revisions address the attributes of the total economy (the realm of macroeconomics). At the end of the chapter, we will summarize, using a global diagram, how the major variables discussed throughout the chapter interact and affect each other.

NATIONAL INCOME AND PRODUCT ACCOUNTS

Most people would recognize the "bottom line" of the national income and product accounts. It is called the GNP (Gross National Product) or the **GDP (Gross Domestic Product)**. The GDP is the universally accepted measure of how a country's economy is doing. China, for instance, is very proud to proclaim that its economy, as measured by its GDP, has been growing recently at over 10 percent per year. Contrarily, most people may not recognize that the accounting method for the GDP is based on the market model. The conceptual structure of the accounting presentation reflects the model's division into two markets, the market for products and the market for resources. The product accounts record the purchases of goods and services while the income accounts record the amounts that the controllers of resources have been paid for their contributions. As explained in the last chapter, the total monetary value that actors in the market pay for goods and services in a certain period of time equals the monetary income that is paid for making them. The two ways of measuring the economy must be the same. Therefore, the total of the product account must equal the total of the income account. Measuring the same flow from two different perspectives is the principle behind double-entry bookkeeping, and the same principle structures the national income and product accounts.

This national accounting system was developed in the 1930s, when it was realized that analyzing depressed economies was difficult because no systematic record of national economic activity was being kept. In the United States the Department of Commerce took on the responsibility of collecting the necessary data required to measure the performance of the economy and how much different components contributed. The accounting system was further developed during World War II, as it was very useful for wartime planning. After the war the national accounting system was codified for the world by a United Nations agency, and the World Bank began using it as the most important measure of economic performance. Countries have been designated as belonging to the categories of high-, medium-, or low-income based on their GNP. Thus every country has to have a GNP figure, even if it is only an estimate. Since GNP is the total value of economic output, its increase from one year to the next means that economic growth is being experienced. The higher the percentage of growth, the more prosperous the economy is considered to be. Without economic growth countries are not experiencing development and modernization. Many countries in sub-Saharan Africa have been in this situation since achieving independence decades ago. Economic growth is one of the few objectives that all members of the United Nations have agreed on. However, in order for a country's inhabitants to actually experience a higher standard of living, the growth of the economy has to be faster than the growth of population. Only under those circumstances would the **per capita product** increase (value of total production divided by the total population). Of course, per capita product is an average. How persons fare would depend on their position in the distribution of income. In 2002 high-income countries had a per capita product of $27,312, middle-income countries a per capita product of $1,877, and low-income countries a per capita product of $451. One way to measure the extent of inequality in the distribution of income is the ratio of the income received by the top 20 percent to that received by the bottom 20 percent. For example, in 2002 Brazil had the highest ratio of income inequality at 31.5, whereas Japan had the lowest at 3.4.

A more precise *definition* of GDP is the total monetary value of all final goods and services produced in an economy within a specified period of time, conventionally one year. The qualifier "final" is intended to prevent the counting of intermediate stages in the production process, which could lead to counting inputs more than once. The qualifier "monetary" signifies that only economic inputs that are measured by a market price are included. That qualification led to many measurement problems in less developed countries. That is because in less developed countries large segments of the economy, especially in the rural agricultural sector, are not incorporated in the market economy. Even in developed economies significant economic activity may not be counted because it is unpaid. For example, housework, including the raising of children, is mostly not done for monetary compensation. Therefore, it is not included in GDP.

Table 3.1 provides a simplified version of the national product and income accounts for the United States in 2006.

The table makes it clear that Gross National Product (GNP), Gross Domestic Product (GDP), National Income, and Net National Product are different measures. GDP is now the standard measure rather than GNP, so that foreign remissions will not distort the total. Foreign remissions are incomes earned overseas and then sent home. Countries that have large numbers of their citizens working overseas, such as Mexico and the Philippines, have a significant difference between their GNP and their GDP. GDP includes only incomes that are earned within the country. The United States has significant remissions going out and coming in, but in 2006 the net effect was only $30 billion, or just two-tenths of 1 percent of GNP.

The table reveals another fact that is surprising to many, namely that National Income is a noticeably smaller amount than Gross Domestic

Table 3.1 U.S. national product and income accounts 2006 (in billions of dollars)

PRODUCT		INCOME	
Consumption		*National Income*	
Durable goods	1,070	Employee compensation	7,498
Non-durable goods	2,715	Net interest	509
Services	5,484	Rent to persons	77
Total	**9,269**	Proprietors' income	1,015
		Corporate profits	1,616
Investment		Indirect business taxes and	996
Non-residential	1,396	other adjustments	
Residential	767	**Total**	**11,711**
Inventory change	50		
Total	**2,213**		
Government		*Adjustments*	
Federal: defense	621	Statistical discrepancy	−11
Federal: non-defense	306		
State and local	1,601	**Net National Product**	**11,700**
Total	**2,528**	Fixed capital depreciation	1,577
Trade		**Gross National Product**	**13,277**
Exports (11.1% GDP)	1,466	Net foreign remissions	
Imports (16.8% GDP)	2,229	(in: 666, out: 636)	−30
Net	**−763**		
Gross Domestic Product	**13,247**	**Gross Domestic Product**	**13,247**

Source: Bureau of Economic Analysis, U.S. Department of Commerce website.

Product (GDP). The major accounting reason for this difference is *capital depreciation* expense. It is a cost to the productive organization for the assumed lifetime of its capital products, which could be as long as 20 years. Therefore a part of the capital cost is included in the selling prices of consumption products that are made with the capital product over its lifetime. However, depreciation expenses are not income payments to controllers of resources. Those payments occurred when the capital investment was first made, and at that time on the product side, the price of the capital products would have been counted under GPDI (Gross Private Domestic Investment) or under government expenditures. When an enterprise makes a capital investment, it expects to recover its cost over time, not immediately in the first year that it is utilized in the production process. If the firm is run responsibly for the long term, the funds collected in the depreciation expense account should be set aside for the purpose of replacing the capital product as it wears out.

Critics of the GDP note that it has several major accounting problems, raising serious questions about its appropriateness as an economic measure. Some of those criticisms and the alternative measures suggested are discussed in Chapter 5. In the meantime, the market-based, conventional GDP accounts remain the most widely used measure of economic performance in business and public policy contexts all over the world.

Of the four major categories on the product side, one deals with the interaction of the country's economy with the other economies of the world. Exports are definitely produced within the country even though they are sold outside the country. Thus, they count toward the economy's total production. However, every economy imports goods and services that are produced elsewhere. Even though they are sold within the country, they should not count toward the country's production total. The accounting convention, therefore, is to subtract the import value from the export value. However, if the import value exceeds the export value, the figure that goes into the GDP total is negative. For the United States in 2006 the net export figure was a negative $763 billion. The other side of that negative figure is the positive net export figures for countries such as Japan and China. This negative imbalance for the United States has continued for several decades, leading some to question the free trade policy that the United States has pursued since Word War II. The next section discusses free trade and the market.

INTERNATIONAL TRADE AND THE MARKET

The Nobel laureate Milton Friedman, an adviser to President Reagan, while appearing some years ago on the PBS program *News Hour* with fellow economist Paul Samuelson, an adviser to Democratic presidents and also a Nobel laureate, enthused that all economists, regardless of their differences on other policy matters, agreed on the economic virtues of free trade. Samuelson agreed, but then he noted that some qualifications were appropriate. **Free trade** means an open market exchange of goods and services between countries. Proponents of free trade believe that Adam Smith's "invisible hand" should prevail. Any form of government protectionism, such as tariffs—that is, taxes on imports—violates free trade and reduces economic efficiency. In the 2007 *Economic Report of the President* the Bush administration reaffirmed its commitment to free trade:

> The United States derives substantial benefits from open trade and investment flows. Over many decades, increased trade and investment liberalization has been an important catalyst for greater productivity growth and rising average living standards in the United States (Council of Economic Advisers, p. 167).

Protectionism and trade policy in general would not even be an issue if the world were one big global market without national boundaries. However, the world is composed of approximately 200 nation-states, all of which have different government policies on trading with other countries. Since within the market point of view nation-states are presumed to rationally pursue their self-interests, the question arises, how can these states best promote their national economic interests? That is, how can states achieve the optimum allocation of resources and enjoy the highest economic production value? From Adam Smith to today, the unequivocal answer of most economists is free trade.

As mentioned in Chapter 1, Adam Smith argued against the economic inefficiencies of mercantilist protectionism and in favor of free trade. Beyond the obvious and classic basis of trade, that is, exchanging goods that neither country has nor makes at home, Smith argued that countries should trade when the market identifies complementary products. Complementary products are products that both countries want and make, but one country makes one of them cheaper while the other country makes the other product cheaper. In the language of trade, each country has an **absolute advantage** in something the other wants. A market basis for trade exists, and both countries would be made better off by the exchange. But what if one country has an absolute advantage in all tradable products? No basis for an exchange would seem to exist.

A few decades later in 1817, David Ricardo came along and disputed this conclusion with his theory of **comparative advantage**. He argued that even the country with the absolute advantage in all tradable products might gain in total value of production if it turned out that there were differences in the internal production cost ratios between the countries. A basis for mutually beneficial trade would then exist. If each country produced a little more of the product that was relatively cheaper to make domestically (the product in which it had a comparative advantage) and traded it with the other country for the product in which it had a comparative disadvantage, each country, by using its resources more efficiently, would have a larger total value of goods.

This phenomenon is illustrated in Figure 3.1. After trade, both China and the United States end up with a higher total value of goods available within their respective countries. China has a comparative advantage (relatively cheaper resource use) in textiles whereas the United States has a comparative advantage in grain. Even though China has an absolute advantage (cheaper production costs) in both textiles and grain, it can still increase the total availability of both products by trading with the United States. The key market-based argument for free trade, therefore, is that trading countries will acquire more total economic value after trade than before trade. Trade will enable the trading countries to use their resources more efficiently.

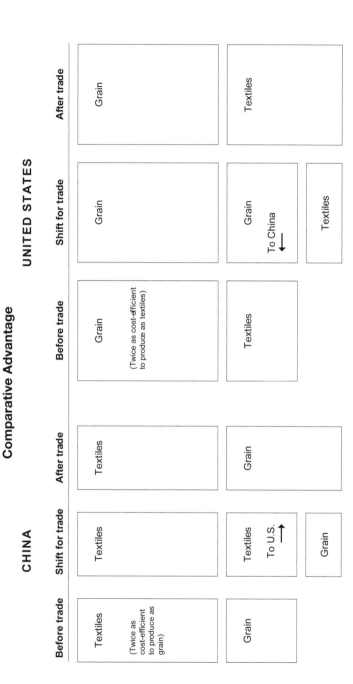

China's costs for producing both textiles and grain are less than those of the United States (width of bars). Thus China has an **absolute advantage** in both products, and on that basis would have no incentive to trade with the United States. But because of different internal cost ratios, China (in this illustration) has a **comparative advantage** in textiles, while the United States has a **comparative advantage** in grain. Thus each country can get more of the products in which it is least efficient by shifting, for instance, one half of the resources used in the less efficient product into making more of its most efficient product and trading it to the other country in exchange for 50% more of its less efficient product. After trade, in this illustration, both countries end up with 50% more of the product in which they have a comparative disadvantage. The process pictured above is intended as a graphical depiction of the possible gains from comparative advantage, not as an exact statement on the actual terms of trade.

Figure 3.1. Comparative advantage.

Of course, according to the free market advocates, the key to the actual, fullest achievement of this greater value for the trading countries would be the existence of an open, competitive market economy within the countries (one that approximates the premises of the market model), because the relative cost of any production process can only be determined accurately when free market supply and demand are fully functioning. Classical political economists, including Ricardo, believed that the essential cost differences between countries would be determined by the relative productivity of labor. They recognized that labor's productivity would be affected by the other resources available to the production process within the different countries, such as fertile soil and technology. But their cost comparisons focused mainly on the relative number of labor units required to make the products being considered for trade. Looking at these labor cost differences, for instance, Ricardo observed that Portugal had a comparative advantage in wine, whereas England had a comparative advantage in cotton textiles. Each country would gain by trading these commodities (Edwards, *The Fragmented World*).

However, Ricardo's trade model recognized that in order for the mutual gains to be realized and maintained over time between trading countries—a necessary element in any politically successful argument—the following additional conditions had to hold:

1 Most importantly, there should be no shifting of capital and technology between countries. That is, there should be capital immobility between countries. Shifting capital and technology would eventually change the internal cost ratios and the basis for comparative advantage in the first place. Ricardo, in agreement with Smith, was not in favor of his home country giving up its comparative advantage.

2 There must be full employment. If not, the price of labor would be misleading, and the accuracy of the internal cost ratios would be questionable.

3 Trade must be balanced. If not, one country would be, in effect, draining resources from another (Daly and Cobb, *For the Common Good*).

Notice that the first condition contradicts one of the premises of the neoclassical market model: mobility. The second condition is a predicted outcome of the pure market, but seldom do real nation-states achieve full employment. The third condition is also difficult to achieve. The United States, as noted above, has had a trade deficit for 30 years.

Ricardo's necessary conditions for achieving mutually positive results from comparative advantage trade play the same role as the premises of the market model. That is, they must be fulfilled if the "win–win" outcomes are to actually happen. Yet the contemporary discourse promoting the superior qualities of market economies and free trade seldom mentions these qualifications. In fact, capital mobility, even though in direct contradiction to Ricardo's first condition, is now considered a key component of free trade by the promoters of free market approaches. For example, the free flow of capital is built in to the provisions of the 1994 North American Free Trade Agreement (NAFTA), and it would have been built in to the charter of the International Monetary Fund (IMF) if the 1997 Asian financial crisis had not happened: The proposal was on the agenda of the upcoming 1997 IMF meeting in Hong Kong, but it was pulled because many observers believed that the IMF-promoted free flow of financial capital was a major contributing cause of the crisis (Stiglitz, *Globalization and Its Discontents*).

Ironically, in order to demonstrate that free trade continues as a "win–win" strategy within the neoclassical market approach, the trade theorists Heckscher, Ohlin, and Samuelson (HOS) in the 1920s and 1930s came up with an even more complex model with even more restrictive conditions than Smith and Ricardo. The *HOS model* includes the three factors of production of the neoclassical market model: land, labor, and capital—not just labor. Similarly to Ricardo's, the HOS model assumes immobility between countries for all three resources, yet somehow, at the same time, all nations are expected to have access to all available technology. Second, these neoclassicists had new objectives to meet; one objective was that no one within any country should be worse off after trade than before it (the *Pareto Optimum*). Consequently, their model presumes that the winners from trade within a country will compensate the losers. The winners will be those businesses whose products have a comparative advantage. Their production will increase as they produce for export markets as well as domestic. On the other hand, businesses whose products have a comparative disadvantage will have to cut back, meaning idle factories and unemployment, at least temporarily. Even if they were to find other products to make for which there is a demand, the returns would probably be less. Making sure that these losers from trade are "held harmless" might require some type of government intervention such as taxing the winners and sharing the proceeds with the losers. This type of intervention, which many governments practice today, can be perceived as another violation of the premises of the market model.

Another objective of Heckscher and Ohlin was to demonstrate that despite the lack of resource or factor mobility between countries, their prices would tend to converge across the globe. For example, they believed that eventually there would be the same payment for a particular labor specialty in all countries. Optimists see this theoretical outcome of "factor price equalization," or similar wage, rent, and interest levels across the world, as a positive development. It provides theoretical justification for restrictions on immigration. Pessimists are more likely to see the lowering of wages in the advanced industrialized countries to Third World levels as definitely negative.

If there were a global free market as envisaged in the market model rather than protected nation-states, everything, including labor, would be fully mobile, and resources would be optimally allocated by market standards. The total of global production value would then be greater. Unfortunately, these free market results would also create gainers and losers, unequal distribution, and volatility. Markets can be efficient, but they are not necessarily beneficial to all participants. Consequently, governments feel obliged to intervene to protect their economic interests as they perceive them. This policy is called strategic trade intervention or **neomercantilism.** Sometimes it involves imposing tariffs so that less developed local industry can be allowed to improve its efficiency and lower its costs while being protected from foreign competition. The United States followed this protectionist strategy from the late 1700s until 1947. Another strategy that governments use is subsidizing local production, allowing products to be sold below market cost. Agriculture subsidization is probably the most salient current example, with expensive programs in Europe, the United States, and Japan. They cause trade conflicts with other countries who believe that these market-distorting policies hurt them economically, especially poor countries whose only export potential may be in agricultural goods. One of the unresolved disputes that contributed to the failure of the 2003 trade negotiations in Cancun, Mexico, was one pitting the cotton-subsidy program of the United States against small-farmer cotton exporters in Africa. Another neomercantilist strategy is the positioning of non-tariff barriers, usually justified by health, safety, or security policies. The United States estimates that its economy loses as much or more from non-tariff barriers as it does from tariff barriers (Council of Economic Advisers, *Economic Report of the President,* 2007, pp. 169–170).

Since the end of World War II, governments have been trying to reduce the extent of neomercantilism. Free trade has been the principle driving international efforts to lower protectionism, starting first with the General Agreement on Tariffs and Trade (GATT) in 1947. From 1947 to 1994 GATT member countries held a series of negotiating rounds in which they lowered tariffs on the international trade of manufactured products. On average, tariffs came down substantially between the major trading partners, from approximately 40 percent to 5 percent. Not surprisingly, the rationale was the expected increase of economic value for all countries through both increased efficiency of production from trade specialization and economic growth from import competition and export promotion. The basic free trade principle underpinning GATT was "no discrimination." If two member countries negotiated a tariff-reduction arrangement, they had to offer that same reduction to all other members of GATT. In this respect, to each other, all the members of GATT were "most-favored nations" (Hoekman and Kostecki, *The Political Economy of the World Trading System*).

The last completed negotiating round of GATT was the Uruguay Round, which lasted for seven years and resulted in a treaty that came into effect in 1995. That treaty created the World Trade Organization (WTO). Besides incorporating GATT, the WTO also covered some new areas:

1 Starting in 2006, trade in agricultural products and textiles was supposed to be covered by the same free trade principles that had previously guided the GATT approach to trade in manufactured products. In 2007 WTO members were still negotiating how to implement this agreement.

2 Intellectual property (patents, copyrights, trademarks, etc.) is now protected through this trade treaty. The rules are called TRIPs (for Trade Related Intellectual Property).

3 Disputes over all the rules of the WTO are now resolved through a dispute settlement mechanism that allows for real sanctions: legal tariffs against the offending country in proportion to the economic damage caused by the unfair discrimination.

4 Trade in services was also added to the treaty's jurisdiction. Services include major areas such as financial, telecommunications, and transportation. This section is known as the General Agreement on Trade in Services (GATS). U.S. estimates are that the elimination of national restrictions on the provision of services could generate an additional $575 billion in annual income for the United States, or 4.3 percent of GDP. That compares to only $16 billion of income gain that further openness in agriculture and manufacturing would generate (Council of Economic Advisers, *Economic Report of the President*, 2007, p. 174).

5 Investment in other countries is another activity that has come under the umbrella of the WTO. The operating principle is that foreign firms should receive the same treatment as domestic firms. Naturally, it has its acronym: TRIMs, for Trade Related Investment Measures (Lal Das, *The WTO and the Multilateral Trading System*).

The specific rules and commitments in all of these areas are still under negotiation, and some have progressed further than others. The latest round of negotiations, known as the Doha Round, was supposed to have been completed in 2006, but in mid-2008 discussions were still continuing. Reaching agreement is made difficult by two circumstances: the necessity of achieving consensus, and the intractable nature of the different national interests involved. In contrast to the IMF and the World Bank, WTO decision-making processes require consensus among all of its 150 members. In actuality, that means consensus among the major blocs. Previously that could be accomplished among the G-7 states (the United States, Japan, the United Kingdom, France, Germany, Italy, and Canada), but now some other major players (Brazil, China, and India) must be included. As soon as Russia becomes a member, it will take its place among the major players. The key issue creating the impasse in the Doha Round has been the dispute over the terms of the trade-off in which less developed countries lower their tariffs on manufactured goods on the one hand, and developed countries lower their agricultural subsidies on the other.

Regional free trade agreements have appeared on every continent, the most notable being the one in Europe. Starting in 1957 with six countries (Belgium, France, Italy, Luxembourg, the Netherlands, and West Germany), the pact had expanded to 27 countries in 2007, with more countries seeking membership. The European Union now encompasses cooperative agreements in many other areas than trade, the most significant being the sharing of a common currency, the euro, among about half of the members. NAFTA—the North American Free Trade Agreement between Canada, the United States, and Mexico—was mentioned above. Mercosur, which originally comprised Argentina, Brazil, Paraguay, and Uruguay, has recently been expanding its realm. Other free trade agreements exist in Asia and Africa. Some have speculated that if the WTO falters in the Doha Round, the regional trade agreements will increase their influence over trade policy. Another development has been the proliferation of *bilateral trade agreements*. The United States and the European Union have been especially active in the pursuit of these agreements; agreements with Colombia, Panama, and South Korea were pending before the U.S. Congress in 2007. All of these trade agreements are ostensibly based on the principles of free trade.

Historically, as countries became organized into states, one of their first administrative tasks was to keep track of the trade flows that crossed their territories. There was ample prior experience in this endeavor, as for centuries levies on trade had been one of the best sources of tax revenue for governments. Every walled city had its toll gate for the collection of customs duties on traded goods. Tariff revenues were the main source of funding for young nation-states even in the modern era. Consequently, record-keeping systems for international trade were developed much earlier, for instance, than the national product and income accounts. The current cross-national accounting system incorporates relatively modern innovations such as double-entry bookkeeping, commercial concepts of capital, and expanded types of market flows. We will discuss this system, the balance of payments, in the next section.

BALANCE OF PAYMENTS

The financial flows between countries are recorded in a system of accounts known as the **balance of payments**. Flows are recorded as they come in and as they go out. The accounting presumption is that the flows will match, so that the net balance is zero. That is, the total monetary value of payments-in will equal the total monetary value of payments-out. Table 3.2 provides a simplified presentation of the U.S. balance of payments for 2006. The first flow measured is trade in goods. Exports result in financial flows coming in as foreign purchasers pay for the goods while imports result in payments-out. The net figure is called the **balance of trade**, even though exports and imports are seldom exactly equal. When a country has more imports than exports, as in the recent experience of the United States, the financial flows from trade are negative. After the trade figures come the flow amounts for the buying and selling of services. In 2006 the United States had a net positive flow in services, but nowhere near enough to compensate for the huge deficit in trade. To the net results from exchange of goods and services the accounts system adds the net amount from the payments on overseas earnings such as dividends on foreign stock. The resulting net figure from all three of these components is known as the **current account**. The current account is the most important measure of how a country is doing in its economic exchanges with other countries. Note how this accounting system also mirrors the market model categories.

Table 3.2 U.S. balance of payments 2006 (in billions of dollars)

Activity	Amount in	Amount out	Balance
Exports of goods	1,023		
Imports of goods		1,861	
Balance of trade			**−838**
Exports of services	423		
Imports of services		343	
Balance of goods and services			**−758**
Income receipts (profits, dividends, interest, etc.)	650		
Income payments		614	
Net transfers (government and private)		90	
Current account balance			**−812**
Capital asset transfers – in (short- and long-term, government and private)	1,860		
Capital asset transfers – out		1,055	
Net financial derivatives	29		
Net capital account transfers		4	
Statistical discrepancy		18	
Balance of payments			**000**

Source: Bureau of Economic Analysis, U.S. Department of Commerce website.

A country that like the United States has a deficit in its current account will have to cover that liability by borrowing saving from other countries that are running surpluses, such as Japan or China. The transfer of saving from one country to another is recorded in the next major component in the balance of payments: the **capital account**. The way the term **capital** is used in the balance of payments accounting system is somewhat confusing, because all transfers of saving, whether temporary shifts of cash or permanent capital investments, are called capital. As noted earlier, financial specialists employ the term *capital* in this broad way. When economists use the term *capital*, they are referring more narrowly to real tangible investment in the productive capacity of the society. However, the balance of payments accounts do make a distinction between short-term and long-term capital. Short-term capital flows involve the rapid movement of liquid funds. These days that usually happens with a click of the computer mouse. Speculators move these funds from one country to another in response to changing return possibilities, especially differences in short-term real (inflation-discounted) interest rates. Because these funds are "footloose and fancy-free," they are generally known as *hot money*. Short-term flows can involve the buying and selling of financial assets, even bonds. In other words, they are not just cash. China, for instance, has used its surplus dollars to purchase large amounts of U.S. Treasury bonds. Long-term capital flows generally involve *foreign direct investment*. FDI can be the actual construction of a physical facility, such as a factory, in another country or it can be an acquisition of a substantial share of a foreign facility through stock purchase.

The balance of payments accounting system relies on using the nation-state as the basic unit. As the world's economy becomes increasingly integrated, the relevance of that assumption comes into question. Transnational corporations have product chains that may involve dozens of countries. Or corporations may ship product parts over a border, have them assembled, and then bring them back in for sale. That happens regularly, for instance, between Mexico and the United States. The exports and imports involved in this transaction are recorded in both countries' balance of payments accounts. Another anomaly occurs within regional trade groupings, such as the European Union. The balance of payments accounts are still kept by the individual member countries.

Despite these reservations, the balance of payments accounts do keep track of which countries are spending more than their revenue and are therefore accumulating obligations to those countries that are financing the excess spending. This overspending behavior is especially characteristic of the United States. The U.S. current account deficit in 2006 approximated 6 percent of the value of the total economy (GDP), about twice the generally acceptable percentage. Only the United States could get away with such a large, continuing external deficit over many years. That is the case because the U.S. dollar is still the most commonly held currency in other countries' foreign exchange reserves. That does not mean, however, that the United States can accumulate extraordinary amounts of debt to foreigners without limit.

Other countries with large deficits in their current accounts include Greece (8.4 percent of GDP), Turkey (7.0 percent), South Africa (6.0 percent), and Hungary (4.7 percent). Predictably, on the other side of the ledger are those countries with significant surpluses in their current accounts: Saudi Arabia (21.4 percent of GDP), Switzerland (14.4 percent), Norway (14.3 percent), Malaysia (13.5 percent), Hong Kong (9.8 percent), Venezuela (9.8 percent), and China (8.1 percent). It's not surprising that three of the top surplus countries in this selected list are oil exporters ("Economic and financial indicators", *The Economist*).

All of these payments between countries are mediated through the foreign exchange markets. How foreign exchange affects these transactions between countries is the subject of the next section.

FOREIGN EXCHANGE

When U.S. dollars are acquired and held in central bank accounts in other countries, they are considered a part of those countries' *foreign exchange reserves*. The larger the foreign exchange reserves relative to the size of a country's economy, the greater the depth of financial protection possessed by that country against foreign claims. If necessary, that country can defend the value of its currency in international markets. Should any short-term deficit occur in its international financial accounts, the country would have the means to meet its obligations. Because more U.S. dollars are held for this purpose around the world than any other currency, the dollar, in effect, serves as the global currency. It has fulfilled that role since the end of World War II, when it replaced the British pound, which had served as the dominant currency from the latter part of the nineteenth century through the beginning of the twentieth.

Other currencies from strong, highly industrialized, politically stable national economies, the so-called hard currencies, also serve as foreign exchange reserves. Examples of *hard currencies* include the Japanese yen, the Swiss franc, the British pound, and the euro—the currency of the 15 (as of 2008) countries of the European Monetary Zone, or "Eurozone." These currencies are called "hard" because other countries will accept them in payment of bills and debt. There is the general belief that these currencies will not lose their value through rampant inflation or other serious attacks on their integrity. Soft currencies do not have that reputation, so banks that operate internationally are reluctant to make soft currency loans. When Mexico, for instance, has had to borrow internationally, it has agreed to repay in U.S. dollars. For the first few decades after World War II the largest holders of U.S. dollars in their foreign exchange reserves were European countries. In fact, a whole financial market was created for Eurodollars. During the oil crisis of the 1970s, oil-exporting countries, such as Saudi Arabia, became large holders of U.S. dollars. As will be explained below, the availability of these petrodollars in the world's commercial banks played a role in the Third World debt crisis of the next decade. In the 1980s, Japan, thanks to its large trade surplus with the United States, became one of the largest holders of U.S. dollars. Now, at the beginning of the twenty-first century, the country with the largest trade surplus with the United States is China. China, therefore, has become a major holder of U.S. dollars or U.S. dollar–denominated financial assets in its foreign exchange reserves.

The hard currencies of the world achieve their value in relationship to each other via global financial markets. For example, when there is more demand for the U.S. dollar in reference to the Japanese yen, then the value of the dollar will go higher vis-à-vis the yen. That is, it will cost more yen to buy a dollar, or one dollar will buy more yen when the exchange occurs. A valuable dollar is an advantage for American tourists visiting Japan. However, it is a problem for American companies hoping to export to Japan, as their goods become relatively more expensive. On the other hand, imports from Japan are less expensive. In the early 1980s this scenario became a reality, and the United States began importing from Japan much greater quantities of goods, especially automobiles and consumer electronics. The shift in the foreign exchange ratio in favor of Japan was a major factor in the United States' developing a large trade deficit with Japan. A trade deficit with Japan still exists today, even though the dollar is not as valuable in reference to the yen. The continuation of the deficit suggests that other factors are at play. For instance, the United States no longer makes many of the products it formerly exported. Consumer electronic products, such as televisions, are an example. Furthermore, Japanese consumers tend to prefer Japanese products, even when they cost more. Nevertheless, the Japanese government has been worried about the relatively high value of the yen, as it does reduce export earnings. Its strategy has been to intervene in the global foreign exchange market, where it sells yen and buys U.S. dollars with the intent of lowering the value of the yen in reference to the U.S. dollar (Strange, *Mad Money*).

Currencies that are allowed by their governments to find their value in relationship to other currencies in the free market are called *floating* or *flexible currencies*. When a floating currency goes up in value, it is said to *appreciate*, and coming down in value is called *depreciating*. Many factors enter into the market's determination of relative exchange values between countries. These include the current account situation, different rates of inflation, the relative strength of the nation's economy, government policies (especially those affecting interest rates), and even the behavior of currency speculators. When a country runs a continuing deficit in its current account, usually one would expect downward pressure on its exchange rate with other currencies, especially in relationship to countries that are running surpluses. Countries with comparatively high rates of inflation (increases in the average level of prices) will also experience downward pressure on their exchange rates. Countries with relatively weak economies will tend to have their currencies decline in value in relationship to countries with stronger economies. Countries that have lower real interest rates will tend to see a decline in the demand for their currency and thus a likely decline in its value (Eatwell and Taylor, *Global Finance at Risk*).

Predicting how the interaction between all these factors will come out in the market is extremely difficult. Even professional speculators win some and lose some. As long as the U.S. dollar has the dominant place among the world's currencies, it can withstand all the usual pressures on its value because other countries will want to hold dollars in their foreign exchange reserves. They are useful for paying foreign obligations, especially for such purchases as oil, which is still mostly priced in dollars. However, the euro is currently mounting a challenge to the dollar as the dominant currency. When leaders of oil-exporting countries wish to challenge the hegemony of the United States, they switch the pricing of their oil exports from dollars to euros. That is what President Saddam Hussein of Iraq did before the U.S. invasion, and that is what President Chàvez in Venezuela is doing. If the euro takes over global currency leadership from the dollar, the ability of the United States to finance its continuing deficits will be severely curtailed. The value of the dollar would then undoubtedly fall significantly, and the American standard of living would fall as imports become noticeably more expensive. Even shopping at Wal-Mart would become more expensive.

Since the market for currency values can be volatile and unpredictable, many countries opt for setting their currency values by government decree. These are called *fixed rates of exchange*. This approach may bring some stability, but it also introduces rigidity into the economy that may backfire. In the financial crises involving the Mexican peso in 1994 and the Thai baht in 1997, their currency values were set too high, that is, they were overvalued. In the early 2000s Argentina made the same mistake. All of these countries had pegged the value of their currency to the U.S. dollar at ratios that were too high to sustain under market conditions. In an effort to rectify the situation, the governments had to precipitously lower the value of their currencies, that is, *devalue* them. The ensuing loss of confidence in the economies of these countries by the international financial markets exacerbated their problems. Because of the phenomenon of financial contagion, other countries were affected by the pessimism that spread throughout the global markets (Stiglitz, *Globalization and Its Discontents*).

It is also possible to undervalue one's currency. Some economists and policy-makers believe that China's great success in its exports to the United States and elsewhere in the first part of the twenty-first century is at least partially due to an exchange rate that is fixed at a below-market rate, making Chinese products about 25 to 40 percent cheaper than they would be under free market conditions. This kind of manipulation of foreign exchange ratios is another neomercantilist strategy. The U.S. government has been trying to get China to increase the value of its currency in relationship to the U.S. dollar. However, the amount of pressure that the United States can exert is limited by its dependence on Chinese purchases of U.S. debt. Nevertheless, there is a movement away from fixed foreign exchange rates to flexible rates. In 1980 more than 75 percent of countries had a fixed target for their exchange rates. By 2005 that had dropped to 55 percent (Council of Economic Advisers, *Economic Report of the President*, 2007, pp. 160–161).

Because of all the variables that affect foreign exchange relationships, it's very difficult to tell how accurately they portray comparative economic conditions. Yet they have been used conventionally when comparing economic performances. If one wishes to compare the GDPs of different countries and their per capita incomes, it is necessary to translate their local currency values into one standard measure. That is usually the U.S. dollar. However, the conversion ratios used are the prevailing foreign exchange ratios. But, as we saw above, some currencies are overvalued and others are undervalued, especially if one presumes that the ratios between currencies should reflect comparable living costs. One effort to overcome the foreign exchange distortion is called **purchasing power parity** (**PPP**). In order to determine a PPP ratio, researchers first have to find comparable baskets of commodities, then get the purchase prices in the local currencies, and finally calculate a ratio that reflects spending essentially the same value for the same commodities. None of this is easy, but the World Bank makes an effort to provide PPPs for all the world's countries, despite the many differences between them. For instance, in 2005 the PPP ratio between the United States and China was 1.8, that is, one dollar equaled 1.8 yuan in purchasing power. However, the foreign exchange ratio was 7.9, creating a per capita GDP for China of $1,800. Using the PPP ratio, China had a per capita GDP of $7,204—a huge difference (World Bank website).

The Economist magazine has viewed all these efforts with considerable skepticism, so it has created its own PPP index based on the "Big Mac." It compares the dollar cost of a Big Mac in the United States with its local currency price in other countries. That provides a ratio that should be the same as the foreign exchange ratio between the United States and the other country. If the country's foreign exchange ratio is higher, then it is overvalued. If it is lower, then it is undervalued. By this admittedly facetious measure the most overvalued currencies are in Scandinavia: Iceland by 154 percent, Norway by 120 percent, and Denmark by 58 percent. China does come out as undervalued, but only by 55 percent (*Economist* website).

The **International Monetary Fund** (IMF) was established in 1944 with the primary purpose of bringing stability to the world currency markets and helping countries that find themselves in short-term balance of payments crises, that is, bills coming due without the means being there to pay them. Originally IMF assistance consisted of the provision of short-term loans that were intended to prevent countries from defaulting on their debts and losing their international credit rating. In other words, the IMF was intended to play the role of lender of last resort. In the late 1960s, in order to help less developed countries, the IMF created an additional foreign exchange reserve asset, called a **Special Drawing Right** (SDR). Member countries were allocated a certain number of SDRs dependent on their deposits in the Fund. Countries could meet their foreign obligations by the transfer of SDRs, but the amounts authorized have never been large enough to significantly affect the world financial situation. Countries can also borrow SDRs from the IMF. The value of SDRs was originally based on gold, but it is now based upon the market value of a basket of hard currencies weighted by their relative role in international trade. The basket currently (2008) includes the euro, Japanese yen, British pound, and U.S. dollar (IMF website).

International financial markets provide what is probably the best real-life, contemporary example of the free market at work. This market is huge, consisting of about $2 trillion of foreign exchange transactions per day. In dollar magnitudes it takes only about one week's worth of trading in the foreign exchange markets to equal the U.S. GDP for the entire year. Some of the transactions finance current cross-border exchanges of goods and services, but more transactions are involved in futures trading of currencies. Some of these futures trades are done by businesspeople who are trying to protect their international transactions from unfavorable future swings in currency values. At the same time, speculators, who are responsible for the largest proportion of transactions, are actively trying to gain from these swings by making bets on which direction exchange values are going. The interaction of supply and demand actually seems to rule the determination of value. In this context one hears frequent references to market efficiency (Weisweiller, *How the Foreign Exchange Market Works*).

However, according to George Soros, a well-known international financier, in the actual foreign exchange markets the assumptions of the market model are not fully realized. He contends that currency traders' assessments of other currency traders' expectations of future movements influence decisions on futures trading more than the traders' independent determination of value based on their view of economic fundamentals. Quite often a "herd mentality" takes over this decision-making process. Then group psychology rules, not independent analysis (Soros, *The Crisis of Global Capitalism*). In addition, money itself, as classical political economists have observed, is a peculiar commodity. This is especially true when the money is not tied to an underlying value such as gold. The amount of untied money that could be created is theoretically infinite. Even some of the most libertarian neoclassical economists, such as the Nobel laureate Friedrich von Hayek, have worried about too much monetary speculation causing disequilibrium and instability in the financial transactions between countries. Hayek has argued that the world economy would be better off if it returned to fixed exchange rates such as that provided by the gold standard, the subject of the next section (Edwards, *The Fragmented World*, pp. 144–145).

THE GOLD STANDARD

For thousands of years in human societies, gold has played a central role as a symbol and measure of wealth. As long-distance trade became more prevalent in Europe in the late Middle Ages, gold, mostly from Africa, became the internationally accepted means of payment between commercial centers of trade. The search for new sources of gold really got under way in the late fifteenth century with the advent of the age of exploration. The Spanish especially were focused on finding gold so that they could have more monetary wealth with which to pursue their favorite activities, luxurious consumption and wars of conquest. When the islands of the Caribbean, where Columbus first landed, proved not very rich in gold, the Spanish moved on to the Aztec Empire in Mexico and the Inca Empire in Peru, both places where gold was plentiful. The Spanish conquered these empires and began shipping the gold extracted from them back to Europe. So much gold was transferred to Europe that the money supply was doubled and prices increased accordingly. As mentioned in Chapter 1, this great transfer of wealth undoubtedly played a role in Europe's growing economic ascendancy, though ultimately it was not the Spanish but the Dutch, French, and especially the British who benefited the most.

In the eighteenth century, Adam Smith tried to convince his contemporaries that their obsession with gold was distracting them from the real source of wealth: a country's ability to produce. While the British accepted his advice on their way to becoming the world's center of manufacturing, they stuck to gold as the basis of money, both at home and in international trade. In fact, the British established a global monetary system based on gold. This system was known as the **gold standard.** Each participating government established a ratio between gold and its unit of money. Then the amount of money a country could circulate was dependent on the amount of gold it had accumulated. The amount of money in circulation in reference to the volume of transactions (demand for goods and services) would determine the level of average prices in that country. The more money in circulation, the higher would be the average level of prices, and vice versa. Thus, gold was used as a means of disciplinary control so that heads of governments could not wildly issue large amounts of money that was not backed with anything solid. Previously many kings had done exactly that, driving their kingdoms into economic collapse. As the business community gained more political power, it insisted on the gold standard, as businesspeople wanted stability in prices so that future business contracts would have predictability.

The gold standard also provided stability for exchanges between countries. If a nation-state was running a favorable balance of trade (more exports than imports), it would acquire more gold, as the countries with the unfavorable balances had to make up the difference with the payment of gold. More gold meant that the government could issue more money. If the now-possible increase in the money supply exceeded the increase in the supply of products, prices would go up; that is, inflation would occur. Exports would now be more expensive and imports cheaper. Consequently, the favorable trade balance or surplus would most likely disappear. On the other hand, countries with trade deficits, or unfavorable balances of trade, would have the opposite experience. The loss of gold would lead to a reduction in the money supply and a likely decrease in prices. That country's exports would then be cheaper, and its imports, at least from countries that previously had favorable trade balances, would be more expensive. Consequently, the unfavorable balance, or deficit, in that country's trade account should tend to disappear. Therefore, the gold standard system was presumably self-regulating, so that no country would find itself running a continual deficit or surplus. Imbalances would be corrected by the system itself. No country would build up a debt it could not afford to repay (Edwards, *The Fragmented World*).

For the latter half of the nineteenth century and the first part of the twentieth century, this system worked reasonably well for the major trading countries of the world. In fact, the system enabled the first global economy to flourish. As the major trade and financial center of the world, the United Kingdom served as the world's banker. The British pound was as good as gold, and therefore provided the monetary support—the liquidity—that enabled the world trading system to flourish. With the onslaught of World War I the gold standard crashed, it was weakly revived in the 1920s, and then it was thoroughly demolished by the Great Depression of the 1930s. Not wanting to experience unfavorable balances and the ensuing loss of gold, countries began erecting high tariff walls in that same decade. The United States was no exception: it raised its tariff levels from an average of about 40 percent to 70 percent. It's not surprising that international trade collapsed.

Central banks also played a role in exacerbating the situation during the 1930s. In many countries the method of protecting the gold supply was to raise interest rates so that people would keep their money at home rather than seek higher rates overseas. Ironically, from the perspective of the domestic economy, this raising of interest rates was exactly the wrong thing to do because it discouraged businesses from borrowing and expanding their activities. In other words, instead of providing stability, the discipline of the gold standard actually undermined the viability of national economies. It was making the economic downturn worse. Therefore, one of the first acts of the newly elected U.S. president Franklin Delano Roosevelt was to take the country off the gold standard. Within the United States the dollar was no longer as good as gold; gold certificates were no longer legal tender. Dealing with the collapse of the economy became politically more important than maintaining the financial discipline of the golden dollar (Galbraith, *Money*).

Nevertheless in 1944, when the Allies, under the leadership of the Americans and the British, were making their plans for the post–World War II world economy at **Bretton Woods**, New Hampshire, they looked back appreciatively at the stability provided by the gold standard to the pre–World War I global economy. They wanted to recreate a stable basis for international trade because they believed that it was necessary for economic recovery. The British wanted a truly international currency that would be administered by an international organization such as the International Monetary Fund, whose creation this conference proposed. However, the United States wanted the dollar to play the same dominant role that the British pound had played in that earlier time. As the hegemonic world power, the United States got its way. The revival of the gold standard would be dollar-based, and it would be limited to the international arena. As a consequence, while the United States and other countries did not return to the strict gold standard in their internal monetary systems, international transactions were to be conducted on the U.S. dollar standard, which was considered "as good as gold." That was because the dollar was established as convertible to gold at $35 an ounce. International creditor countries were assured that they could exchange their accumulated surplus dollars for gold at that ratio. Since at that time the United States had the world's largest reserve of gold, it seemed that this promise of convertibility was solid. Stability was returned to the world economy, and international trade was revived. The 1944 Bretton Woods Conference that had established the system had provided a winning formula (Galbraith, *Money*).

Throughout the 1950s and 1960s this dollar–gold arrangement worked reasonably well. But it was gradually undermined as the United States began sending more and more dollars overseas. The first large flow of dollars abroad was for postwar reconstruction grants in Europe (via the Marshall Plan) and Asia, perceived as urgently necessary because of the developing

Cold War with the Soviet Union. Then in the 1960s another Cold War venture, the conflict in Vietnam, sent many more dollars overseas. As a result, the world was becoming inundated with dollars, causing global inflation. The fixed rate of $35 to an ounce of gold grew untenable because it greatly overvalued the dollar. In 1971, when many countries—especially France under President Charles de Gaulle—threatened to turn their accumulated dollars into U.S. gold in amounts that the United States could not provide, President Nixon severed any fixed relationship between the dollar and gold. For two years the world's major financial players tried to fashion an intermediate arrangement, but that effort collapsed in 1973. Since then, the value of the dollar has been largely determined by demand and supply in the global financial markets. As noted in the previous section, the dollar's value, along with the rest of the world's major hard currencies, is no longer fixed, or pegged, to a precious metal such as gold or silver; its value is flexible, or market-determined.

However, gold has not disappeared as an element in the financial system. Most countries include it in their foreign exchange assets as it can still be used to settle accounts between countries. Gold is no longer a part of the required deposits for all member countries of the International Monetary Fund, but it can still be used to meet obligations. But the value of gold is now established in the open market. Its value has fluctuated widely since 1973, and is currently (2008) hovering around $1,000 an ounce. And, when monetary assets that no longer have a precious-metal backing appear to be in trouble, some people shift a part of their wealth into gold as a hedge against financial uncertainty. But no longer does gold control the value of any major currency, either domestically or internationally. The market has taken over, and some of the supporters of the free market approach are delighted.

MONETARY POLICY

All modern states intervene in their economies via the exercise of **monetary policy**. Monetary policy involves affecting the country's financial circumstances, usually through the actions of the central bank, with the purpose of achieving economic objectives. In today's interconnected world, monetary policies have international implications. Monetary policies in countries whose currency is used by other countries as a foreign exchange asset have major spillover effects around the world. This is especially true of the United States, but also of the Eurozone, the United Kingdom, and Japan. It has even been debated whether the most powerful governmental person in the world is the president of the United States or the head of the U.S. central bank.

Monetary policy as practiced today is a twentieth-century invention. In the United States, for instance, the legislation initiating monetary policy and the establishment of the U.S. central bank was enacted in 1913. Great Britain has had a central bank for hundreds of years, but it was not really a public institution until after World War II, and its status as an independent public policy maker was not achieved until 1997. The European Central Bank was not established until 1999. Conceptually, monetary policy is based on neoclassical economic conceptions, while its contemporary practice owes a great deal to the ideas of Nobel laureate Milton Friedman.

Understanding monetary policy requires knowledge of the modern system of banking. Banks have been around for a long time, just like trade. Modern Western banks were developed first by the Italian city-states in the fourteenth century and are believed to have evolved from goldsmith shops. Gold was the most prevalent form of money in Europe at that time. It played all three of the roles discussed earlier: medium of exchange, measure of relative value, and store of value over time. Goldsmith shops were the safest place to store gold. Eventually, people became comfortable exchanging goldsmith-issued receipts for gold deposits rather than the gold itself. These receipts were the forerunner of today's bank notes. Goldsmith shops became even more like banks when they began making loans based on the gold that was stored in their vaults. That worked fine as long as the goldsmith-cum-banker did not get too greedy. Unfortunately, some did, and their liabilities far exceeded their gold supply. When that weakness was discovered, the depositors rushed to the bank to withdraw their gold, creating a run on the bank. Since the depositors' demands were much greater than the bank's supply, the bank went broke, or "bankrupt."

One would think that we would have learned some lessons of prudence from these bankruptcies and their unhappy fallout for individuals and businesses. We did learn that a national currency is a better idea than letting every private bank issue its own bank notes. On the other hand, we also learned that banks could get away with lending out most of their deposits most of the time for significant interest returns. Thus banks to this day need keep only a fraction of their actual deposits in the bank. The rest they can lend out. That's why what we have today is called the fractional reserve banking system.

The **fractional reserve banking system** has the ability to create or destroy money. Even people who work in banks may find that statement incredible. The kind of money we are talking about, however, is bank money. Most of us use "bank money," only we call it our checking account. Checking accounts are also called demand deposits, because we have the right to withdraw on demand a part or all of what we have deposited in the account to pay our bills or to go shopping with cash in our pockets. Banks today, just like the old goldsmith banks, put most of the money deposited with them to work earning a return. That is, they lend it out to consumers, small businesses, homeowners, corporations, and governments. Banks keep only a small part of their deposits on reserve; enough, they hope, to handle their daily transactions and obligations.

One way to show how the fractional reserve process works is through what is known as a *T account*. T accounts are based on the principle of double-entry bookkeeping. Just like in the market model and the national product accounts, the monetary flow is measured at two different points from two different perspectives. In the case of banks, as in most businesses, the two perspectives are assets and liabilities. On the right, or liability, side, the bank lists its demand deposits or checking accounts. The bank is liable to its depositors as it is the temporary holder of its customers' money. The same funds are reflected on the asset, or left, side of the T account as the bank's assets, the outstanding loans it owns, and its reserves. The loans in a bank's portfolio can have been issued by another lending or borrowing agency and purchased by the bank in the open market. Besides auto loans and home mortgages, the bank can hold bonds issued by corporations and governments. Table 3.3 illustrates a commercial bank T account.

In order to demonstrate how the fractional reserve banking system can create money, let us use a simple T account sequence that assumes that (1) all banking transactions, involving money both deposited and lent, stay within the banking system, and that (2) all banks in the system keep 20 percent (one-fifth) of their deposits in reserve and lend out the remaining 80 percent (four-fifths)—that is, the **reserve ratio** is 20 percent.

Let us start with a new deposit to the banking system, say $100,000 to a commercial bank such as the Bank of America. This first bank in the sequence will set up a $100,000 checking account—bank money—on the liability side, and on the asset side they will record the same flow as reserves and loans. Thus, $20,000 (one-fifth) of the $100,000 will go in reserve and the remaining $80,000 will be lent out to a borrowing customer. When the bank makes a loan, it gives the borrower a check with which he or she may set up or add to a checking account either in that bank or in some other bank. Let us imagine that the borrower takes the check to another bank, say Wells Fargo, and opens an account for $80,000. Wells Fargo, following the assumptions above, will put 20 percent, or $16,000, on reserve and lend out the $64,000 remaining. This $64,000 is now available to another borrower who could put the proceeds in an account at, say, Chase Manhattan. Of this new deposit, Chase puts $12,800 on reserve (20 percent) and lends

Table 3.3 Commercial bank T account

Assets		Liabilities
Reserves		Demand deposits (checking accounts)
Loans (mortgages, bonds, etc.)		
Total	=	**Total**

out 80 percent, or $51,200. That $51,200 now goes to the next bank, say, Sumitomo. Of its new deposit it puts $10,240 in reserve and lends out $40,960. This process is illustrated in Figure 3.2.

This progression continues, with the amount getting smaller each time, until the limit is reached. You have just witnessed the process by which bank money is created. Every time a new checking account is opened in the sequence, new money is being created. In order to determine how much new bank money is created in this process, one could add up all new checking accounts, which would be a rather arduous process. Or one could use the algebraic formula for this type of progression, which provides the potential multiple of expansion. That formula is 1 over 1 – % going forward. In this case, that is $1/(1 – 4/5)$. Thus, 1 over 1/5 equals 1 times 5, or 5. The multiplier is 5. Therefore, if the assumptions are followed perfectly, a new deposit of $100,000 will create $500,000 of new bank money.

The key to this expansion is the reserve approach. Only 20 percent of all deposits are kept in the bank; the other 80 percent is lent out. It is recirculated. If one were to add up the amounts in the reserves of all the banks at the end of the sequence, it would be the original deposit, in this case $100,000. Since the reserve ratio is 20 percent, or one-fifth, another way to look at the potential expansion of bank money would be to ask, "What amount is $100,000 20 percent, or one-fifth, of?"

This potential multiple expansion of money from the fractional reserve banking system is both a facilitator and a threat to the modern economy. It is a facilitator because through the expansion of credit it helps consumers and businesses acquire a greater ability to purchase consumer or capital products. The demand for these products is what keeps the economy rolling. This available-credit machine provides the liquidity, the financial means, for lubricating the driving wheels of the economy. On the other hand, there is the risk that the banks could get carried away or act irresponsibly and create more money than the economy needs. If the money supply grows faster than the economy's transactions, overall prices will rise, and the economy will experience inflation.

Fractional Reserve Banking Expansion

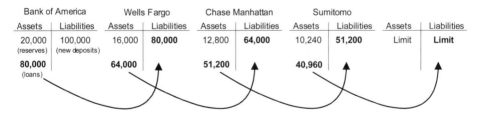

Figure 3.2 Fractional reserve banking expansion.

Inflation is the rate of increase in the overall, or average, level of prices. One possible way to generate inflation is to excessively lower the fractional reserve rate. As the fractional reserve rate is lowered, the multiple-expansion potential of the money supply is increased. For instance, if the reserve ratio were to be lowered to 10 percent, the multiplier would be 10. If it were to go down to 5 percent, the multiple-expansion potential would be 20. And if banks were to keep no reserve, the possible expansion would be infinite. Out-of-control monetary expansions have indeed happened in a number of countries. In the 1920s Germany experienced rates of inflation in the thousands of percent, so that even buying a loaf of bread involved going to the store with a wheelbarrow full of cash. After World War II many Latin American countries had similar inflationary explosions. In 2007 Zimbabwe experienced an inflationary spiral of over 20,000 percent from excessive monetary creation.

In all modern economies this potentially volatile nature of the fractional reserve banking system has engendered a public concern that has resulted in the creation of some type of regulatory system, usually involving a *central bank*. In the United States that regulatory system is called the **Federal Reserve System** or, simply, the **Fed**. In Japan it is the Bank of Japan; in Great Britain it's the Bank of England; in the Eurozone it's the European Central Bank. Not surprisingly, the term "reserve" in the Fed's formal title refers to the reserve accounts of banks. The term "federal" relates to the traditional tendency in the United States to avoid too much centralization at the national level. Thus, the 1913 Federal Reserve legislation divided the country into 12 Federal Reserve districts, each with its own Federal Reserve Bank. However, there is a national board of governors.

The Board of Governors of the Federal Reserve System is appointed by the president of the United States with the consent of the U.S. Senate. There are seven Governors, each of whom serves a 14-year term. The Chair of the Board is not elected by the other Governors but is also appointed by the president for a four-year term with the consent of the Senate. The Fed is a largely independent regulatory body with immense influence on the world's political economy. Not all central banks in the world are as politically independent as the Fed. However, the European Central Bank (ECB) does follow the independence pattern. Its Governing Council includes six public members with eight-year terms along with the presidents of all the Eurozone member countries' central banks (15 in 2008). Each Governing Council member has one vote. The Fed's Board of Governors and the Governing Council of the ECB, as well as comparable groups in other countries, are responsible for monetary policy (Board of Governors, *The Federal Reserve System*; Hosli, *The Euro*).

The 12 individual Federal Reserve Banks are actually owned by the member commercial banks as shareholders. This mixture of private ownership and public policy responsibility has resulted in some observers calling the Fed a "quasi-public institution." The Federal Reserve Banks serve many functions. They:

1   assist in the clearing of checks between banks;

2   hold the reserve accounts of member banks and other depository institutions;

3   manage an account for the U.S. Treasury;

4   issue bank notes (all U.S paper currency is in the form of Federal Reserve Notes);

5   carry out the monetary policy promulgated by the Board of Governors and its Open Market Committee;

6   inspect member banks to make sure that they are operating prudently and legally; and

7   carry out important research on the economy.

The same T account picture that we used above for commercial banks also works for the Federal Reserve Banks—the banks' banks. Table 3.4 describes the T account.

The Board of Governors of the Federal Reserve System is responsible for the nation's **monetary policy.** The primary objective of monetary policy is the maintenance of stability in the price level. The Governors are especially concerned with keeping inflation to a minimum. Other central banks, such as the ECB, also have price-level stability as their primary assigned policy objective. The Fed has additional, secondary objectives that are spelled out in its governing legislation. The Governors must attend to stability in the economy, defined as maximum employment and moderate long-term interest rates. They also need to consider the implications of any policy decisions for the value of the U.S. dollar vis-à-vis other currencies (Board of Governors, *The Federal Reserve System*).

Table 3.5 summarizes the tools of intervention used by the Fed, the variables affected by them, and the outcomes they are intended to achieve.

Table 3.4 Federal Reserve Banks' T account

Assets		Liabilities
Loan portfolio (mostly U.S. Treasury securities)		Reserve accounts (commercial banks and other depository institutions)
Gold		Federal Reserve bank notes
Foreign exchange		U.S. Treasury account
Total	=	**Total**

Table 3.5 Instruments of monetary policy

Tools of the Fed	Major variables affected	Outcomes pursued
Reserve ratio	Money supply	Price-level stability
Federal funds rate	Short-term interest rate	Price-level, economic, and foreign exchange stability
Open market operations (buying and selling U.S. securities)	Interest rates, money supply, credit availability and exchange rates	(same as Federal funds rate)
Discount window	Bank liquidity	Bank and economic stability
Margin rates on stock purchases	Bank exposure and stock prices	(same as Discount window)

The whole approach of monetary policy in mostly market-run systems is to influence the market, but not to control it. In other words, the Fed does not set prices, as it would if it its tools included wage and price controls, but indirectly influences price determination through actions that affect supply and demand in the market.

Let us explain what each of the tools is and how it works. As explained in the discussion of the fractional reserve banking system, the percentage of deposits that banks keep on reserve determines how much money they can create, that is, the multiple-expansion potential. Since bank money is a major component of the money supply, and money supply in reference to the transactions in the economy determines the level of prices, the authority to set the **reserve ratio** gives the Fed a basic control over the money supply and the level of prices. This set of relationships seems self-evident, but it is actually based on the *quantity theory of money*, which is the rationale for believing in the effectiveness of monetary policy. This theory is, in turn, based on the market conception of how an economy works. The theory states that the price level in the economy will be determined by the supply of money in reference to the demand for it. If the supply is growing faster than the transactions demand, prices will tend to increase as more money chases proportionately fewer products. According to this theory, that's how inflation occurs.

Inflation is considered undesirable because it destabilizes business decisions dependent on future expectations. Furthermore, inflation decreases the value of the currency, making creditors and people on fixed or relatively fixed incomes unhappy as the purchasing value of their incomes declines. The policy solution is to decrease the potential increase in the money supply. Raising the reserve ratio will have exactly that effect. For example, raising the ratio from 10 to 20 percent would lower the multiple-expansion potential in bank money from ten times to five times the deposits. Of course, the actual percentage changes are much smaller in magnitude. The ratio imposed on large-scale depository institutions is usually around 10 percent. In fact, the reserve ratio is seldom changed, as moving it to a different level has major long-term repercussions. In more recent legislation the Fed has been given broader jurisdiction than just member commercial banks, so that all depository institutions, such as savings and loan associations and credit unions that can also create money, must have their reserves monitored by the Fed. The Fed pays close attention to the reserve balances, and it uses that information in implementing its responsibilities (Board of Governors, *The Federal Reserve System*).

The second tool or instrument of monetary policy is setting the **federal funds rate**. It is probably the most important and most prominent of the monetary policy tools utilized by the Fed. The federal funds rate is an overnight interest rate. An important and similar rate exists in the United Kingdom, called the LIBOR (London Inter-Bank Offer Rate), although this is a three-month rate. The designation "federal" in "federal funds rate" comes from the fact that short-term borrowing and lending often involves funds that are deposited as reserves in the Federal Reserve Banks. The Fed actually sets a "target rate" and then uses the tools available to it to nudge the market rate to the preferred rate. When the Fed perceives an unacceptable inflationary move in the economy, it raises the federal funds rate. When the economy is flat or potentially deflationary, the Fed lowers the federal funds rate. The Fed countered the decline in the American economy after the terrorist attacks of September 11, 2001, with a series of reductions in the federal funds rate, bringing it down from 5 to 1 percent (Board of Governors, *The Federal Reserve System*).

The Fed's decision on the federal funds target rate is actually made by the *Federal Open Market Committee* (FOMC). The FOMC is composed of the Board of Governors and five presidents of Federal Reserve Banks. One of the five Bank presidents is always from the New York District Bank, and the other four rotate among the remaining eleven districts. The bimonthly meetings of the FOMC are followed very closely by members of the financial community. They even parse the language of FOMC press releases very carefully to determine the likely future behavior of the Committee.

Though the Fed's focus is on the short-term interest rate market, it expects that changes in this market will diffuse throughout the entire interest rate structure. Interest rates are very important to the economy because they have a pervasive impact on borrowing and spending decisions, especially by businesses, but also by consumers. Mortgage interest rates, for instance, have a significant effect on home purchase decisions. The more borrowing there is in the financial or banking system, the more bank money is being created. And the more money that is created, the greater the inflationary potential becomes. Furthermore, stock prices always take into account current and anticipated interest rates. Higher interest rates are expected to lower the level of economic activity and the rate of profit, whereas lower interest rates are expected to have the opposite effect.

Generally speaking, therefore, there is an inverse relationship between interest rates and stock prices.

The structure of interest rates, mentioned above, is depicted in Figure 3.3. Normally, the lowest interest rate would be the federal funds rate, and they go up the ladder in the order presented. In recent U.S. experience the interest rate ladder starts at around 3 percent and then ascends to 30 percent or higher. Long-term rates are usually higher than short-term rates because they need to cover the possible degradation of purchasing power from inflation, the longer period of consumption denial, and the greater risk involved. However, it does not always work that way. In mid-2007, for instance, the federal funds rate was higher than the market rate of return (the effective interest rate) on a ten-year U.S. Treasury Bond.

The federal funds rate becomes especially pertinent when commercial banks borrow or lend overnight from each others' reserve accounts in the Federal Reserve Banks. The borrowing is usually done by banks with shortages in their reserve accounts and the lending by banks with excess amounts in their reserve accounts. Banks with excess reserves are pleased to lend them to banks with shortages, because commercial banks do not earn any interest from the Fed on the funds they have to keep on reserve.

As noted earlier, interest rates are important internationally as well as domestically. Foreign exchange assets tend to move to those countries having the highest real interest rates. *Real interest rates* are the inflation-discounted rates. To determine the real interest rate, take the actual interest rate that can be earned (known as the "nominal rate") and subtract the inflation rate. For example, if the nominal interest rate is 15 percent and inflation is 10 percent, the real interest rate is 5 percent. It is quite possible to have a negative real interest rate. A negative rate would please

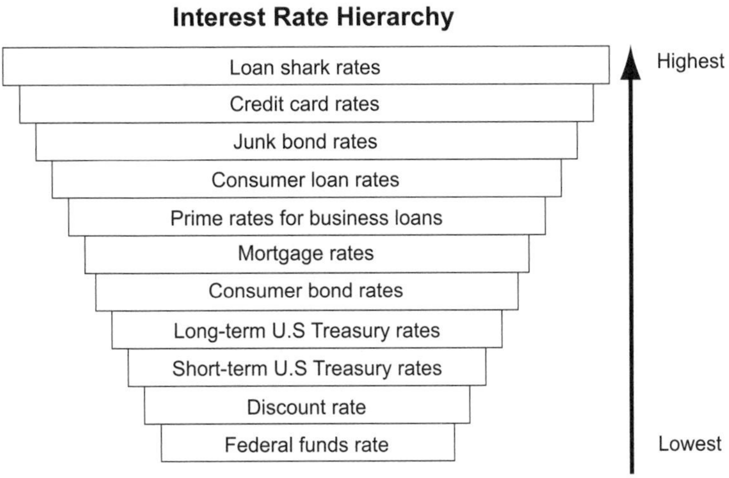

Interest Rate Hierarchy

Figure 3.3 Typical hierarchy of interest rates.

the borrower, but not the lender, who, over the course of the loan, would actually be losing real monetary value.

When a country has a relatively high real interest rate, the demand for financial assets denominated in its currency increases and the value of the currency most likely increases. It is simply a matter of supply and demand. If the currency significantly increases in value, exports become more expensive and imports become cheaper. The trade balance is negatively affected and may even move into deficit. When monetary authorities, such as the Fed, raise interest rates in order to fight inflation, they need to be aware of the potential impact on foreign exchange values. An expensive currency means fewer jobs and lower business revenue in export industries. If the decline in export sales are widespread, it can have a very negative effect on the entire economy. In order to maintain or achieve a desired foreign exchange rate, some central banks, such as Japan's, intervene in the foreign exchange market. However, neither the Fed nor the European Central Bank follows a policy of intervening in foreign exchange markets. Their focus is on domestic policy, where they do intervene in money markets.

The Fed intervenes in domestic money markets through **open market operations**. Although the FOMC has legal authority to buy and sell various types of debt securities as well as equities (stocks) in the private open market, for decades it has largely limited its market interventions to the buying or selling of U.S. Treasury debt securities. Except for special issues such as U.S. Savings Bonds for individuals, U.S. Treasury securities are transferable—that is, they can be bought and sold in the market. Since they are marketable, their prices go up and down according to changes in supply and demand. As the price fluctuates, the yield, or effective interest rate, also fluctuates, as explained in Chapter 2. There is an inverse relationship between the price of the security and its effective interest yield.

The Fed plainly states that "Open market operations are conducted to align the supply of balances at the Federal Reserve with demand for those balances at the target rate set by the FOMC" (Board of Governors, *The Federal Reserve System*, p. 33). The operations are conducted daily, usually in the over-the-counter New York market. Purchases of securities increase the balances in the reserve accounts whereas sales or redemptions lower the balances. The reserve balances are actually bigger than the reserve ratio would suggest because the depository institutions also keep in the Federal Reserve Banks contractual clearing balances. The amounts in these balances can be even bigger than the amounts in the basic reserve accounts. They are used to assist in the clearing process between banks, and they do earn credits that can be used to pay for the services of the Federal Reserve Banks.

At the **discount window** the Fed lends to depository institutions that have temporary shortages in their reserve balances and are not able to acquire the funds in any other way. The interest rate, called the **discount rate**, is usually one percentage point above the federal funds rate. Nearly all the central banks of the world have a similar discount window. Commercial banks and other depository organizations make use of these central bank loans because there are heavy fines for not maintaining the required or contractual reserve balances. On the other hand, the Fed's discount window has not been used very often in recent years, as banks were reluctant to openly admit their need to borrow. That changed somewhat in 2007–2008 when the Fed aggressively used the discount window to facilitate the injection of liquidity into weak credit markets. Credit markets were in trouble because of the crisis in the subprime mortgage sector. The Fed lowered the discount rate several times and strongly encouraged banks, both commercial and investment, to take advantage of the discount window for loans of up to three months (Guha, in *Financial Times*).

Finally, the Fed has another regulatory instrument available to it: the ability to set the **margin**, or the cash down payment percentage, on the purchase of stocks. This instrument was added to the Fed's arsenal after the disastrous connection between the stock market crash of 1929–1930 and the failure of many banks. In the 1920s when it was believed that stock values would keep going up forever, many banks made loans for the purchase of stocks with no money down. The only collateral was the stocks themselves. A provision in the loan contracts stipulated that if the stock value dropped below a certain percentage of the purchase price, the loan was called in for payment. The holders of the loans would then have to sell the stocks, as these would be the only assets available to them. The outcome of this arrangement is probably immediately evident. When the unexpected happened, namely, that all stocks started losing value precipitously, all of these loan contracts were triggered. That initiated another round of widespread selling, which sent stock prices plummeting even further down. These stock-loans then became uncollectible for the banks, and, consequently, many of the banks failed. Today, if the Fed perceives a state of "irrational exuberance" in the stock market, it can raise the percentage that borrowers must put down in cash when they use loans for the acquisition of stock. Raising the margin in these circumstances is an effort to protect both the lender and borrower from reckless behavior, and in the process protect the economy from financial deterioration. Ironically, a loan situation similar to the Great Depression has occurred in 2006–2008 with subprime home mortgages, rather than stocks, serving as collateral. A similar set of regulatory controls is being recommended.

For much of U.S. history, monetary policy was conducted without paying too much attention to the international repercussions. After the experience of the early 1980s, that narrowness of focus became less likely. One could make a plausible case that U.S. monetary policy was one of the major causes of the **Third World debt crisis** in that period. The situation unfolded as follows. In the late 1970s the United States developed a serious inflation problem. Both political parties labeled this double-digit yearly increase in prices as "Public Enemy #1." As a part of his strategy to deal with this problem, President Carter appointed Paul Volcker, a tough inflation-fighter, as Chair of the Federal Reserve's Board of Governors. Volcker set out to use all of the instruments of the Fed to get inflation under control. The first noticeable impact was a growing recession in the United States, as businesses were discouraged by very high real interest rates from borrowing and investing. The international consequence of the U.S. recession was a reduction in imports, especially from Latin America. The second impact of the exceptionally high U.S. real interest rates was the inflow of "hot money" from all over the world. As a consequence, the U.S. dollar value rose significantly against other currencies. Both of these developments had disastrous consequences for many Third World countries, especially in Latin America. Third World countries had borrowed heavily in the late 1970s as interest rates were very low, even negative in real terms, thanks to the flood of petrodollars. However, their borrowing had to be in hard currencies, especially the dollar, and at variable rates tied to the dollar market. As U.S. monetary policy dramatically increased U.S. interest rates and then the value of the dollar, previously cheap debt now became very expensive. At the same time the recessionary U.S. economy bought less of the indebted countries' export products. Yet it was the revenue from these export products that these countries were depending upon for the funds with which to pay their international debt. Consequently, the debt service obligations (required yearly payments) of many Third World countries grew far beyond their means. A crisis ensued, starting with Mexico. In order to prevent major defaults, the major lending countries, such as the United States, and international financial organizations, such as the International Monetary Fund, had to come up with refinancing solutions to alleviate the immediate emergency. The decade of the 1980s in Latin America is known as the "lost decade," because most countries in the region were forced to spend their resources fulfilling their inflated debt obligations rather than growing their economies. Even though it is not appropriate to blame the entire Third World debt crisis on U.S. monetary policy, even Paul Volcker admitted later that it played a major role. The Fed was so focused on fighting domestic inflation that it paid insufficient attention to the significant international ramifications.

The strategy of monetary policy relies on markets responding appropriately to the indirect interventions of policy-makers. It presumes that, given some not-too-intrusive, indirect interventions, markets will adjust and facilitate the resolution of whatever problems are occurring. Monetary policy relies on the self-regulating quality of markets. The economic philosophy that relies heavily on monetary policy to achieve stability and better market outcomes is called **monetarism**. Its major proponent is the late Nobel laureate Milton Friedman. He even cautioned the Fed against becoming too active in trying to influence the economy. In most instances, Friedman argued, "the market knows best." The treaty that established the European System of Central Banks sets forth its market-oriented philosophy in very straightforward language: "The ESCB shall act in accordance with the principle of an open market economy with free competition, favoring an efficient allocation of resources" (Hosli, *The Euro*, p. 56). The European Central Bank is not allowed to financially assist member governments in raising funds for their budgetary needs. In other words, there should be no direct connection between the monetary realm and the fiscal realm. The Fed is not similarly restricted, as will be discussed in the next section on fiscal policy.

THE KEYNESIAN REVISION AND FISCAL POLICY

John Maynard Keynes (1883–1946), the famous English economist, did not agree with Milton Friedman. Keynes believed that speculators could undermine the efficiency of financial markets, and that markets did not always achieve optimum equilibria. The periodic downturns in market economies demonstrated to him that something was amiss. Furthermore, he believed that monetary policy was not always effective in achieving its objectives. Keynes presented his views in his 1936 treatise, *The General Theory of Employment, Interest and Money.* Since at that time both the United States and the United Kingdom were deep in the Great Depression, the greatest relevance of Keynes's work was his analysis of how the economy had collapsed and what to do about it.

JOHN MAYNARD KEYNES
1883–1946
British economist and key participant at the 1944 Bretton Woods Conference. Inventor of macroeconomics and promoter of government intervention to compensate for market failures such as depressions. His major work was *The General Theory of Employment, Interest and Money* (1936).

Keynes argued that the conventional market model was inherently flawed. He took aim at the weakest link in the logical chain that culminated in the necessity of full employment. That link was the role of the interest rate, the price of money, in bringing savers and investors together in a full-utilization equilibrium. As explained in Chapter 2, the conventional market model presumes that the supply of savings, or that part of production capacity not used for consumption, will be fully utilized or demanded by managers of productive organizations for capital investment.

If production managers had less of a need to expand their firms or increase their productive efficiency, they would lower their demands in the savings market, which would result in a lower price for savings. According to the market model, that lower price, a lower interest rate, would discourage savers from providing the same supply as before. Savers would then cut back enough to compensate for the decline in demand, and no productive capacity would go unused. In other words, the interest rate would mediate between savers and investors, clearing the market, and assuring full utilization of all resources. Keynes did not believe that the market actually worked that way.

Keynes argued that the interest rate played no such role. He contended that the interest rate was not the main motivator for either saving or investing. Based on empirical evidence, Keynes believed that "saving is a function of income," not the interest rate. It should be evident that poor people cannot afford to save. Wealthy people save because they cannot spend all the income they receive. Thus, Keynes observed, the more skewed the distribution of income toward the rich end, the more saving there will be, almost regardless of the interest rate. On the other hand, businesses are not primarily motivated to invest by changes in the interest rate. What drives investment decisions is anticipated profit. If businesses do not expect any forthcoming profitable sales, they will not invest, no matter how low the interest rate. In the midst of a major depression in the economy, no rational business person will make any major capital investments. The role of the interest rate, as the special cost of investment, is to set the floor for sensible investment decisions. That is, it makes no sense to make a capital investment if the businessperson believes that the rate of return will be less than the cost of borrowing. But, to reiterate, even if the interest rate is lowered to zero, private decision-makers will not invest if they perceive no profitable investment opportunities. That is why Keynes did not believe that monetary policy could be effective in a depressed economy.

Keynes pointed out that as a consequence of this "disconnect" between the motivations for saving and investment, the amounts of each that people would like to make could diverge substantially. Income recipients might like to save much more than investors need, but since neither are paying that much attention to the interest rate, it will not serve to bring these decisions closer together. Thus a gap could open up between what people would like to save and what investors believe they need to pursue their perceived opportunities for profit. However, in a dynamic economy that gap cannot persist. The economy will close the gap by lowering the income and the output until a new equilibrium is reached. If people are withdrawing more demand for productive capacity (saving) than investors want, a part of the economy's productive capacity (land, labor, and capital) will cease to be used. These unused or idled resources will not be paid. Thus the income that they previously received will not be generated. Therefore, the total income of the economy will be less than what could have been achieved if the economy's full productive capacity were demanded (Heilbroner, *The Worldly Philosophers*).

This downward fall of the total income will not stop until the amount that people want to save equals the amount that investors want spend on capital products. The key identity that needs to be achieved for the economy to reach equilibrium and not decline further is the equality of saving (demand removed) and investment (demand replaced). That equilibrium, however, may be far below full employment. As long as none of the key players (consumers, savers, and investors) change their behavior, the economy will stay stuck at that point. Keynes called it the "**low-level equilibrium trap**." He believed that he had provided an explanation of how a capitalistic market economy falls into a depressed state. Simply put, the explanation is excess saving or inadequate investment. According to Keynes, full employment is not the necessary outcome of the market. Table 3.6 demonstrates through a hypothetical case how this process works.

The first column represents different levels of national income in billions of dollars (set at $30 billion intervals.) The next two columns make assumptions about the amount of consumption spending and saving that people wish to engage in at different levels of income. The column on investment stays at $10 billion throughout, as it is assumed that investors only perceive $10 billion worth of profitable investment opportunities available to them. The fifth column shows the income consequences of the prior set of decisions on consumption, saving, and investment. People receive income for making consumption products (goods and services) and capital investment products. Thus in the first row people receive $220 billion for making consumption products and $10 billion for making capital products, for a total of $230 billion. Income has declined by $30 billion because people wished to save that much more than investors needed. Income will continue to decline until what people wish to save equals what investors want to invest. In this table that level of income, where equilibrium is reached, is $170 billion.

Table 3.6 Demonstration of Keynes's "low-level equilibrium trap"

Starting income	Consumption	Saving	Investment	Ending income	Direction
260	220	40	10	230	↓
230	200	30	10	210	↓
200	180	20	10	190	↓
170	160	10	10	170	stable
140	140	0	10	150	↑
110	120	−10	10	130	↑

Keynes deduced that capitalistic market economies go into **depression**—that is, serious declines in income, production, and employment—when there is not enough demand to keep the economies' productive (supply) capacity fully utilized. If no major actors change their behavior, stagnation will prevail. Economies experience boom periods when investors want to invest more than savers are currently saving. Their increased demand, which is financed essentially by bank borrowing, drives the economy up, as can also be seen in Table 3.6. In fact, in boom periods investors tend to get overenthusiastic and initiate more capital spending than a prudent analysis of actual profitable sales would suggest. That leads to more capacity than demand warrants. From Keynes's perspective that is exactly what happened in the 1920s. The 1920s was the first real consumer-product decade of the modern age. It was the age of mass-produced automobiles, radios, refrigerators, and toasters. When investors realized they had overdone it, they drastically cut back on investment. In the meantime, also in the 1920s, income inequality increased dramatically. In 1920, after World War I, the top 5 percent of income recipients in the United States accounted for 20 percent of the national income. By 1930 they had 33 percent. It was the "perfect setting" for a collapse of the economy due to excess saving and inadequate investment. Therefore, the stock market crash in 1929 was not the primary cause of the depression but the reflector of this more basic illness in the economy (Heilbroner, *The Making of Economic Society*).

Keynes not only came up with an analysis of what caused the ups and downs in capitalist economies, or what has been called the business cycle, but also came up with a solution. In doing so, he had to confront a strong moral and ideological belief that contradicted his solution. Until Keynes it was believed in Anglo-American capitalist circles that governments should have no role in managing the economy. The market was promoted as the decision-making mechanism of choice. After all, the market process resulted in the optimum allocation of resources and the full utilization of all resources—full employment. Government was supposed to have a neutral effect on the economy. It should not do anything that would interfere with the supply–demand relationships. That meant that the government's budget, its revenue and expenditures, should be balanced. Revenues come from taxation, which removes some ability to demand products from consumers and productive organizations. But government expenditures return that demand back into the economy. If the budget is balanced, then the overall impact on total demand should be neutral. Historically, however, governments have shown a proclivity to spend more than their revenues—sometimes considerably more—and their injection of demand beyond the ability of the economy to supply it have created serious inflation problems. Thus the moral injunction of the **balanced budget** was not only consistent with market reasoning, it also served as a disciplinary rule for potentially irresponsible governments. Both Herbert Hoover and

Franklin Delano Roosevelt, the major-party presidential candidates in the midst of the Great Depression in 1932, vowed never to break the sacred trust of the balanced budget.

Keynes's willingness to think "out of the box" showed his intellectual courage and creative genius. As a consequence he was called several unflattering names. His radical solution was for the government to have an *unbalanced budget*. He reasoned that the problem of the depressed economy was insufficient demand to fill the savings gap. As long as consumers, savers, and investors did not change their behavior, the only source for an injection of new demand in the economy was the government. And the only way that the government could do that was by spending more than it took in. In other words, the national government had to put more demand into the economy than it took out. The budget *had* to run a deficit. The sacred principle of the balanced budget had to be discarded if the economy were to be brought out of the low-level equilibrium trap. Keynes demonstrated that the market was not all that self-correcting. On occasion the invisible hand needs an assist from the government. Keynes provided a rationale for government intervention in the economy, for which the true believers in the market have never quite forgiven him (Yergin and Stanislaw, *The Commanding Heights*).

Keynes even proposed a means of determining how large the deficit needs to be in order to bring the economy back to full employment. He pointed out that the deficit does not need to be as big as the gap between the depressed level of national income and the full employment level. The reason for this fact is the existence of the **multiplier effect**. Deficit spending injects new demand and income into the economy. The first people to receive that income will spend most of it, thus making it income for someone else, who in turn spends it, and so on. The same type of progressive series that occurs in the expansion process within the fractional reserve banking system is put into play. Only this time, instead of the percentage in reserve determining the extent of the multiplication, it is the percentage set aside for saving. Keynes labeled the percentages that people spent and saved of their new income their "marginal propensities to spend and save" (Heilbroner, *Understanding Macro-economics*).

Table 3.6 is constructed with the assumption that people spend two-thirds of their additional income and save one-third. For instance, if the full employment level is $230 billion while the economy is stuck at $170 billion, the income gap to be closed is $60 billion. The government deficit needs to be large enough to generate that amount. If the deficit is much smaller than the required amount, full employment will not be achieved. On the other hand, if the deficit is larger than the required amount, demand will exceed supply, and the economy will experience inflation. Since the assumed multiplier in the table is 3, the deficit needs to be $20 billion. On the $230 billion line, the provision of $20 billion of government deficit spending initially plays the same role as private investment, putting to work the previously unused saving. The $30 billion of saving is now matched by $30 billion of investment, $20 billion from the government and $10 billion from the private sector. The equilibrium of the economy, where saving equals investment, is now at full employment. Even though the initial income impact of government deficit–generated demand is the same as private investment, the long-term effect can be different if the government expenditures are of a make-work variety, like raking leaves, rather than a long-term capital investment variety, like building roads or dams. Obviously, from the perspective of long-term growth of the economy, efficiency-enhancing investment expenditures are much better.

A similar point can be made about the multiplier effect of export earnings. If they exceed import expenditures, they will have a net positive effect on demand in the economy. However, their long-term impact will depend on the quality of the economic activity responsible for the export earnings. Revenue from the sale of commodities such as oil, for instance, does not by itself add to the productive capacity of the economy. On the other hand, revenue from capital investment, whether physical (capital goods) or human (capital services), does have a long-term positive impact on economic growth. There are two major current examples of these different long-term growth strategies: China has been emphasizing the physical capital investment strategy (manufacturing) for exports, whereas India has been emphasizing the human capital investment strategy (information technology).

Even though Keynes made a special trip to Washington to persuade President Roosevelt of his views, he was not able to convince the president of the correctness of his analysis and its deficit spending solution. Roosevelt did, however, support very limited deficit spending with the hope that it would encourage private businesses to start investing again. It didn't work. In fact, in the late 1930s Roosevelt approved a budget that nearly eliminated the limited deficit because of the revenue from the new Social Security tax. The economy responded exactly as Keynes would have predicted, by contracting. But the event that really proved Keynes was right was U.S. involvement in World War II in the 1940s. When there is a war to fight, almost no one cares about balanced budgets and the size of the deficit. With huge government deficits and massive amounts of new demand being injected into the economy, the United States not only climbed out of the depression, it started experiencing the usual consequence of more demand than its economy could provide: inflation. The problem was no longer inadequate demand, but too much demand. The solution was government intervention in the form of price controls and rationing (Heilbroner, *The Making of Economic Society*).

Whenever government spending exceeds revenue, the government must find a way to finance the deficit spending. The most responsible way is to borrow in the financial markets. The irresponsible way is to just order the central bank to create the money. In essence the government, specifically the Treasury Department in the United States, issues and sells bonds in the open market. The government is then committed to repay the face value upon maturity and interest every year to the bondholders. When people buy U.S Treasury Bonds, they dedicate some of their saving to assisting the government cover its overexpenditure. When this deficit spending on a large scale first began during World War II, the major bond purchasers were U.S. citizens, businesses, and even other government agencies such as the Federal Reserve Banks. Thus, in effect, U.S. citizens owed the debt to each other.

The experience of World War II convinced most economists and policy-makers that Keynes was right. Keynes had invented a new type of economics: **macroeconomics.** Macroeconomics deals with the economy-wide measures of performance: total production, total income, total employment, total saving and investment, and the price level. The national income and product accounts became the means of keeping data on these variables. Keynes had also invented a new type of public policy. **Fiscal policy** was no longer just a matter of how much to spend on different programs and what taxes to use in raising revenue. Now it was also a matter of using the budget to manage the economy so as to reduce the volatility of the business cycle inherent in capitalism. Managing the economy meant ensuring the right amount of demand in reference to the supply capacity. Because of Keynes's emphasis on the demand side of the equation, his approach has often been called **demand-side economics**. The federal government's responsibility to seek economic stability, especially to pursue "maximum employment," was affirmed in the Employment Act of 1946, just ten years after the publication of Keynes's *General Theory*. The Act also established the Council of Economic Advisers and committed the president to provide an annual economic report to the Congress (Galbraith, *Economics in Perspective*).

The first U.S. president to explicitly identify himself as a Keynesian was John F. Kennedy, a Democrat, in the early 1960s. Ten years later, President Richard Nixon, a Republican, said, "We are all Keynesians now." However, just ten years after that, President Reagan, in a return to the conventional free market approach, rejected Keynesianism, at least ideologically, and called for a constitutional amendment requiring a balanced budget. In his belief in the superiority of the free market approach, Reagan was joined by Prime Minister Margaret Thatcher in the United Kingdom and other world leaders in the 1980s (Yergin and Stanislaw, *The Commanding Heights*).

Keynesianism has run into two political problems. The first is the somewhat unfair criticism by advocates of the free market approach that labels all excessive and inept government forays into the economy as "Keynesianism." It's true that Keynes argued that government had an important role to play in a healthy economy, but he also believed in the efficacy of markets in most circumstances. The second problem involves the political difficulties in implementing Keynesian fiscal policy. Keynes called for a **compensatory fiscal policy**—deficits when the economy is depressed and surpluses when the economy is overheated. The debt incurred during the deficit years could be paid off by the surpluses collected during the boom years. However, generating surpluses sometimes meant raising taxes, a politically difficult task. Consequently, from the end of World War II to the Clinton administration in the late 1990s, most federal budgets were in deficit. After surpluses appeared in the Clinton years, the next Republican administration found the political temptation to lower taxes overwhelming, and deficits reappeared.

Some analytical distinctions are important to keep in mind. A **deficit** occurs when expenditures exceed revenues in a particular fiscal year. As deficits occur year after year they become part of the accumulated debt. **Debt,** therefore, is the summation of the unpaid borrowing liabilities. At present the total debt of the U.S. government exceeds $9 trillion. Because the 2007–2008 federal budget is running a deficit, it will add about $400 billion to that debt.

It is important not to confuse federal or national government budget deficits and debt with that other deficit and debt category, the international current account. As previously explained, a country experiences a current account deficit when its payments for goods and services to other countries exceed the payments from those countries. As these deficits accumulate, the country's overseas debt, both public and private, adds up. Ongoing deficits in the U.S. international current accounts have resulted in a debt to foreigners in other countries of over $4 trillion. That makes the United States the world's biggest international debtor. The situation does get a little confusing as some of the debt owed to foreigners is the debt of the U.S. government. In fact, some argue that national government deficits are a major cause of deficits in the international current accounts. That is especially the case for those countries that like the United States have virtually no domestic saving.

Lord Keynes was not only the father of modern fiscal policy, he was also the intellectual parent of the major international financial organizations that were established after World War II. Keynes had written extensively on the form these organizations should take, and he represented Great Britain at the 1944 *Bretton Woods Conference* where they were actually created. The purpose of the meeting was to design the international financial architecture that would provide order and stability in the international economy after the war was over. Two organizations were proposed and created: the *International Monetary Fund* (IMF) and the International Bank for Reconstruction and Development (IBRD, or *World Bank*). The IMF was discussed earlier in this chapter. The purpose of the

World Bank is to provide needed capital investment funds, initially for countries devastated by the war and thereafter for poor countries in need of economic development. Both organizations are located in Washington, D.C. Even though they are affiliated with the United Nations, the decision-making procedures of these institutions are not based on a one-country, one-vote basis. Voting is weighted by the percentage of contribution that a country makes to the institution's funding. More than 60 years after the founding of the IMF and the World Bank, the United States still accounts for approximately 17 percent of the funding and thus has 17 percent of the votes. Since major policy decisions require a supermajority of 85 percent, the United States effectively still has a veto. There is a current effort to change that situation, but it is uncertain how long it will take.

At the end of the Bretton Woods Conference Keynes was given a standing ovation, but he was disappointed with some of the meeting's results. For example, Keynes had recommended the creation of a truly international currency, not connected to any national currency, but the United States insisted on having its dollar become the international currency. Yet, despite some deficiencies in structure and implementation, the IMF and the World Bank did successfully facilitate, for several decades after World War II, many of the Keynesian economic objectives, such as global economic development. In fact, the capitalistic world economy did so well after World War II, mainly by following his prescriptions, that Keynes was called by some the "savior" of capitalism.

GLOBAL CONNECTIONS

Keynes provided a framework that enables us to understand the functioning interrelationships between the major economic variables, at both the national and global levels. Figure 3.4 portrays how the major macroeconomic variables that have been discussed in this chapter relate to each other. The saving activity is central, because it provides the means for supporting capital investment in the private sector, the deficits in government budgets, and deficits in international flows as measured by current accounts. The more the world globalizes, the more likely it is that these flows involve large amounts across national boundaries. The activity in the private, government, and foreign sectors determine the level of production as measured in the national product accounts. Decisions in these realms are affected by the prevailing interest rates, which are determined in the bond markets, which in turn are influenced by monetary policy. Foreign exchange ratios are affected by interest rates, but also by the balance of payments situation and the overall state of the economies. In a complex way, everything affects everything else. That includes the level of prices, which is an issue of stability for both national economies and

Global Connections

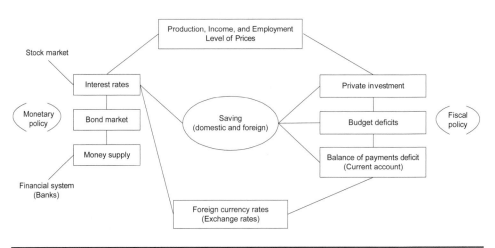

Figure 3.4 Global connections (macroeconomic variables).

the global economy. All of the other variables, through the mediation of markets, as modified by government policy, determine the level of prices.

If the price of a major world commodity, such as oil, goes up, it affects everything else. In fact, in just a few years the price of oil has gone from $10 a barrel to over $100 a barrel. Since the United States imports more than half of the oil it consumes, the higher price of oil contributes to the deficit in the U.S. current account balance. In 2007 more than two-thirds of the savings accumulated by countries with surpluses were being absorbed by the United States to finance its current account deficit. Big surplus countries include Saudi Arabia, China, and Japan. If for some reason they decided to stop buying and holding U.S. debt (mostly U.S. Treasury securities), the price of the securities would drop, the rates of interest would climb, and the value of the dollar would fall. The United States would undoubtedly experience a severe recession and an accompanying decline in its standard of living. Everything is connected to everything else.

The market world view holds that the best way to understand these complex interactions is by understanding the functioning of markets. And that understanding is based in the underlying market model. Those who believe that the market is the superior way to organize an economy strongly promote the implementation of certain policies that are consistent with market decision-making. Policies they support include free trade, flexible exchange rates, full capital mobility across borders, limited government intervention, deregulation, privatization, non-existence of public enterprises, weakening of unions, competition, elimination of subsidies, and so on. During the 1980s and into the 1990s, both the IMF and the World Bank aggressively pushed these policies on all the recipients of their loans, essentially the Third World countries. The market-friendly conditions they placed on loans were known as *structural adjustment programs* (SAPs). As a package these policies were labeled the *Washington Consensus* because the impetus came from the United States, which effectively controlled the Washington-based IMF and World Bank during that period. The critics of these programs called them neoliberalism or market fundamentalism. The next chapter will discuss these criticisms and an alternative model for understanding how the global political economy works.

REVIEW QUESTIONS

1 How does the accounting system of the national product and income accounts reflect the structure of the market model?

2 Explain why National Income is a smaller figure than Gross Domestic Product (GDP).

3 Explain the difference between absolute and comparative advantage as reasons for countries trading with one another.

4 What are the conditions that David Ricardo specified as necessary in order for comparative advantage to result in mutual economic benefit for the countries engaged in trade with one another? Which one of those conditions is not only systematically violated in current flows between countries, but also now considered by many free market supporters as actually part of free trade?

5 Present the objectives and scope of the World Trade Organization (WTO).

6 What is the composition of the current account in the balance of payments, and why is it the most important figure?

7 What composes the capital account, and why does its net total equal the net total of the current account?

8 Discuss the processes by which the ratios between different national currencies are established.

9 What are foreign exchange reserves, and why does the United States have a privileged position in that financial arena?

10 What is the problem that the use of PPP is trying to resolve, and why is it not a perfect solution?

11 What are the advantages and disadvantages of the gold standard in the international trade and financial arena?

12 What role was the International Monetary Fund (IMF) designed to play in the international economy?

13 How does knowledge of the market system help in understanding trade and payments between countries?

14 Explain how a fractional reserve banking system can "create" or "destroy" money.

15 Explain what is meant by price stability and why central banks around the world have it as their primary concern.

16 Explain how the Board of Governors of the U.S. Federal Reserve System uses the reserve ratio, the federal funds rate, and open market operations to achieve its monetary policy objectives.

17 By using the Third World debt crisis as an example, discuss the connection between domestic monetary policy and the global political economy.

18 Discuss the relationship between monetary policy and a market economy.

19 Explain how the "disconnect" between saving and investment observed by Keynes could lead to a "low-level equilibrium trap" for an economy.

20 Explain how Keynes's proposed "compensatory fiscal policy" was intended to alleviate this problem.

21 Discuss how the IMF and the IBRD, at least in their first two decades, were a reflection of Keynesian philosophy.

22 Using the U.S current accounts deficit as an example, describe how the global macroeconomic variables are interconnected.

BIBLIOGRAPHY

Board of Governors, *The Federal Reserve System: Purpose and Functions*, 9th edn. (Federal Reserve System: Washington, D.C.) 2005.

Council of Economic Advisers, *Economic Report of the President* (U.S. Superintendent of Documents: Washington, D.C.) 2007.

Daly, Herman E. and John B. Cobb, Jr., *For the Common Good: Redirecting the Economy toward Community, the Environment, and a Sustainable Future* (Beacon Press: Boston) 1989.

Eatwell, John and Lance Taylor, *Global Finance at Risk: The Case for International Regulation* (New Press: New York) 2000.

"Economic and financial indicators," *The Economist*, July 7, 2007, pp. 93–94.

Edwards, Chris, *The Fragmented World: Competing Perspectives on Trade, Money and Crisis* (Methuen: London) 1985.

Friedman, Milton and Rose Friedman, *Free to Choose: A Personal Statement* (Harcourt, Brace, Jovanovich: New York) 1980.

Galbraith, John Kenneth, *Money: Whence It Came, Where It Went* (Houghton Mifflin: Boston) 1975; revised edition 1995.

Galbraith, John Kenneth, *Economics in Perspective: A Critical History* (Houghton Mifflin: Boston) 1987.

Guha, Krishna, "Fed brings relief to markets," *Financial Times,* August 18, 2007, p. 1.

Heilbroner, Robert, *The Making of Economic Society* (Prentice-Hall: Englewood Cliffs, New Jersey) 1986; first published in 1962.

Heilbroner, Robert, *Understanding Macro-economics* (Prentice Hall: Englewood Cliffs, New Jersey) 1965.

Heilbroner, Robert, *The Worldly Philosophers: The Lives, Times and Ideas of the Great Economic Thinkers,* 6th edn. (Simon and Schuster: New York) 1986.

Hoekman, Bernard and Michel Kostecki, *The Political Economy of the World Trading System: From GATT to WTO* (Oxford University Press: Oxford) 1995.

Hosli, Madeleine, *The Euro: A Concise Introduction to European Monetary Integration* (Lynne Rienner: Boulder, Colorado) 2005.

Keynes, John Maynard, *The General Theory of Employment, Interest, and Money* (Harcourt, Brace and Company: New York) 1958; first published in 1936.

Lal Das, Bhagirath, *The WTO and the Multilateral Trading System: Past, Present and Future* (Zed Books: London) 2003.

Soros, George, *The Crisis of Global Capitalism* (Public Affairs: New York) 1998.

Stiglitz, Joseph, *Globalization and Its Discontents* (W. W. Norton: New York) 2002.

Strange, Susan, *Mad Money: When Markets Outgrow Governments* (University of Michigan Press: Ann Arbor) 1998.

Weisweiller, Rudi, *How the Foreign Exchange Market Works* (New York Institute of Finance: New York) 1990.

Yergin, Daniel and Joseph Stanislaw, *The Commanding Heights: The Battle for the World Economy,* rev. edn. (Simon and Schuster: New York) 2002.

CHAPTER 4

The Multi-Centric Organizational Model and World View

As discussed in Chapter 1, a major alternative world view to the market traces its origin to another of the classical political economists, **David Ricardo** (1772–1823). Whereas Adam Smith focused on the production side of economic activity, David Ricardo focused on distribution. His analysis led him to a depressing conclusion: in contrast to Adam Smith's optimistic belief that economic growth would make workers and industrialists continuously better off, Ricardo concluded that, because of competition and plentiful labor supply, the incomes of most workers would not rise above the subsistence level. Hence, he agreed with those who had pronounced the "iron law of wages," that is, wages would trend toward subsistence. Industrialists would not fare any better as competition would result in non-profitable operations. The only winners would be the owners of relatively scarce and well-located prime agricultural land who would receive a special premium simply because of their land's higher fertility and/or its proximity to the population concentrations in cities. Essentially, Ricardo believed that even though the more specialized division of labor and the application of more capital might be useful for increasing production, it did not provide concomitantly increasing rewards for most participants. In other words, there is a disconnect between who is responsible for production gains and who gets the rewards in the distribution of income. From this insight a distinct school of thought has emerged (Heilbroner, *The Worldly Philosophers*).

As also mentioned in Chapter 1, the world view presented in this chapter is an amalgamation of two schools of thought that are intellectual descendants of Ricardo. Both schools were developed as counterpoints to the market world view that was discussed in Chapters 2 and 3. One school of thought is known as *institutionalism*; the other has been called *neo-Ricardianism*. The major American academics responsible for the articulation of institutionalism are Thorstein Veblen (1857–1929) and John Kenneth Galbraith (1908–2006). Both authored bestselling books that widely circulated their criticisms of the "conventional wisdom." The scholar who is probably most responsible for providing the sophisticated theoretical foundation of the neo-Ricardian school of thought is little known outside specialist circles. He is Piero Sraffa, an Italian economist, who spent most of his professional career at Cambridge University in the United Kingdom. For extending this approach to the international arena, major credit should be given to Raul Prebisch (1901–1986), a Latin American economist, and Susan Strange (1923–1998), an English journalist and academic. Probably the most active current popular author in this school of thought is David Korten.

This chapter first will discuss the challenges of institutionalism and neo-Ricardianism to the market world view. After presenting the critiques of Veblen, Karl Polanyi, and Sraffa, the chapter will focus primarily on the critique of neoclassical economics by John Kenneth Galbraith. Second, the chapter presents Galbraith's alternative conceptualizations of the modern political economy as a model with premises, interactions, and outcomes, similar to the structure used in the discussion of the market model in Chapter 2. Finally, the chapter compares the basic attributes of the market model to that of the Galbraith-inspired multi-centric organizational model. The next chapter will present the contributions of Prebisch, Strange, and Korten, as well as others.

THE VEBLEN AND POLANYI INSTITUTIONALIST CHALLENGE TO THE MARKET MODEL

Thorstein Veblen mounted the first major intellectual challenge to the dominance of neoclassical economics even though one of his teachers, John Bates Clark, was one of its founders. Instead of the benign, harmonious, efficient market that is central to neoclassical economics, Veblen saw an excessive, wasteful, and predatory system. His first major book, *The Theory of the Leisure Class,* captured so much of the popular resentment of the robber barons of the time that it became a bestseller at the turn of the nineteenth into the twentieth century.

Veblen directly challenged the realism of the neoclassical model. He believed, for instance, that contemporary society could be understood

THORSTEIN VEBLEN
1857–1929
Norwegian-American founder of the institutionalist school of Political Economy. Brilliant writer and social critic but unintelligible lecturer. His most famous book is *The Theory of the Leisure Class* (1898) in which he lampoons "conspicuous consumption."

only within its historical and cultural context. This **institutionalist view** directly contradicted the ahistorical, economics-only approach of neoclassical economics. Veblen saw capitalists as modern manifestations of the ancient warrior class, seeking to gain wealth and power through predatory manipulations. He called them "captains of industry" or "captains of finance." Veblen contended that men such as John D. Rockefeller, the oil tycoon, and J. P. Morgan, the banker, were out to win the wealth and power game in any way possible. Usually that meant destroying competition, that is, Adam Smith's self-regulating market (Knoedler, in *Introduction to Political Economy*).

Veblen was also highly skeptical of the neoclassical economists' assumption of the free and rational individual consumer. According to his observations, people were more interested in showing off their wealth in as ostentatious a fashion as possible, which he called *conspicuous consumption*. He felt that people are always emulating those who are richer than they are, exhibiting culturally induced, "irrational" behavior. Consistent with irrationality, not rationality, consumers are prepared to endanger their health and their families' economic viability in order to show off their presumed material success. Recent examples of conspicuous consumption would include those individuals who are willing to sacrifice basics, such as health insurance, in order to have that luxury vehicle, even though a less expensive one would serve the same functional purpose, or those individuals who tear down perfectly serviceable houses in order to build bigger and more impressive mansions, just to show that they are wealthy enough to do it.

From Veblen's perspective, capitalists are obsessed with amassing profits, not seeking more efficient production. Capitalism is all about driving for monopoly control, destroying all possible competitors, short-term time horizons, manipulating the financial system—all in an effort to maximize wealth accumulation. Veblen contended that engineers and scientists provide the only countervailing force to these proclivities. They are dedicated to the rational use of technology in the production process. They are the ones trying to build the efficient capacities of the economy, whereas the captains of industry and finance are quite prepared to sabotage it if they believe that they can acquire a short-term financial gain by doing so.

Veblen believed that neoclassical economists were simply apologists for the dominant capitalist class. The harmonious, non-political market analysis was used as a means to obscure from the public the actual predatory and unstable nature of the system. Because the capitalists controlled the higher educational system in the early twentieth century through their control of the purse strings and politicians, they made sure that the capitalist-supportive market-oriented economists got most of the jobs in the academy and that critics like Veblen, especially those who supported the interests of labor, were a small minority (Veblen, *Higher Learning in America*).

Another important institutionalist is **Karl Polanyi** (1886–1964). In contrast to Veblen, who put major emphasis on technology as the driver of social change, Polanyi focused on the cultural idea of the market itself. In Polanyi's major work, *The Great Transformation*, he argues that the most pervasive and devastating change that triumphed in the nineteenth century was the imposition of the market decision-making system on all aspects of society. Up until modern times, decisions about production and distribution were made by custom or central authority. Most transactions were not monetized. In Polanyi's view the injection of market-based monetary valuation into most societal exchanges profoundly changed the nature of society. As discussed in Chapter 1, this shift was associated with the Industrial Revolution that began in Western Europe and then spread to North America and elsewhere. More and more people began to work for monetary wages in city factories rather than producing for themselves in largely self-sufficient villages. Land and natural resources in general were converted from control by the community in common into something to be privately bought and sold. People shifted their allegiance from their community commitments to their individual material gain. All of this transformation was justified by the philosophy of *laissez-faire*. Presumably that meant that the government, both local and national, was supposed to get out of the economy (keep its "hands off") and let the monetary values in the market, as determined by supply and demand, make the decisions. The advocates of this Smithian approach, who strongly believed that it was the path to economic freedom for individuals and businesses, were called "liberals." Polanyi argued that the liberalization policy prescription was actually part of a strategy by businessmen to gain the upper hand over the resistance of workers, the clergy, and landowners. Therefore, the *laissez-faire* policy, according to Polanyi, was in fact imposed by the government on behalf of the capitalists so that they could make more profit. *Laissez-faire* really meant the removal of restrictions on merchants and industrialists. Veblen would have agreed, but not the neoclassical market-believing economists who accepted *laissez-faire* as a necessary and natural condition for the implementation of Adam Smith's "invisible hand."

KARL POLANYI
1886–1964
An Austrian-Hungarian economic anthropologist who migrated to England and then the United States in order to escape Nazism. His most well-known book is *The Great Transformation* (1944), in which he argues that the market is embedded in the broader cultural and political context and that, furthermore, the market's transformation of workers, nature, and monetary gold into "fictional commodities" is responsible for the destruction of community, the environment, and democracy.

Instead of the market serving as a liberalizing institution, Polanyi argued that over the course of the nineteenth and early twentieth centuries the market actually turned real things into **"fictional commodities"** that had harmful consequences. Once something has been turned into a commodity, it can be bought and sold for whatever price comes from the market process. From the perspective of the market, all other attributes of that which has been commodified are irrelevant. The structure of the capitalist market of this period required the transformation of humans, nature, and gold into unprecedented states. These new conditions of existence Polanyi called "fictions" because they were human inventions, just like novels. Human beings are transformed into a fictional state called "wage labor." Capitalists wanted cheap labor in their factories, so they turned workers into fictional commodities that could be bought and sold. Individual workers were torn from their community roots and thrown into the atomistic "satanic mill," the impersonal, uncaring market for wage labor. The market did not care about the horrible working or living conditions, only the wage. The same was done to nature. Nature was made into a fictional commodity in order for it to be more easily exploited. Previously nature and land were considered sacred trusts. In many cultures and religions severing that stewardship relationship was akin to blasphemy. But the market turned nature into consumable commodities by extracting salable parts from ecosystems so that they could be bought and sold without regard to depletion, pollution, or environmental destruction. In terms of political consequences, the most dangerous fictional commodity was money. Polanyi argued that the rigid adherence to the monetary gold standard in the 1920s and 1930s was disastrous. The monetary gold standard had been given a superior, almost untouchable, status. Upholding its requirements was more important than the overall health of the economy. Consequently, many economies collapsed into the Great Depression, bringing their governments down with them. In many countries, Germany being the most salient example, democracies were replaced with fascist dictatorships. These fascist regimes then initiated World War II. This sequence of events led Polanyi to conclude that the rigid commitment to the gold standard was a major cause of the rise of fascism and, therefore, of the Second World War. For Polanyi, the "free" market with all of its fictions was both a "cultural and political catastrophe" (*The Great Transformation*). The harmful consequences of market capitalism's fictional commodities will be discussed further in the next chapter.

SRAFFA'S NEO-RICARDIAN CRITIQUE

Though not well known, **Piero Sraffa** made many important intellectual contributions in the first part of the twentieth century. One author called him "the outstanding Italian economist of his generation" (Caspari, in *Routledge Encyclopedia of International Political Economy*, p. 1444). Sraffa's initial work was in monetary policy and in critiquing the Marshallian competitive model of neoclassical economics. Because of the high quality of his work, he was invited to Cambridge University by John Maynard Keynes in the mid-1920s. Sraffa accepted the post for a number of reasons, one of which was his personal safety. His publication on Italian monetary policy had already been criticized by the Italian dictator, Benito Mussolini, and his good friend Antonio Gramsci, a famous Marxian scholar and activist, had just been jailed by Mussolini. While at Cambridge Sraffa was asked to become editor of the collected works of David Ricardo. The task occupied over 40 years of his life and made him the unrivaled expert on Ricardo. Throughout his life Sraffa was critical of analysis that relied on atomistic or individualistic approaches. Sraffa believed that all things were connected and interdependent. That led him to be critical of neoclassical economics and the early philosophical works of Ludwig Wittgenstein. Wittgenstein admitted in his later publications that Sraffa's arguments were responsible for a total revamping of his entire philosophical system (Caspari).

PIERO SRAFFA
1898–1983
Italian economist who joined Cambridge University in the 1920s at John Maynard Keynes's invitation in order to escape imprisonment by the fascist dictator Mussolini. Besides Keynes, Sraffa also personally knew and influenced the Italian Marxist Antonio Gramsci and the philosopher Ludwig Wittgenstein. After editing Ricardo's papers, Sraffa wrote a small but influential book, *The Production of Commodities by Means of Commodities* (1960), which is the foundation of the neo-Ricardian school of thought.

Based on his own scholarship in the 1920s and his careful reading of Ricardo, Sraffa published in 1960 a slim volume that would become the founding treatise of a new school of thought, **neo-Ricardianism**. The book was titled *Production of Commodities by Means of Commodities*.

Succinct and highly mathematical, it single-handedly reestablished the credibility of classical political economy and its associated value theory. Sraffa demonstrated that with his Ricardian-based theory it was possible to construct a set of equations that would result in a single set of consistent prices. He also demonstrated that neoclassical economics could not do the same. In a small review article in the early 1930s, Sraffa defended Keynes against an attack from the neoclassical Nobel laureate economist Friedrich von Hayek. Sraffa noted that Hayek's own argument was logically inconsistent. Hayek was embarrassed, but his theory still endures (Caspari, in *Routledge Encyclopedia of International Political Economy*).

Sraffa contended that the price-setting theory (or **value theory**) of neoclassical economics was flawed because it assumed the impossible, namely that the values of resources or factors of production (land, labor, and capital) were determined independently in the market. In agreement with a long lineage of classical political economists from pre-Smithians to John Stuart Mill, Sraffa argued that the values of labor and capital were set by interdependent socio-historical processes. The value of capital cannot be determined until the profit rate is known, and it is not possible to know the rate of profit until the wage rate is known. Capitalists and workers are in a struggle over the division of the net product. Until the outcome of that struggle at any particular historical point is known, it is impossible to know what the relative prices will be. The issue is further complicated by the realization that prior determinations of the struggle between labor and capital are reflected in the input prices of the current means of production. Sraffa's equations are based on the assumption of economic reproducibility. He presumes that the current structure of production will seek to reproduce itself. Therefore, once information is known about that structure of production, a set of long-term relative prices can be determined. The three components of the structure of production are (1) level of aggregate income and activity, (2) technical conditions of production (input–output relationships), and (3) distribution of social product among the classes. Because all the necessary information for determining relative prices comes from the production component of the economy, Cole, Cameron, and Edwards call Sraffa's theory of value the **cost of production theory**. Notice that determining relative prices does not rely on any notions of resource scarcity, marginal productivity of factors of production, or consumer preferences—all central to the value theory of the market model. In fact, the market itself plays a subordinate and minor role in the cost of production approach (Cole et al., *Why Economists Disagree*; Sinha, in *Encyclopedia of Political Economy*).

In an article titled, "Piero Sraffa and the Rehabilitation of Classical Political Economy," Robert Paul Wolff agrees with this argument and then notes its most significant implication: "What is more, it is easy to show that the wage rate and the profit rate vary inversely to one another, thus exhibiting the objective basis for the unending conflict between labor and capital" (in *Alternatives to Economic Orthodoxy*, p. 169). The distribution experience of the United States over the last 30 years demonstrates this insight. The real incomes of workers have stagnated even though the increases in labor productivity have been above historical averages. On the other hand, and predictably, from a Sraffian perspective, profit rates and thus the share of the social product going to profit have significantly increased.

The Sraffian analysis essentially establishes an alternative value theory. As noted earlier, each model, or world view, has a different idea about how things traded in the political economy receive their relative values, and ultimately their prices. The market model relies on supply and demand to determine relative values, whereas the cost of production model relies on production costs plus the outcome of the distribution power struggle to determine relative values. Of course, the pure forms of the models make logical and quite abstract arguments, often relying on mathematics. John Kenneth Galbraith, on the other hand, believed that mathematics was often used to obfuscate institutional reality. Consequently, his books were conceptual and institutionally descriptive as we shall see in the rest of this chapter. It is interesting to note that while Galbraith was in Cambridge in the 1930s he studied under both Keynes and Sraffa.

THE GALBRAITH CRITIQUE AND ALTERNATIVE

Professor **John Kenneth Galbraith** combined the ideas of Veblen, Polanyi, Keynes, Sraffa, and many others, along with many of his own ideas, to develop a comprehensive alternative perspective. He was one of the first American economists to embrace the insights of John Maynard Keynes. Even though Galbraith served as Director of the Office of Price Administration during World War II and then wrote a well-regarded theoretical book on the experience, he was still denied an expected appointment at Harvard because of his unorthodox views. Eventually Harvard relented, "rescuing" him from Princeton University and *Fortune* magazine. Galbraith then devoted the next 25 years to developing his alternative to the purely competitive model of neoclassical economics. His three key books are *The Affluent Society* (1958), *The New Industrial State* (1967), and *Economics and the Public Purpose* (1973). Galbraith died in April 2006 at the age of 97, still hopeful, but very disappointed at the revival of free market capitalism and attacks on the programs of the New Deal, President Franklin Delano Roosevelt's efforts to combat the Great Depression of the 1930s. Nevertheless, Galbraith firmly believed that the institutional changes that have occurred in capitalism, especially since World War II, have increasingly made the conventional market model an obsolete analytical tool. He believed that his approach provided greater insight into contemporary reality, especially that part of the political economy dominated by large private corporations. Galbraith observed that already in the 1960s the large corporate sector represented more than half of the U.S. economy. However, in contrast to the believers in the market model who see the market as an ideal-type system and a preferred means of decision-making, Galbraith was critical of the system that his analysis more realistically portrays (Parker, *John Kenneth Galbraith*).

JOHN KENNETH GALBRAITH
1908–2006
Canadian-born but spent most of his academic life at Harvard University and became a U.S citizen in 1937. Prolific and popular advocate of institutional political economics. Follower of Thorstein Veblen and John Maynard Keynes and opponent of Milton Friedman. Held high positions in the Roosevelt and Kennedy administrations. Major books that presented his alternative views are *The Affluent Society* (1958), *The New Industrial State* (1967), and *Economics and the Public Purpose* (1973).

Galbraith was not a believer in the practical usefulness of the tightly deductive model that serves as the basis of the neoclassical economic approach. His more discursive approach involved presenting attributes of the contemporary political economy as he saw it, contrasting them with the market model, and then showing how his approach illuminated issues more realistically. The discussion below will first look at some of those attributes; second, present how those attributes can be formulated into a simple model, analogous to the market model, with premises, interactions, and outcomes; and third, compare the qualities of the multi-centric organizational model with the market model.

Galbraith noted that the evolution of capitalism from multiple small firms into a system with larger and more powerful business organizations was greatly facilitated by the development of the modern **corporation**. The legal features of the modern corporation that assisted this development were indefinite lifetime, unlimited size, limited liability for stockholders, and an enormous capacity for mobilizing savings through the issuance of shares. Thomas Jefferson and others in the early nineteenth century had presciently warned against the potential of this type of corporate form to facilitate the concentration of wealth and power, but the advance of industrial capitalism, especially after the Civil War, overwhelmed the populist resistance.

In Galbraith's view, developments in *technology* were primarily responsible for production being carried out in increasingly bigger organizations. Complex technologies in both products and manufacturing processes are most effectively facilitated in large organizational settings.

They require massive capital investments, major research and development capacities, and large, highly specialized professional workforces. Developments in communication and transportation technologies allow rapid coordination across many units without geographical limitation. While technology does not require corporations to grow as big as Toyota or ExxonMobil or Microsoft, modern technology does enable very big corporations to function effectively on a global scale.

Galbraith contended that *power* is the corporation's number-one objective. Corporations want to control everything affecting their operations, including supply and demand for their products. However, firms in a competitive market cannot control either of these. They see themselves as at the mercy of the market. Business leaders in this uncomfortable situation quickly figured out that if they wanted to escape from the uncertainties of the market, they had to undermine market competition and gain control over supply and demand. In other words, they needed to acquire **market power**. Starting in the late nineteenth century, corporate leaders set out to acquire market power through any possible means. Some of the names of the first generation of American businessmen to successfully follow this strategy are well known: Andrew Carnegie, John D. Rockefeller, J. P. Morgan. Galbraith believed that any model of the economy that doesn't recognize this historical reality is thoroughly irrelevant. Of course, he was referring to the purely competitive market model, which avoids the issue of power altogether.

Galbraith noted that in the early stages of a new corporation's development—its entrepreneurial stage—decision-making is very hierarchical. But as corporations mature and get bigger and more complex, managers take over from the founding entrepreneurs. That process is beginning to happen now at Microsoft, the same way that it happened in the past at U.S. Steel and General Motors. Galbraith believed that in the next stage of corporate evolution, teams of knowledge specialists would become more influential in the decision-making processes. Those specialists would include scientists, engineers, lawyers, accountants, marketing specialists, government liaison officers, and so on. In the mature corporations these professional teams would actually run the corporation. Galbraith dubbed them "the **technostructure**." This group is very similar in composition and function to Veblen's "engineers." Both authors saw this group as the source of rational constraint on rampant capitalism. So far the technostructure has not achieved the decision-making dominance anticipated by Galbraith; but there does seem to be a continuing tension between the technostructure's efforts at rational long-term planning and the risk-taking, short-term profit behavior of the captains of finance.

Galbraith argued that most of the important decisions for the political economy are made by large corporate organizations, not isolated individuals, as the market world view claims. But, by a strange historical twist, U.S.

corporations are considered under the law as **"artificial persons"** with all the legal rights and obligations of individuals. This interesting fiction was not passed by any legislature. It is usually attributed to a Supreme Court decision in 1886 (*Southern Pacific Railroad* vs. *Santa Clara County*); however, it turns out that the Court made no such decision. The statement that corporations were "persons" and therefore subject to the protections provided by the Fourteenth Amendment was put into the head notes on the 1886 case by a government official who had connections to the railroad. The reference was to testimony given in an earlier case by former Senator Roscoe Conklin. Conklin claimed that the Senate had intended the concept of persons in the Fourteenth Amendment to include corporations. Many years later a researching professor actually read the transcript of the committee meeting that Senator Conklin had used as evidence for his claim. To his surprise the transcript makes no such reference. However, the Senator's subsequent employer, the Southern Pacific Railroad, had made such an argument. Despite the dubious authenticity of the head note statement, it has subsequently been referenced in later Supreme Court decisions and has become part of the received legal doctrine. A significant recent application of this legal doctrine was the Supreme Court decision in 1978 that declared that, as "persons," corporations are protected by the free speech clause of the First Amendment, and any limitation on their expenditures in a political campaign is a violation of their personal free speech rights. Not only does that decision carry the corporations-are-persons fiction to new heights, it also gives large corporations immense spending advantages over most individuals in the political process (Nace, *Gangs of America*, chapters 8–10).

Galbraith recognized that as technology changes, individual corporations as well as entire industrial fields go through phases of development. When a new product is introduced, there are usually many small firms competing for a place in this new industry. But eventually, through the process of drop-outs, mergers, acquisitions, buy-outs, takeovers, even vicious practices, the number of firms gets smaller and smaller. That happened in steel, railroads, and oil in the first phase of the Industrial Revolution. The most successful predator would end up as "king of the mountain." That meant a monopoly (one seller) and the power to control production and price. That extreme was eventually considered politically unacceptable, so anti-trust legislation was introduced to prevent the construction of monopolies through predatory practices. The effect of this legislation has been to prevent consolidation of one industrial field under one corporation, but it does allow consolidation under a few corporations. For instance, the U.S. automobile industry started out with scores of producers, but eventually only three major ones were left (General Motors, Ford, and Chrysler). With the advent of globalization in the 1980s, the number of major automobile manufacturers selling cars in the United States expanded beyond the big three. The most successful companies were based in Japan. But now these multi-national companies are all merging with one another transnationally, just as Galbraith had foreseen.

When fewer than ten corporations control most of the production in an industrial field, a special type of decision-making structure exists. It is called an **oligopolistic market** (few sellers). Since the participants are aware of each others' decisions and can gauge their effect, pure competition as the market model defines it does not exist. The firms are not small, independent actors who must accept whatever prices the aggregative market provides. Because they have market power, corporations singly or in tacit collusion pursue efforts to control both production and distribution. Consequently, oligopolistic corporate managers follow different kinds of strategies than managers would under purely competitive market conditions. In his book *The New Industrial State* (1967), Galbraith identified eight likely controlling strategies:

1 *Control of consumer demand*. Galbraith argued that big corporations seek to convince consumers of what they really need. That way, their production schedules are not dependent on the "whims" of consumers. The method for "brainwashing" consumers into buying what the corporations want them to buy is, of course, advertising. The more this approach works, the more "sovereignty" shifts from the consumer to the producer. Galbraith dubbed this phenomenon the **"revised sequence."** In other words, the direction of control over what is produced is shifted so that it originates with the producers, not the consumers, as the market model presumes. In fact, by turning the major market model premise of "consumer sovereignty" on its head, Galbraith thoroughly undermined one of the major rationales of the market world view. Naturally, producers do not want the general public to believe that they are being manipulated. Consequently, producers insist that they only make products that consumers want.

2 *Control over profit*. Galbraith believed that big corporations would prefer to have a steady profit flow over time. Therefore, they would not seek maximum profit in the short run, a practice that would almost always create volatile ups and downs in revenues. Instead they would seek a consistent target profit year after year. The target rate would have to generate enough profit to satisfy the dividend expectations of stockholders, and it would have to generate enough retained earnings so that the corporations could reduce their borrowing from outsiders, such as investment banks. So, instead of engaging in profit-maximizing, the corporate managers would practice "profit satisficing." Oligopolistic control over both demand and supply would give corporate managers within their national boundaries the means to

pursue this strategy. However, because of the economic globalization that began in the 1980s, the degree of oligopolistic control required for the effective implementation of this control strategy no longer exists. That could change if producer market power were to be reestablished globally.

3 *Control over labor.* Galbraith thought that collective bargaining between trade unions and large corporations was a means of gaining control over worker behavior. Union representatives would promise worker passivity in return for continuously increasing pay and benefits. As long as corporations had market power, that is, the ability to control the prices of their products, they could make these promises to the unions. However, Galbraith noted that corporations were not happy with these arrangements, and he expected them to try to escape them. In the 1960s the most likely strategy seemed to be more automation, that is, more capital machinery and less labor. The movement toward full robotization of the automobile assembly process was an example of this labor-reduction strategy. This presumption by Galbraith was consistent with his emphasis on the role of technology.

In developments not foreseen by Galbraith, the 1980s brought globalization and anti-union governments, both of which further undermined the strength of organized labor. Corporations got more control over labor through the strategies of shifting or threatening to shift jobs overseas as well as significantly reducing the percentage of the labor force that was unionized. Therefore, the extent of corporate control of labor changed, but the strategic objective remained the same.

4 *Control over prices.* Galbraith thought that big corporations would try to take control over the determination of prices away from the market by using their market power to "administer" prices. By controlling consumer demand, corporations would administer the prices in the product market. But the corporations would also try to control prices in the resource market. The previously mentioned control over the price of labor was one aspect of this strategy. Another aspect of the strategy was the domination of resource supply prices through vertical integration. If the corporation owned or otherwise controlled the whole production process from beginning to end, then it could determine what the supply prices would be. For instance, J. D. Rockefeller set out to own and control the production of oil from the oil wells to the gasoline station. His Standard Oil Corporation succeeded in doing that so well that his resultant monopoly was the first major "trust to be busted." Recently vertical integration has been accomplished through chains of subcontractors.

5 *Control over growth.* Capitalism and its corporations thrive on economic growth. In fact, growth is the essential nutrient for the viability of capitalism. The success of the economy is measured by its growth, but so is the success of each corporation. Each corporation is out to increase its share of the market. Therefore, according to Galbraith, one of the objectives of market power is to expand one's corporate share in a production area. Various strategies are utilized, hostile takeovers being one of the most predatory. Expanding overseas in order to increase market share is a standard corporate strategy now. The business news regularly reports on which transnational corporation has the largest market share. In 2007 Nokia, a Finnish-based corporation, was first in cell phone sales, while Toyota, a Japanese-based corporation, was about to pass General Motors, an American-based corporation, as first in motor vehicle sales.

6 *Control over the universities.* The corporate "technostructure" requires a steady flow of professionally trained specialists who will smoothly accommodate themselves to corporate organizational expectations. Furthermore, universities also provide venues for basic scientific research and technological innovation. The society's universities provide both of these essential functions without the corporations having to directly pay for them.

Galbraith was especially worried about this corporate strategy of controlling universities, as it undermined his hope for a progressive reform movement. Galbraith looked to the universities for independent intellectual leadership in enabling society to regain control over the big corporations. Unfortunately, as he recognized, that leadership is not likely to come from MBAs or even biochemists whose research is paid for by large pharmaceutical corporations. As Galbraith ruefully recognized, even his own discipline of Economics seems more interested in rationalizing the current distribution of power than challenging it.

7 *Control over the government.* The modern state is a major player in the political economy. Policies established in the legislative process go far beyond simply determining the rules of the business game as envisaged in the market model. Government revenues depend on a large and complex tax system, and budgeted expenditures range over thousands of programs. Numerous areas of regulation are established, ranging from drug safety to environmental protection, to fair business practices, to labor organizing, to health standards. All the players in the system have an interest in getting the most favorable results from the political process. Because of their wealth, corporations have the greatest success in controlling these government processes. They want government policies, budgets, and interventions that favor their

interests, and they usually get what they want. The military–industrial complex is the most egregious example of corporate-controlled government. But there are many other corporate-friendly government programs, the subsidies for agribusinesses and energy companies being two salient examples.

8 *Control over the popular culture.* Corporations understand the importance of a receptive public as the public both consumes and votes. Therefore, it's highly desirable that the prevailing social norms support corporate-friendly views. Ironically, in Galbraith's opinion, the competitive market model of neoclassical economics provides ideological cover for the power-driven behavior of large corporations. Galbraith argues that the public is told through the corporate-controlled media that any government intervention or regulation that business does not like interferes with market competition; never mind that no real competition exists in most of the economy in the first place. Corporate propaganda justifies high profits and low wages as the "natural outcome" of market processes rather than being brought about by the realities of market power. Furthermore, corporations argue that taxes should not interfere with this "natural outcome" as it would be bad for business, the economy, and, therefore, jobs. In this prevailing corporate view, expenditures in the private sector are inherently more valuable than public sector expenditures. Therefore, taxes (especially taxes on business) should be cut along with social expenditures. Galbraith believed that this anti-government and anti-tax attitude along with its political implementation have led to a serious public–private imbalance in the society. Or as he colorfully put it, we get "private opulence and public squalor."

MULTI-CENTRIC ORGANIZATIONAL (MCO) MODEL

Using the preceding discussion of Galbraith's views as background, this section constructs an institutionalist model of the political economy, using the same framework used to structure the market model in Chapter 2, with premises, interactions and outcomes. Because this model is my own construct from several sources, it is given a name unique to this text: the **multi-centric organizational model.**

Premises

1 *Basic actors are organizations.* Organizations make the major decisions in the political economy, not individuals as in the market model.

Corporations with thousands of employees and billions of dollars of revenue are the central players. However, big corporations are not the only organizations playing important roles; government agencies also play significant roles. In most modern economies *governments* are directly involved in 30 to 50 percent of the transactions. *Labor unions* can also be key organizational players, though their significance varies from country to country. Other groups, usually classified together as *non-governmental organizations* (NGOs), are sometimes also significant players. Examples of NGOs include religious organizations, professional organizations, advocacy organizations, and philanthropic foundations. Even a large portion of criminal activity is done through organizations. Because organizations of several types take center stage in this model, it seems appropriate to call it the multi-centric organizational model, or MCO for short.

In their internal decision-making, organizations are certainly different from individuals. As organizations become mature and bureaucratized, the model presumes a rational process of decision-making. However, the elements involved in decision-making, though regularized, become more complex. Besides financial measures, other matters influencing decisions are politics, status, future advantage, and so on.

2 *Choices are made through the exercise of organizational power.* Since power is exercised in a relational manner, decisions are made via inter-organizational struggles. As organizations seek to achieve their objectives, they must strategize about how to outwit and out-muscle other organizations that have contending objectives. This is a totally different dynamic from that of the market, in which isolated individuals express preferences that are aggregated via the power-free mechanisms of supply and demand.

Even though the MCO process differs significantly from the market model, the term **market power** is often used to describe both the means and the objective of organizational actors. The MCO model does have prices, but they are administered by the organizational players through the exercise of power. Thus "negotiated outcomes" would be the term that probably best describes the process of value determination in this model much more accurately than supply and demand.

3 *Money represents power.* In contrast to the market model, in which money is a neutral go-between, money in the MCO model takes on the role of an institutional power broker. It is issued, controlled, and manipulated by organizations on behalf of specific interests. Having access to money means having access to capital. Having preferred access to money means greater control over wealth allocation. Central

banks in collaboration with large private banks determine the supply and cost of money (interest rates). The establishment of interest rates has a political component. Besides political processes internal to countries, countries are also potentially subject to formal and informal controls from external sources. Formal controls could come from international organizations such as the International Monetary Fund, whereas informal controls could come from organizations such as the Bank for International Settlements, an informal association of central banks located in Basel, Switzerland. The currencies of some countries, such as the U.S. dollar and the euro, have more financial power than others. Financial power will be discussed further in the next chapter.

4 *Wealth and power are the driving objectives.* By separating economics from politics, the market model analytically isolates the two classic objectives of wealth and power from each other. The MCO approach brings them back together again, recognizing their interdependence. Organizations are assumed to seek more wealth primarily through the exercise of power. Wealth consists of income and accumulated capital. The term *capital* is popularly used to refer to both the physical and financial sides of the capital investment–saving relationship. Capital products are both goods and services. Capital services include research and development that results in knowledge. Knowledge refers specifically to the ideas or technologies that bring innovation in products and production methods, thereby enhancing productivity.

Power is important because it determines how successful the organizations can be in the exercise of the controlling strategies that Galbraith outlined. For example, one means of controlling access to knowledge is the legal strategy of patents, copyrights, and trademarks. As previously discussed, the World Trade Organization provides a means of enforcing this strategy via its intellectual property provisions (Trade Related Intellectual Property, or TRIPs). The exclusive ownership of intellectual property provides the type of monopoly control that directly contradicts the freely available information assumption of the market model.

5 *Power rivalries characterize interaction.* From the MCO perspective organizations are engaged in direct power rivalries over things that matter. In the vernacular these interactions are often labeled "competition," but they do not in any way resemble the form that competition takes in the pure market model. When two big corporations are struggling over market share, say, a telephone company vs. a cable company, they are engaged in a direct power rivalry. Virtually none of the conditions required for true market competition exist. For instance, as stipulated in Chapter 2, true competition requires so many sellers and buyers that market participants have only the prevailing,

aggregated prices upon which to base their decisions. Instead, in the MCO model, the few corporations involved in a particular industry are dealing directly with each others' business strategies, not the impersonal set of market-determined prices that would prevail in truly competitive conditions.

Corporations struggle with each other, with labor unions, and with governments in order to acquire more wealth. NGOs also try to influence the outcomes. NGOs represent a great range of civil society interests from the environment to guns. Because none of these sectors are monoliths, the power struggles can get quite complicated. Different corporations, especially in different product fields, have different interests. Different government agencies and levels of government have different agendas. Even among NGOs with the same concerns, differences exist. Degrees of effective power change over time. For example, labor unions in the United States have lost power over the last few decades. As technology changes, leadership power shifts from the companies involved with the old technologies to those involved in the new. For instance, over the last few decades, leadership power has been shifting from steel and automobile corporations to information technology corporations such as Microsoft. The allocation of power within organizational sectors also differs from country to country. Organized labor is more powerful in Western Europe than in the United States. Government agencies are more powerful in Japan than in the United States. All of these complex interactions are best characterized as *power rivalries*.

6 *Institutional power controls access.* Although equal opportunity for all individuals presumably sets the stage in the market, the MCO model presumes that access to all things of value is a matter of relative organizational power. The biggest corporations, such as ExxonMobil, have a much better chance of getting access to government decision-makers. Big corporations such as Wal-Mart can coerce smaller suppliers into providing products at rock-bottom costs. Governments can control labor mobility through immigration and other regulations. The IMF controls the access of small indebted countries to credit. Some large foundations, such as the Gates/Buffet Foundation, dominate the global philanthropic agenda. Wealth is concentrated in some countries, in some corporations, and in some other organizations; thus a few have much greater access than others. The MCO model recognizes that institutional barriers of unequal wealth and power thoroughly undermine the egalitarian myth associated with the market world view.

7 *Government is a major organizational player.* In contrast to the market model, in which government is understood as a background

player, in the MCO model government is a major player. The U.S. military–industrial complex is a combined operation between the Pentagon, private corporations, and relevant congressional committees. Galbraith said that Lockheed, General Dynamics, and other defense corporations might just as well be public enterprises, but the fiction is maintained that they are private so that their stockholders and top managers can benefit. In fact, there has been a system of rotation of top officials among private corporations and public bureaucracies, especially in the military–industrial complex. Government provides subsidies to businesses in preferred industries such as those in energy exploration, agribusiness, transportation, and mining. Government decides how oligopolistic the economy can be even in crucial areas such as the news and entertainment media where only five conglomerates own and control most of the U.S. industry, including movies, radio, television, music production, magazines, newspapers, sports teams, and theme parks. The government also runs major pension and medical programs. Law-making and regulatory processes are an arena of power rivalry among the major organizations of the society. In the United States, as elsewhere, it is not surprising that the most powerful players, the big corporations, tend to win most of the power struggles. Sometimes, as noted above, big corporations fight among themselves. That happens not only in the economic arena, but also in the political arena, that is, in legislative bodies, government enforcement agencies, and the courts.

Interactions

The above discussion of the premises and attributes of the MCO model, or world view, telegraphs the nature of the interactions that make the political-economic decisions. Power is exercised by the major players in the overlapping arenas. The struggle of participants to maintain and preferably increase their shares of income, wealth and control characterizes the system. In fact is is the driving dynamic of the system. Big corporations seek advantage by using all the control strategies mentioned above, that is, by engaging in extensive product advertising, practicing price administration, containing labor costs, buying up rivals, acquiring patents, obtaining government contracts, seeking favorable government laws and rulings, attempting media manipulation, outsourcing to cheaper providers at home or abroad, and so forth. The winners of the power struggle have the most influence over the distribution of income, which in turn influences the prices of products, as Sraffa demonstrated.

Non-governmental organizations enter into the power struggle on behalf of specific interests. For example, the AARP (formerly the

American Association of Retired Persons) seeks legislation that would require corporations and governments to provide better medical assistance to the elderly. Business-funded think tanks might lobby legislatures to reduce business taxation, thereby increasing profits. Environmental groups propose legislation or file lawsuits in order to induce governments and businesses to behave in environmentally friendlier ways. Sometimes, as a consequence, the offending parties have to absorb the costs that they were previously passing on to others.

Susan Strange points out that the most powerful actors not only win in relation to other players, but also establish the structure in which the power game is played, usually setting up a built-in advantage for themselves. For instance, the major media corporations greatly influence the rules that are established by the U.S. Federal Communications Commission, not to mention the guiding legislation. Major energy-producing countries and companies establish the framework in which energy supplies are controlled, made available, and priced. The Bretton Woods Conference, discussed in Chapter 3, is an example of the U.S. government exercising structural power. The United States essentially imposed the global financial architecture that was to exist for the next 60-plus years (Strange, *States and Markets*).

Figure 4.1 outlines the interactions among the major players in the MCO model. Designating corporations as the most powerful players certainly identifies contemporary American capitalism as the obvious context. On

Multi-Centric Organizational World View

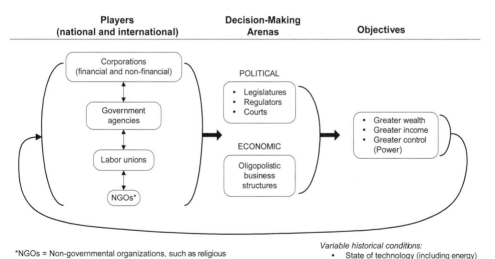

*NGOs = Non-governmental organizations, such as religious groups, professional associations, advocacy groups, etc

Variable historical conditions:
- State of technology (including energy)
- Relative organizational power
- Basic labor costs

Figure 4.1 Multi-centric organizational (MCO) world view.

the other hand, the model as pictured applies to many other countries. That would include all the countries that are members of the OECD, the Paris-based Organisation for Economic Co-operation and Development, which counts among its 30 member countries most of the industrialized countries of Europe and North America as well as Japan and South Korea. It can also be applied usefully to most emerging economies, such as those of Brazil and India. With some adjustments it could even be applied to government-dominated economies, such as China and Russia. In contrast to the market model, which claims detachment from any specific historical or geographical situation, the MCO model recognizes the institutional context as an important variable.

Outcomes

Unlike the market model, the multi-centric organizational model is not purely deductive. Therefore, there are no logically necessary outcomes. However, it is possible to deduce likely outcomes from the power-negotiation interactions that flow from the premises and the changing historical circumstances. Based on their observations and analytical framework, institutionalist authors, such as Veblen and Galbraith, have proposed a number of likely outcomes. Six of the major ones are presented below. The next chapter discusses some of them in greater detail.

1 *Inequality.* The unequal possession of power leads to unequal distribution of income, wealth, and knowledge. Galbraith observed this process both within the United States and around the world. As over the last few decades power in the United States shifted to major corporations and away from labor unions and workers, increasing inequality was a predictable consequence. Union membership in the U.S. private sector has declined from about 35 percent in the 1950s to approximately 9 percent today. As a consequence, over the last 30 years incomes going to workers have stagnated while incomes going to the well-off have significantly increased. According to U.S. government figures, inflation-adjusted incomes for the lowest 20 percent of households have increased only 2 percent over the 1979–2004 period, while incomes of the top 20 percent have increased 63 percent. The top 1 percent income recipients are the real winners, with an increase of 154 percent over this same period. Both the share of income going to the top 1 percent and the share of national income going to profits have returned to where they were in 1929. All of the improvements in income distribution that occurred in the three decades after World War II, thanks to New Deal policies, have largely been eradicated (Miller, in *Dollars and Sense*).

Another measure of inequality is the ratio of difference between the average working person's pay and that of corporate CEOs. In 1980 the U.S. ratio was 40. By 2006 that ratio had increased to 364. The average U.S. CEO earned $10.8 million. The big winners, however, were CEOs of private equity and hedge-fund companies; in 2006 the top 20 received an average of $657.5 million in compensation. The top 20 CEOs of U.S. publicly held corporations received an average of $36.4 million, with the CEO of Yahoo being at the top with $71.7 million. European CEOs seem to be catching up with their American counterparts, but the compensation of the top 20 averages about one-third of the U.S. top 20 (Anderson et al., *Executive Excess 2007*).

Another manifestation of inequality is the gap between rich and poor in the world. In general terms, 20 percent of the world's people have 80 percent of the income, wealth, and technological knowledge. A United Nations University study found that in 2000 the bottom 50 percent of the world's adults owned only 1 percent of the wealth whereas the richest 1 percent owned 40 percent of global assets. Wealth is defined as land, buildings, other tangible property, and net financial assets. Wealth ownership is heavily concentrated in North America, Europe, and high-income Asia-Pacific countries such as Japan. The Gini coefficient measure of inequality is 89 percent for the world's adults. As the authors of the study state in reference to this figure: "The same degree of inequality would be obtained if one person in a group of ten takes 99 percent of the total pie, and the other nine share the remaining 1 percent" (Davies, Sandström, and Wolff, *The World Distribution of Household Wealth*). Since 2000 the situation has become even worse. According to a report on global wealth from the Boston Consulting Group, from 2001 to 2006 all households with financial assets of less than $100,000 (83.5 percent) experienced a decline in their assets' value while those with assets above that level experienced a 64 percent increase in value. Worldwide poverty has been declining, primarily due to economic growth in the world's two most populous countries, China and India. However, the growth in these big Asian countries has been accompanied by increasing inequality (McGregor, in *Financial Times*).

2 *Market-defying movements in price levels.* Occasionally overall price levels move in ways that would not have been predicted by conventional market analysis. In the 1970s the world experienced a general inflation. Many causes have been identified, such as supply restrictions by oil-exporting countries, grain shortages, and large U.S. dollar expenditures for the war in Vietnam. However, there was one component of the inflationary experience in the United States in the

late 1970s that was puzzling. Domestic prices kept increasing despite declines in demand for major durable goods such as automobiles. Major manufacturers kept increasing prices while they were selling fewer products and laying off workers. This combination of increasing prices and economic recession was such a new phenomenon that it was given its own name, "stagflation." The term combined stagnation and inflation. From a conventional market perspective, it was an impossible combination. How was it possible to experience rising prices when demand was curtailed by rising unemployment? The competitive supply–demand approach of the market model could not give a satisfactory answer. However, Galbraith and the MCO model had an explanation. Stagflation was the culmination of the process of "cost-push" labor–management bargaining agreements. Unions pushed for regular wage increases, whether or not justified by increases in productivity. The corporations were prepared to grant the increases in order to avoid strikes, because they had the oligopolistic market power to pass on the increased costs in the form of increased final-product prices to consumers, regardless of falling demand. From the MCO perspective, the policy response that was used to counter the stagflation was all wrong. The Federal Reserve in the late 1970s and early 1980s used conventional market-based monetary policies that were designed to fight excess-demand inflation. The serious decline in the economy that resulted had a very discriminatory impact. The burden of high interest rates and scarce credit fell heavily on small business borrowers and consumers who had not created the problem in the first place, whereas the tight monetary conditions did not seriously affect the large corporations because they were partly insulated from the credit markets, thanks to retained earnings from profits. Galbraith was particularly disdainful of those economists who were so wedded to the market world view that they refused to even consider his analysis, even though it not only provided a persuasive explanation of stagflation but also gave a sensible guide to appropriate policy interventions. Since stagflation was caused by those industries in cost-push oligopolistic markets, the appropriate policy response should have been some type of government intervention in those industries (Edwards, *The Fragmented World*).

3 *Symbiotic relationship between major corporations and government.* Corporate managers expect the government, through its fiscal and monetary policies, to maintain a satisfactory and stable business environment. Government has a reciprocal interest in a positive business climate, since its stable tax revenues are dependent upon it. As mentioned before, the corporations in the military–industrial complex are totally intertwined with the Pentagon bureaucracy and

the congressional armed services committees. Most of the funding for important research and development comes from the government. The Internet, for example, was originally a Defense Department project. Corporations in energy, agriculture, and other fields expect and rely upon their government subsidies. Corporations expect that the government will represent their interests in the World Trade Organization. In fact, these symbiotic relationships easily become transnational, forming the basis of the process known as globalization. The U.S. government has the major influence over the activities and policies of the International Monetary Fund, which have supported transnational banking corporations and foreign corporate investors in general, the largest number of which are based in the United States. Paradoxically, by encouraging U.S.-based corporations to move their manufacturing, banking, and other activities overseas, the U.S. government has facilitated the loss of its own regulatory and taxing power.

4   *Chilling effect on democracy.* Today, small elite groups of corporate leaders, who are essentially unaccountable to the general public, are making many of the major political-economic decisions for the world. Galbraith observed that corporate management, not the general citizenry, was determining what gets produced, where it gets produced, and who gets the benefits. It was neither the individual consumers nor the workers, as imagined by the market model, nor was it the individual voters of a pluralistic democracy. The amount of resources allocated toward providing services for the general community vs. providing wealth to the privileged elites was moving noticeably in the direction of the elites. Big corporations have increased their control over the political arena through their financing of political campaigns. Because of the access that funding buys, corporate lobbyists have increased their influence in the legislative process, sometimes to the extent that corporate-funded lawyers actually write the legislation. Increasingly government departments are headed by individuals who come from the industries they are supposed to be regulating (Korten, *When Corporations Rule the World*).

In his younger years Galbraith thought that government would be an independent countervailing power to both corporations and unions. In fact, he even wrote a book in 1952 that presented that thesis: *American Capitalism: The Concept of Countervailing Power*. But the unions have lost much of their power, and the government has been significantly co-opted by corporations, so that there isn't much countervailing power left. Since the corporations also control the media, neither is there much independent public criticism of the corporate-controlled system on their networks. Even though there is a lot of critical dissent on the Internet, most people still get their information from corporate-friendly television.

Our democracies are also threatened with the loss of university-based independent social critics. Galbraith located them primarily in institutions of higher education. As noted above, he saw universities being compromised as they accepted large grants and contracts from corporations and affiliated government agencies, especially those in the military–industrial complex. Because universities are now able to share in the proceeds from patented inventions, even those that originated from publicly funded research, universities share private-property interests with cooperating corporations, such as those in biotechnology, information technology, energy, chemicals, and pharmaceuticals. Universities, especially the major research universities, manifest an interest in defending the corporate-centered status quo rather than criticizing it.

Robert Reich, a public intellectual and institutionalist like Galbraith, carries Galbraith's pessimistic analysis of his later years even further, proclaiming that democratic capitalism in the United States is dead. It has been replaced by "supercapitalism," in which the entire political process has been hijacked by the corporate bottom line, especially as measured by shareholder value. Nearly all concern for the common good has been obliterated. Corporate money, lobbyists, lawyers, and public relations professionals dominate the political process. Business calculations overwhelm concerns for inequality, health care for all, civil and human rights, global peace, viable communities, democratically responsive government, and a healthy environment (Reich, *Supercapitalism*).

5   *The natural environment is abused and overused.* The objective of growing wealth through profitable operations results in the denigration of the environment. As Polanyi argued, the market capitalist system turned nature into a "fictional commodity." Consequently, for example, timber companies practice clear-cutting because from the market-pricing perspective it's the least-cost approach. They do not have to pay for the damage to the ecosystem. Following market signals, motor vehicle corporations only have to pay for the materials that go into making the automobile, but not the associated pollution that is dumped on the ground or in the waterways or released into the air. Some of nature's resources are non-renewable, but that fact is ignored by the market-pricing system. Some of nature's resources are renewable, but the limits of their renewability are ignored by the market system. Nature's ability to absorb waste and pollution is limited, but those limits are also ignored by the market system. Environmental neglect in the capitalist system is facilitated by the market world view

because it considers all of these environmental matters as external to the market-pricing process. This oversight is recognized as a market failure, but the only way to mitigate this failure is government intervention. The degree of environmental protection is then up to the political process. Corporations resist environmental legislation that they believe will reduce their profits. Those who are deeply committed to the superiority of the decision-making process of the market, like Milton Friedman, also resist government intervention on behalf of the environment as they believe that the government's incompetence will actually make things worse. The MCO model incorporates this power struggle over the environment and looks to the government to provide sensible environmental protection. In his essay "Economics as a System of Belief," Galbraith predicted that "producer sovereignty" would overwhelm the community's "ecological preferences" (in *Economics, Peace and Laughter*).

6 *The highest social goal is the production and consumption of more "stuff."* Over 100 years ago Thorstein Veblen observed that the overriding social goal of capitalism was becoming "conspicuous consumption." Polanyi believed that the obsession with the individual acquisition of material goods and services undermined interest in and dedication to community values. Galbraith similarly expressed his concern that the adoration of private wealth meant that public goods upon which the long term viability of a community depends were being shortchanged. The more recent version of preferring private consumption over public goods is the antipathy toward taxes. Galbraith believed that the corporate search for more sales, more market share, and thus more profit and wealth, were responsible for these developments. Of course, free market advocates will argue that producers are simply responding to consumers' desires. The MCO skeptics, however, will respond that people are not really born with a built-in need for the fastest, biggest, most gas-guzzling automobile that their credit rating will allow them to acquire. Their desires are created by the popular culture in which corporate advertising plays a major role.

The outcomes presented above are quite different from those of the market model. They are political and social as well as economic. The market model focuses only on economic outcomes, and the only economic outcomes that count are those that can be priced in the market. The market model provides a logical and quantitative rigor that the MCO model cannot possibly match. On the other hand, proponents of the multi-centric organizational model would contend that their approach is more empirically based and, therefore, much more relevant to understanding

Table 4.1 The MCO and market models compared

	MCO model	Market model
Outcomes are determined by	power	market efficiency
"Sovereign" player is	corporate management ("producer sovereignty")	consumer ("consumer sovereignty")
Central actors are	organizations	individuals
Interactions are	power rivalries	competitive
Access is	controlled and unequal	open and equal
Government role is	as major player	limited
Economy is	prone to instability, requiring government intervention	naturally stable, with full employment
Wealth concentration is	inevitable	limited by competition
Resource allocation is	for optimum gain of big corporations, not the public or the environment	optimum in response to consumer preferences
Price (value) is established by	power negotiation process	interaction of demand and supply

the way things actually work. Since the model is historically variable, the interactive dynamics and outcomes change over time. Many of the observations that Galbraith made in the 1960s have been superseded by events. However, the model has enough flexibility to incorporate newer developments, including the process of special interest to International Political Economy, the globalization of the last 30 years.

Table 4.1 compares key attributes of the multi-centric organizational model and the market model.

A better way?

As mentioned earlier, Galbraith was unhappy with many of the real-world consequences of the corporate-dominated multi-centric organizational system that he described. But he remained optimistic that improvements were possible within the current system. In other words, he, like others of this school of thought, advocated reform, not revolution. The key strategy is *redistribution*, the basic principle of President Franklin Roosevelt's New Deal, which opponents of interventionist government continue to resist. Redistribution implies progressive taxation, which takes wealth from those best-off and shares it with those not so fortunate, both nationally and internationally. The Scandinavian countries have been much more effective in the use of this strategy than has the United States. But in order for this vision to assert itself, significant restrictions have to be imposed on the acquisition of too much power by any segment of the political economy. Currently, corporate power is in the ascendant. For reform to occur, corporations need to come under global, democratic control. In order for that to happen, effective democracy needs to more fully permeate many organizations around the world, including many governments.

Historically, the political-economic systems that end up dominating are those that are favored by the winners in the changing allocations of power. The private market replaced government-led mercantilism when business owners acquired more power. When small businesses were transformed into megacorporations, corporate agendas began to dominate. MCO reformers need to identify what groups could emerge that would challenge the current power structure. The MCO model gives considerable insight into how the current system works, but it does not provide much guidance as to how it might actually be reformed, though there is no shortage of wonderful visions for the future. At the end of the next chapter, we will look at the content of some of these reform agendas.

REVIEW QUESTIONS

1 How did Thorstein Veblen's institutionalism inform his critique of neoclassical economics?

2 What did Karl Polanyi mean by "fictional commodities," and how did this concept inform his critique of neoclassical economics?

3 Describe the essence of Piero Sraffa's cost of production value theory.

4 Explain the concepts of revised sequence, technostructure, and oligopolistic markets.

5 Explicate the eight corporate-control strategies that Galbraith identified in *The New Industrial State* (1967).

6 Discuss how the premises of the multi-centric organizational (MCO) model interact in order to create the projected outcomes.

7 Compare the outcomes of the MCO model with those of the market model.

BIBLIOGRAPHY

Anderson, Sarah, John Cavanagh, Chuck Collins, Sam Pizzigati, and Mike Lapham, *Executive Excess 2007: The Staggering Social Cost of U.S. Business Leadership* (Institute for Policy Studies and United for a Fair Economy: Washington, D.C.) 2007.

Caspari, Volker, "Sraffa, Piero (1898–1983)," in R. J. Barry Jones (ed.), *Routledge Encyclopedia of International Political Economy* (Routledge: London) 2001.

Cole, Ken, John Cameron, and Chris Edwards, *Why Economists Disagree: The Political Economy of Economics* (Longman: London) 1983.

Davies, James, Susanna Sandström, and Edward Wolff, *The World Distribution of Household Wealth* (United Nations University: Helsinki) 2006.

Edwards, Chris, *The Fragmented World: Competing Perspectives on Trade, Money and Crisis* (Methuen: London) 1985.

Galbraith, John Kenneth, *The Affluent Society* (Riverside Press: Cambridge, Massachusetts) 1958.

Galbraith, John Kenneth, *American Capitalism: The Concept of Countervailing Power* (Riverside Press: Cambridge, Massachusetts) 1952.

Galbraith, John Kenneth, *Economics in Perspective: A Critical History* (Houghton Mifflin: Boston) 1987.

Galbraith, John Kenneth, *Economics and the Public Purpose* (Houghton Mifflin: Boston) 1973.

Galbraith, John Kenneth, "Economics as a system of belief," in J. K. Galbraith, *Economics, Peace and Laughter* (Houghton Mifflin: Boston) 1971, pp. 60–87.

Galbraith, John Kenneth, *The New Industrial State* (Houghton Mifflin: Boston) 1967.

Heilbroner, Robert, *The Worldly Philosophers: The Lives, Times and Ideas of the Great Economic Thinkers,* 6th edn. (Simon and Schuster: New York) 1986.

Knoedler, Janet, "Thorstein Veblen on the predatory nature of capitalism," in Charles Sackrey and Geoffrey Schneider (eds.), *Introduction to Political Economy* (Dollars and Sense: Cambridge, Massachusetts) 2002, pp. 20–31.

Korten, David C., *When Corporations Rule the World,* 2nd edn. (Berrett-Koehler Publishers: San Francisco) 2001.

McGregor, Richard, "China's prosperity brings income gap," *Financial Times,* August 9, 2007, p. 2.

Miller, John, "Mind boggling inequality: Enough to make even Adam Smith worry," *Dollars and Sense,* January/February, 2007, pp. 9–11.

Nace, Ted, *Gangs of America: The Rise of Corporate Power and the Disabling of Democracy* (Berrett-Koehler: San Francisco) 2003.

Parker, Richard, *John Kenneth Galbraith: His Life, His Politics, His Economics* (Farrar, Straus and Giroux: New York) 2005.

Polanyi, Karl, *The Great Transformation: The Political and Economic Origins of Our Time* (Rinehart: New York) 1944.

Reich, Robert B., *Supercapitalism: The Transformation of Business, Democracy and Everyday Life* (Alfred A. Knopf: New York) 2007.

Sinha, Ajit, "Surplus approach to political economy," in Phillip Anthony O'Hara (ed.), *Encyclopedia of Political Economy* (Routledge: London) 1999.

Sraffa, Piero, *The Production of Commodities by Means of Commodities: Prelude to a Critique of Economic Theory* (Cambridge University Press: Cambridge, United Kingdom) 1960.

Strange, Susan, *States and Markets* (Pinter: London) 1988; 2nd edition, 1994.

Veblen, Thorstein, *Higher Learning in America: A Memorandum on the Conduct of Universities by Business Men* (B. W. Huebsch: New York) 1918.

Veblen, Thorstein, *The Theory of the Leisure Class* (Macmillan: New York) 1899.

Wolff, Robert Paul, "Piero Sraffa and the rehabilitation of classical political economy," in Randy P. Albeda, Christopher E. Gunn, and William Waller (eds.), *Alternatives to Economic Orthodoxy* (M. E. Sharpe: Armonk, New York) 1987.

CHAPTER 5

The Multi-Centric Organizational World View

Critical applications

Many scholars and practitioners analyze the global economy from the perspective of the multi-centric organizational (MCO) world view. Of course, they do not use the MCO label since the construct of an "MCO school of thought" is unique to this text. This chapter will apply the MCO perspective in greater depth to some of the issues previously raised. The central topics are: problems of "free trade," the global financial "casino," ecological degradation, and "corporate colonialism." The final section of the chapter will present some of the reform proposals that members of this school of thought have put forward.

PROBLEMS OF "FREE TRADE"

"Free trade" is put in quotation marks because proponents of the MCO perspective believe that actual trading practices are neither free nor mutually beneficial for the participating countries. However, those few countries and corporations that have been benefiting from the trading regime rationalize their gains as the consequence of "free trade." Presented below are some of the problems with the so-called "free trade" approach that have been identified by different MCO thinkers.

Static vs. dynamic orientation

The conventional market theory of trade, consistent with neoclassical economic assumptions, is ahistorical (static). That means that free trading countries should follow their current comparative advantages in their importing and exporting decisions, regardless of their stage of economic development (dynamic). The basic rules of the General Agreement on Tariffs and Trade (GATT) follow this static principle. The central rule states that there should be no tariff discrimination among members of GATT. If some members negotiate a reduction in tariffs between them, then they are supposed to apply those same reductions to all other members. Members of GATT are not supposed to favor some members over others. All members of GATT (now incorporated into the WTO) are each others' favored nations. Therefore, the principle is known as the MFN, for "most favored nation."

MCO adherents point out that this approach ignores the implications of countries being at different stages of economic development. It inherently provides the more developed countries with a built-in comparative advantage in technologically advanced industries. Trade will then serve as a means of maintaining the existing differentials between the less and more industrialized. Many poorer or less developed countries who follow or are forced to follow their static comparative advantage will continue to export primary raw materials while importing technologically sophisticated products rather than developing their own industrial capacities. Yet, historically, nearly all the currently highly industrialized countries recognized that they had to protect their own domestic manufacturing when it was struggling to achieve technical parity with countries that had developed ahead of them. In other words, they protected their own "infant industries" with tariffs in opposition to the principle of free trade. This group of countries includes, among others, France, Germany, and the United States before World War II and Japan, Taiwan, and South Korea after World War II. The GATT rules do recognize several different kinds of exceptions to the "no discrimination approach" but, especially since the 1980s, the pressure has been to make all countries lower their tariff barriers. Free traders believe that following this policy will help countries develop, while MCO'ers believe that it will prevent many countries from developing. They cite the devastation of existing local industries that occurred in the 1980s and 1990s under the free trade structural adjustment policies of the World Bank and the IMF. Senegal, for example, lost one-third of its manufacturing jobs from trade liberalization. Similar or worse collapses of manufacturing capacity occurred in the Ivory Coast, Nigeria, Ghana, Tanzania, Peru, Ecuador, and elsewhere. Despite these experiences, the current round of WTO negotiations (the Doha Round, which started in 2001 and continues in 2008) includes proposals for tariff reductions in less developed countries. The less developed countries are resisting as they consider this free trade approach to be inherently unfair to them, since it undermines their development aspirations. They believe that free trade rationalizations, based on static as opposed to dynamic comparative advantage, are being used to push policies that discriminate against them (Cavanagh and Mander, *Alternatives to Economic Globalization*).

Terms of trade

A related MCO critique of the free trade approach is the terms-of-trade analysis associated with Raul Prebisch, a Latin American economist. He argued in the 1950s and 1960s that the structure of international trade was inherently biased against the economic interests of the less developed countries. For Prebisch the manifestation of that bias was the deteriorating terms of trade for the poor countries in relationship to the rich. **Terms of trade** refers to the value ratio of exports to imports, that is, the ratio of the amount of export sales that is required to purchase a certain amount of imports. A country's terms of trade are declining when it takes an increased amount of exports sales to buy the same amount of imported goods and services. For example, Prebisch calculated that over the period from 1880 to 1938, the terms of trade turned against poor countries so much that by 1938 poor countries had to increase their export sales by 58 percent just in order to get the same value of imports that they could have received in 1880. This decline in trading position was due to the fact that poor countries were mostly exporting primary commodities (agricultural and mineral products) while importing mostly manufactured goods. Prebisch used a multi-centric organizational approach to explain this long-term disparity. He argued that the state of technology, labor conditions, and oligopolistic markets in the rich countries enabled them to keep their manufactured goods export prices relatively higher than raw material imports, which were subject to greater competition. Prebisch added that rich countries magnified their advantage by subsidizing agribusiness via either direct payments or tariff protections (Edwards, *The Fragmented World*).

This terms-of-trade problem still seems to exist for some commodities and countries. For instance, the terms of trade for coffee exporters have fallen approximately 50 percent from 1965 to 2000. The agriculture subsidy problem has not gone away either. An effort is being made in the current WTO trade negotiations to lower these multi-billion dollar subsidies in Europe, Japan, and the United States. In mid-2008 the negotiations remain stalled. Even though the rich countries had agreed in the Uruguay Round that within ten years of 1995 they would significantly lower their agricultural subsidies, not only has little been accomplished, but some subsidy programs have actually increased.

Another economist in the 1970s, by the name of Arghiri Emmanuel, took the Prebisch analysis one step further. He argued that all types of products exported from less developed countries, not just primary products, face declining terms of trade. Therefore, even when countries manage to succeed at exporting manufactured goods, such as textiles, they will still experience unfavorable terms of trade. The reason for that, according to Emmanuel, was the weakness of labor in the poor countries, which have large numbers of under- and unemployed laborers with little bargaining power. Consequently, wages are very low, even when worker productivity increases. Free trade advocates tend to overlook this labor situation when they proclaim the great gains that will be forthcoming from increased liberalization of trade. That's the case even though the theory behind the predicted mutual gains from free trade is premised on the existence of full employment. China, the great export-growth success story of the last 20 years, has experienced this weak-labor phenomenon. Most of the manufacturing capacity added in the last 20 years in the Third World has been in China. As a consequence, China's export revenues have jumped substantially, yet the price ratio terms of trade have declined approximately 20 percent, primarily because of cheap labor. China still has millions of peasants moving from the countryside to the cities willing to accept any employment that's available (Kaplinsky, *Globalization, Poverty and Inequality*).

Capital confusion

This phrase refers to a serious flaw that MCO proponents believe exists in the neoclassical theory of free trade. As noted in Chapter 3, the theory was developed by two Swedish economists, Eli Heckscher and Bertil Ohlin, and modified by the American economist Paul Samuelson. The theory argues that relative factor endowments (land, labor, and capital) will determine comparative advantage and whether, therefore, a country will specialize in labor-intensive or capital-intensive production for export. Presumably, a country with relatively cheap capital will specialize in exporting products that use more capital and less labor. But how does one know that capital is relatively cheap? Well, by the price of course. But how does one isolate the price of capital? Unfortunately, the theory doesn't differentiate between financial capital (saving) and physical capital (investment). Yet one is dependent on the other. Physical capital prices reflect rates of return. But, as Sraffa demonstrated (see Chapter 4), rates of return are dependent on the distribution struggle between capital and labor. Thus, there is no means of independently ascertaining the factor price of capital. Therefore, comparative advantage cannot be determined by a natural market process (per neoclassical economic theory), but only by an institutional expression of relative power between labor and capital (per MCO theory) (Edwards, *The Fragmented World*).

Conditions contravention

As pointed out in Chapter 3, the achievement of mutual gains from comparative-advantage free trade between countries depends on certain conditions being satisfied. Those conditions include full employment, balanced trade, and capital immobility. MCO proponents note that not only are these conditions ignored by most advocates of "free trade," but they even promote the contrary when it suits their interests. The most outstanding example of contravention behavior involves capital. Both classical (Ricardo) and neoclassical (Heckscher–Ohlin) theories of comparative advantage have a condition of capital immobility, that is, capital stays in its home country. Only under that restriction can a confident prediction of mutual benefit be made. However, when a country sends its capital overseas, it transfers a part of its comparative advantage to another country. If the capital-recipient country has a large supply of cheap labor, its absolute advantage (cheap prices across the board) also increases. Usually that situation creates trade imbalances. In the last 20 years China has exemplified this pattern. China has been the biggest beneficiary of foreign direct investment among the less developed countries. Much of that investment has gone into manufacturing capacity for export. As a consequence, large trade surpluses have been generated by China, meaning large trade deficits for other countries, such as the United States. Chinese workers have yet to see much benefit, but owners of Chinese businesses are doing very well. Customers of corporations such as Wal-Mart also benefit from low-priced goods. Wal-Mart alone accounts for 15 percent of the U.S. trade deficit with China.

The most extreme version of capital mobility would be the unregulated transfers of short-term speculation money around the globe that financial services corporations and free traders pushed strongly in the 1980s and 1990s ("hot money"). When the bottom fell out of the speculative bubble in the late 1990s, the bankers were bailed out by the IMF, but not the workers and small businesses of the affected countries. (These financial crises will be covered in more detail in the section on the "global casino.") MCO analysts were not surprised by any of these events because they were consistent with the MCO model. They represent, however, clear contraventions of the market model conditions. Yet, paradoxically, cross-border capital mobility and government bailouts were most strongly advocated by people claiming allegiance to the free market and free trade approaches (Daly, *Beyond Growth*).

Deindustrialization

Another MCO economist, Ravi Batra, argues that the "free trade" program that the United States has pursued since World War II, especially since the severance of the gold–dollar connection in 1973, has been responsible for the income stagnation of non-professional American workers. U.S. income inequality has grown as more than half of the well-paying manufacturing jobs have been sent overseas (**deindustrialization**). At first they went to Western Europe with the Marshall Plan, then to Japan, then to the four East Asian "Tigers" (Taiwan, South Korea, Hong Kong, and Singapore), then to Mexico, and most recently to China. The service jobs that replaced the lost manufacturing jobs receive on average only half the salary of jobs that were moved overseas. Few service employers offer full health and pension benefits. It's not surprising that most service employers are non-union whereas most manufacturing employers are unionized. This income stagnation among the U.S. working class demonstrates to MCO'ers that, since the 1970s, there has been no connection between productivity increases and wages. Batra contends that U.S. trade policy, justified under the banner of "free trade," was responsible for undermining the power of workers and lowering their standard of living. On the other hand, corporations did very well. This shift in income distribution had nothing to do with productivity, as the market might suggest, but everything to do with the success of the corporations over labor in the power struggle between labor and capital (Batra, *The Myth of Free Trade*).

Benefits vs. losses

MCO proponents are deeply skeptical of the claims of free trade advocates such as the World Bank that everyone wins from increased free trade. According to empirical studies using the World Bank's own trade models, 36 less developed countries that adopted the most open trade policies in the 1990s experienced increases in the incidence of poverty. Projections from the likely outcomes of the trade liberalization being pushed in the current WTO negotiations (Doha Round) are similarly instructive: All the countries south of the Sahara except South Africa will experience net losses if the proposed tariff reductions are implemented. Other countries, such as Bangladesh, will also be losers. Many other developing countries will end up net losers when their moderate gains from trade are compared with their substantial losses of tariff revenues. In fact, tariff revenue losses are projected by UNCTAD (the United Nations Conference on Trade and Development) to be almost ten times greater than the trade benefits ($63.4 billion vs. $6.7 billion) (Wise and Gallagher, "Doha Round and developing countries").

These free trade–induced losses happen for some countries because the actual circumstances in their economies do not match the theoretical expectations of the free trade model. Because of the flaws in the free trade theory noted above, price signals might induce countries to shift resources in ways that cost their economies more than they gain. For example, shifting production from machinery used to produce one type of goods to another in response to trade-affected price changes might cost more than it gains, especially if the previously used machinery has no other feasible application. The same could be said for labor. Some workers will end up unemployed. Again the human and economic costs could be greater than the gains from trade. Thus, according to MCO thinking, it is not possible to say definitively that comparative-advantage free trade will result in positive net economic benefits. A further complication that reinforces this conclusion is possible movements in exchange and interest rates. Because shifting a country's production mix in response to trade pressures takes time, the trade deficit may increase in the meantime, potentially causing a decline in the value of the currency. In order to protect the value of the currency, the country's central bank may decide to increase interest rates. Higher interest rates will probably discourage capital investment in the country's economy, but they could encourage unproductive speculative flows. Keynes was worried about scenarios of this type happening as "speculation drives out enterprise" (Edwards, *The Fragmented World*).

Another questionable assumption of the Heckscher–Ohlin free trade theory is that technology or knowledge is equally available throughout the world. The laws that protect intellectual property such as patents and copyrights directly violate this assumption. In fact, the rules of the presumably free trade–oriented World Trade Organization give special protection to intellectual property. The beneficiaries of this protection are the major corporations, who own 90 percent of the valuable technology. It has been estimated that the Trade Related Intellectual Property provision of the WTO (the TRIPs) supports the transfer of $41 billion a year in royalty payments from poor countries to multi-national corporations based mostly in rich countries (Eagleton, *Under the Influence*).

The advocates of the neoclassical free trade theory recognize that there may be losers within the countries involved in trading relationships because of displacements. However, they firmly believe that the overall net result will be positive. Therefore, their solution to this problem is for the winners to compensate the losers. Not surprisingly, the MCO supporters find this solution to be another example of the unrealistic nature of the free market approach.

THE GLOBAL CASINO

Beyond trade, the realm of international finance has also been investigated by members of the MCO school of thought. For many decades the scholar providing the leadership in this endeavor was **Susan Strange** (1923–1998), widely identified as one of the founders of the modern field of International Political Economy. One of the topics on which she focused was the unregulated and volatile global financial market. She considered it the world's biggest short-term problem. Her last book, *Mad Money*, addressed it. Ten years earlier she had authored another book on the same topic, *Casino Capitalism*. In both books she followed in the steps of John Maynard Keynes, who had warned in his 1930s publications about the dangers to capitalism from the "speculative casino" (Lawton et al., *Strange Power*).

SUSAN STRANGE
1923–1998
British journalist and academic whom many consider the founder of modern International Political Economy. Highlighted the decision-making roles of corporations along with nation-states and the importance and dangers of the unanchored global financial system. A few of her important books are *States and Markets* (1988), *Casino Capitalism* (1986), and *Mad Money* (1998).

MCO thinking about money and financial markets is quite different from the market school of thought. Market adherents perceive money as a neutral commodity that serves primarily as a medium of exchange, facilitating supply–demand relationships. The value of money, like any other commodity, is determined by supply and demand. On the other hand, MCO proponents like Polanyi consider these conceptions nothing but "working fictions." To them, money is neither neutral nor a commodity. They agree with Max Weber, the German economic historian and sociologist, who contended that money is a weapon in the struggle between major interest groups in society (Ingham, *The Nature of Money*).

So what then is money from the MCO perspective? In order to answer that question, some financial history is helpful. The MCO story is somewhat different from the tale told in Chapter 3, which started with goldsmith shops. The story begins in Babylonia, 5,000 years ago. From its beginning money has been a unit of account, a measuring stick of relative value whose legitimacy is established by a public authority such as a ruler or a state. The major purpose of this unit of account was to provide a means for calculating relative tax burdens. In Babylonia tax obligations could be fulfilled with a variety of items, such as crops, labor, animals, or handicrafts. But what was the relative worth of all these items? The unit of account was used in ascertaining the relative values. It was a recordkeeping device. It took several thousand more years before this process was facilitated with an intermediate token. Alexander the Great used tokens or coins to pay his troops. But what the coins were worth was established by Alexander, not by any inherent metallic value. A similar situation prevailed in the Roman Empire. After the Roman Empire disintegrated, there were numerous coinages circulating in Europe. In order to transcend this coinage anarchy, Emperor Charlemagne in the eighth century decided to impose a standard unit of account throughout his realm (the Holy Roman Empire). His purpose was the same as the Babylonians—the regularization of the payment of taxes to him and the Church. The money-changers had to come up with exchange ratios between the various coinages so that trade could be conducted, but the comprehensive and abstract units of accounting were provided by Charlemagne. Although the coins contained metal, even precious metals such as silver or gold, the standard unit of account system had no relation to metallic content (Ingham, *The Nature of Money*).

As supplies of silver and gold became increasingly available in Europe, more coins were minted with silver and gold. The big shift to gold began in the thirteenth century with the arrival of large amounts of gold from Africa. Thus began a several hundred year period of European infatuation with gold as the ultimate symbol of wealth. As noted earlier, the Spanish set out in the fifteenth century to conquer the world in the search for gold. They succeeded in confiscating huge stores of gold from the Aztecs (in Mexico) and the Incas (in Peru). Eventually, as also discussed earlier, the gold standard of financial settlement was established within Europe and ultimately for the trading world. According to Polanyi, gold was elevated to this central monetary role by financiers, with the support of the state, who believed that gold's scarcity was a way of protecting the value of the claims due them from borrowers. It was an expression of power by creditors over debtors, whether public or private. The gold standard went into decline because of the disruption of the two world wars and the Great Depression. It was not fully abolished until 1973.

This centrality of gold during the development of the modern economic system led people to believe that gold, the commodity, was the basis of money. However, according to members of the MCO school of thought, this conception confuses the means of payment with "moneyness." **Moneyness** is constructed as a social relation by a public authority, such as the state, when it determines the unit of account in which debt will be paid, especially taxes owed to the authority. Logically and chronologically, this determination of abstract relative values must precede the creation of vehicles, such as coins, which are used as means of payment. The Florentine florin, or the English pound, or the U.S. dollar is the unit of account. It could have 100 parts, or 16 parts, or whatever the public authority decides. Even during the heyday of the gold standard, it was still the state that decided how much gold there was to the currency unit (Ingham, *The Nature of Money*).

The advent of capitalism brings the whole issue of what money is to a new level of complexity. In capitalism private bills of exchange become monetized. And private institutions known as banks are eventually allowed to create money "out of thin air" with their ability to issue credit that is acceptable as money. **Bills of exchange** are promises to pay between parties, usually based on some underlying store of wealth such as a shipload of spices due to arrive in two months. These bills were used by Arab merchants, and the practice was copied by merchants in the Italian city-states as a means of fulfilling debt obligations. In the sixteenth century the bills became transferable and thus served as a form of private money. In fact, banks can probably trace their origins to medieval money-changers who made their living exchanging between multiple coinages and units of account, not goldsmith shops. Even the word *bank* comes from the Latin word for bench, the location where the changers plied their trade in the town square. The first public banks were in the Italian city-states in the fourteenth century. They monetized credit–debt relationships between members of the ruling oligarchy, and they accepted deposits. In the late seventeenth century the Dutch and then the English integrated the private and public credit–debt relationships into general banks, and the transferable bills of exchange evolved into checks. The banks were then able to issue checks and notes. These were depersonalized notations of credit–debt relationships that served as money (Ingham).

As discussed in Chapter 3, general banks hold only a percentage of their deposits on reserve, so that they can make loans or credit money, which cumulatively adds to the money supply. As discussed in Chapter 1, the British were the first to pull it all together with the creation of a national monetary system that included a central bank. In 1697 the Bank of England was given the right by Parliament to take deposits, issue bank notes, and discount bills of exchange. The bank as a lending institution was made more credible by the commitment of Parliament to approve the taxes required to pay off the public debt with interest. Even though the Italians and the Dutch had invented all of the components, the English were the first to have the internal political balance that provided the necessary foundation for a national, capitalist-style banking system. The balance of power between the monarchy, Parliament, merchants, financiers, and landowners was made possible by the "glorious revolution" of 1688. In contrast, during the same period the French monarch took full power and abolished the private banking system (Ingham).

As capitalism spread from Great Britain to Western Europe and the Americas in the nineteenth and early twentieth centuries, the power of the financial segment of the society grew along with it. Financial markets, "the headquarters of capitalism," become ever more prominent in the economies of the more industrialized countries. The banking system created more credit-money, and the stock market created more equity value. But any financial house of cards can just as easily collapse, as they periodically have in the history of capitalism. Sometimes monetary and equity values are created that exceed the underlying economic capacities. The capitalist financial system allows overly enthusiastic players to create a speculative "bubble" that inevitably bursts. When the stock market speculative bubble of the 1920s crashed down to earth in 1929–1930, it greatly exacerbated the Great Depression of the 1930s. During high-flying financial booms, such as the 1920s, income inequality inevitably increases as returns to credit and equity soar while wages stagnate. It's the capitalist financial system that allows this expansion of income and wealth for the rich. During the 1920s, the top 20 percent of income recipients increased their share from one-fifth to one-third of national income. However, when the bursting bubble is economy-wide, it has major political implications. In several countries in the period between World War I and World War II, the political consequence was fascism. In the United States it brought the election in 1932 of Franklin Delano Roosevelt as president and his New Deal. He used his political leverage to humble the financiers while giving more power to government, production corporations, and even labor unions. As a consequence income distribution shifted in the direction of these other segments of the society. In the several decades after World War II, thanks to the power shifts associated with the New Deal, incomes for workers actually kept up with productivity increases, and the American middle class was created. Families could own a house and a car and send their children to college with only one income recipient in the household. From the MCO perspective, because of this power shift, the 1950s and 1960s were the "age of the middle class" (Heilbroner, *The Making of Economic Society*).

However, this shift was unacceptable to the financiers (Keynes called them the "rentiers"). After all, they were used to being the dominant power. In order to regain their pre-eminence, the financiers embarked on a series of business and political programs to reestablish their prominence. They urged the government to rescind restrictive regulations and laws; they collaborated with production corporations to reduce the power of organized labor; they promoted globalization, which reduced the power of governments; they invented all sorts of financial strategies that subjected production corporations to the power of the financial markets; and they lobbied the government to lower taxes on the financial sector. They were very successful in all of these endeavors. Ingham references several studies that claim that the financial sector grew from just 2 percent of U.S. GDP in 1950 to over 50 percent by the late 1980s (*The Nature of Money*, p. 158).

Their first major political breakthroughs were the elections of Margaret Thatcher as U.K. prime minister in 1979 and Ronald Reagan as U.S. president in 1980. The Thatcher–Reagan ideological platform was "free market," but their real political objective, according to the MCO analysis, was the "revenge of the rentiers" (Ingham).

To those with an MCO perspective, it is not surprising that the decades after 1980 have been characterized, especially in the United States, by wage stagnation and growing income inequality as the financial sector continues to take an ever-increasing share of the national income. One poignant example of this trend comes from the aftermath of the September 11 tragedy. The government agreed to provide fair compensation to the families of the victims of the destruction of the World Trade Center towers. It was revealed that "fair" was determined by how much the victims were making in annual salaries. That led to big differentials, as cooks in the restaurant were making $40,000 per year while financial traders were making $1 million per year. From the market perspective these large income disparities are appropriate as they reflect market outcomes. They were presumably determined by the neutral process of supply and demand, whereas the MCO world view sees these large income differences as a manifestation of power differentials in social relationships.

The globalization strategy of the financiers started in the 1970s with the demise of the Bretton Woods dollar/gold standard in international exchange. The first big move was the opening of foreign currency accounts in Europe, especially with the U.S. dollar. These so-called "Eurodollar accounts" enabled U.S. and other financial institutions to expand credit operations without close regulatory scrutiny. They were beyond the geographical scope of the U.S. Federal Reserve System, and the European regulators did not keep careful watch over these accounts, as they were not in their home currencies. The extensive lending of commercial banks from their euro petrodollar accounts in the late 1970s to Third World countries, especially in Latin America, was a major contributor to the Third World debt crisis of the early 1980s.

The end of the dollar/gold standard in 1973 meant a movement to floating exchange rates for all the world's major currencies and an explosion in the size of foreign exchange markets. The daily foreign exchange trading expanded from a few hundred billion dollars to $2 trillion. These international currency markets were mostly beyond the regulatory control of national authorities. Before the movement to floating exchange rates, most of the transactions in these markets were related to trade and actual economic investment. Now, approximately 90 percent of the transactions are related to speculative financial activity (Strange, *Mad Money*).

In the early 1980s a wave of free market deregulation swept over the major industrial countries as the Thatcher and Reagan regimes spearheaded "neoliberalism." Within the developed countries that policy meant opening up the financial sector. Regulatory protective barriers that had been put in place during the Great Depression were rescinded. In the United States, for instance, the restriction placed on commercial banks that prohibited them from serving as stockbrokers and insurance vendors was repealed. Ostensibly that was necessary so that American banks could compete with the so-called "universal banks" in Europe and Japan. It also facilitated the greater concentration of financial services, not to mention the assumption of greater risk. For the world, deregulation meant a big push toward "capital mobility." Funds would be allowed to flow freely back and forth across national borders in response to market signals. Capital controls or restrictions on free cross-border monetary flows would be dismantled. At the urging of the United States, the IMF and the World Bank promoted capital mobility, sometimes coercing countries to open their financial markets through loan conditions. This policy was one of the components of the structural adjustment programs of the 1980s and 1990s.

Partly as a consequence of these policies in the 1980s and 1990s, a number of countries experienced financial crises. They had more obligations to foreigners than they had the financial means to satisfy them. This difficulty occurred especially with short-term lending. Mexico had two such episodes, the first in the early 1980s and the second in the mid-1990s. In both instances the United States government played a major role in bailing out Mexico. The motivation for the United States, from the MCO perspective, was not so much being a good neighbor as making sure that the American banks and other financial institutions that had been the major lenders to Mexico were able to collect on their loans in U.S. dollars. The consequence for Mexico was a severe decline in the standard of living for most of its citizens, from 30 to 50 percent. In other words, in order for the financial capitalists to be rescued, other segments of the society had to pay the price. It is another example of how the financial sector exercised its dominant power in the latter decades of the twentieth century. From the MCO point of view, these are not natural processes, as claimed by free market advocates (Strange, *Mad Money*).

Another major financial crisis was the Asian crisis of 1997. It started in Thailand and spread to Indonesia, South Korea, Hong Kong, and other countries. All of these countries had recently implemented the free capital mobility policy. Short-term foreign funds poured in because the returns were higher than elsewhere. This was the flow of "hot money" referred to in Chapter 3. Unfortunately, Thailand maintained a fixed, or pegged, relationship between its currency, the baht, and the U.S. dollar. As it turned out, the peg was too high; it overvalued the baht. When the real estate bubble that had drawn in the foreign funds began to burst, the foreign lenders began to pull out their money. As the foreign creditors pulled out of the Thai baht and moved back into U.S. dollars, the Thai currency came under tremendous selling pressure, lowering its unofficial value far below the peg. The Thai government tried to shore up the value of its currency by buying it with dollars from their foreign exchange reserves. Unfortunately, they had insufficient reserves to match the outward flow, and they were forced to give up the peg and devalue the currency. The Thai financial structure was close to collapsing. The IMF came to the "rescue," but its major concern was making sure that the international creditors were repaid. As in Mexico, it was the ordinary citizens of Thailand who paid the price as the economy was depressed for several years. The plight of Indonesia was even worse (Bello et al., *Global Finance*).

The only countries in Asia that managed to mostly escape the 1997 financial crisis were those, such as Malaysia and China, that did not allow free capital mobility. "Hot money" was not allowed to move freely in and out of their countries. Ironically, before the turmoil in the Asian financial markets, the IMF had been intent on changing its charter at a 1997 meeting in Hong Kong. It would have called on all members to accept full capital mobility so that the "efficient" international markets could determine the movement of funds around the globe. It was the epitome of what the Nobel Prize winner Joseph Stiglitz called "market fundamentalism." Needless to say, the experience of the Asian countries scuttled the proposal. In contrast to the Latin American and African countries that were the major victims of the Third World debt crisis of the 1980s, the Asian economies that got into trouble did not have fiscal or current account deficits. Their economies were sound. They were not, however, prepared for uncontrolled movements of short-term cross-border financial capital. While market believers tried to blame the crisis on "Asian cronyism," MCO analysts knew that claim was nonsense. Rather, the crisis was due to the power overreach of the global financial sector seeking to enhance and protect its returns (Stiglitz, *Globalization and Its Discontents*).

In the first few years of the twenty-first century, these financial crises were followed by the collapse of the dot-com boom in the stock markets. In the 1990s many people were behaving as if it were the 1920s all over again—only now they had computers. Many people gave up their regular jobs in order to stay home and be "day traders." Unfortunately, when the stock markets crashed, the only winners were the brokers who collected the commissions on the transactions and those traders who speculatively bet on the crash happening. But the bursting of the dot-com bubble was only a pause in the rule of Wall Street. Even the biggest corporations found themselves slaves to the short-term profit expectations of "the Street." Long-term planning is subservient to large stockholders' insistence on maximum profits now, not later, in order to maximize immediate stock value. Corporations engaged in downsizing, cutting labor benefits, outsourcing, and shifting production overseas—all in an effort to cut costs and maximize profits. The unforgiving stock markets gave them no choice.

The financial sector's dominance has been facilitated by the lack of regulation in the global markets, the growth of unregulated hedge funds, and the continuous invention of a series of new financial vehicles called **derivatives**. **Hedge funds** are financial organizations that mobilize funds from rich clients, whether individuals or institutions, and then seek to provide them higher returns by taking more risk in global markets. Playing derivatives is a part of their strategy. Derivatives are second-order financial vehicles that derive their value from some underlying asset such as stocks, bonds, commodities, collateralized debt, mortgages, or foreign exchange. Both hedge-fund and derivative purchases can be done with very little money down. The rest is borrowed or promised. Or, as Eatwell and Taylor said, they create "towers of leverage." They agree with Susan Strange that the potential risk for volatility and even profound collapse of the whole financial house of cards is immense. If that happens, as it did in 1929, the rest of the society pays the price. Naturally, the financial capitalists play down the risks and insist that they are increasing the efficiency of the world's markets (Eatwell and Taylor, *Global Finance at Risk*).

In the summer of 2007, at least one part of the global financial house of cards came tumbling down. The values of unregulated, poorly described derivatives based on pools of high-risk mortgages, known as subprime loans, collapsed. Even though the subprime loans were made mostly in the United States, the viability of financial institutions all over the world, from Germany to China, was placed in jeopardy as they had purchased these derivatives. The financial crisis was global, and the ensuing "credit crunch" was also global. Central banks all over the world had to intervene assertively in order to bring confidence back into the financial markets.

From the MCO perspective, the establishment of the euro is another example of rentier dominance. The 15 countries (in 2008) that have abandoned their own currencies and adopted the euro have turned their monetary policies over to the European Central Bank (ECB) in Frankfurt. The overriding purpose of the ECB is price stability, especially the control of inflation. Of course, that is exactly what the creditors want. The countries in the Eurozone have given up the possibility of going to their own central banks and seeking financial coverage of a fiscal deficit that may be required to fight a slowdown or recession in their national economy. In order to borrow for this public purpose, these countries have to go to the private financial markets and take whatever terms are available. Public debt will probably cost more, and that will put continuing fiscal pressure on the European governments to cut back on their social programs (Ingham, *The Nature of Money*).

The MCO model draws attention to the relative degrees of power possessed by the major sectors in the political economy, which can change over time. In the 1950s Galbraith observed that the power of the financial sector was counterbalanced by the possession of power by production corporations, governments, and unions. However, this "countervailing power" has been significantly dissipated by the disproportionate growth of the financial sector in the last few decades. MCO analysts believe the financial sector has reached the point where it has become too powerful. The risks involved in this imbalance endanger the whole of the global economy, especially since most transnational financial activity remains unregulated. MCO scholars are not opposed to a viable financial sector. They recognize its role in the effective functioning of a capitalist society. However, a healthy society requires a balance of interests in which no segment can operate outside community-generated rules. Excessive deregulation is a bad idea, especially in the financial sector. It's important to note that the system of checks and balances can be undermined by excessive power in any of the major sectors. Ingham gives the example of Argentina as a society in which labor became too strong. Under the post–World War II populist Peronist regime, wages became an entitlement, not a payment for work accomplished. Government could not collect taxes, and debt obligations could not be met. The economy began to stagnate. In the 1920s Argentina was the fourth-most productive economy in the world. By the twenty-first century it was the seventieth on the list, and it was responsible in 2001 for the largest national default in world history. The left-leaning governments that have been in office since the default blamed the IMF for aggravating its problems by extending too much credit. Consequently, from being one of the IMF's biggest debtors, Argentina has moved away from reliance on the IMF (Ingham, *The Nature of Money*).

MCO analysts remind us that because money is not a commodity, there is no benchmark for its value other than itself. There are no macroeconomic fundamentals to which the value of any currency in relation to any other can be empirically related. The "virtual credit-money" of the current capitalist system is just floating out there. It has value because some authority such as a central bank says it has, and the traders collectively believe it. It is a "working fiction." As Keynes noted many years ago, values in money markets are driven by the average opinion of what the average opinion will be. Eatwell and Taylor remark, "A floating exchange rate is not a 'price' that adjusts to equilibrate markets. Apart, that is, from the markets in which its own future values are set" (Eatwell and Taylor, *Global Finance at Risk*, p. 57).

Money, the credit system, the banking system, and financial markets are all social constructions, according to the MCO perspective. They reflect the power structure in the society. The economic historian Joseph Schumpeter called the financial markets the "headquarters of capitalism." Those headquarters are now global while regulations are still national. Susan Strange finished her last book, *Mad Money*, with this comment:

Our problem in the next century is that the traditional authority of the nation state is not up to the job of managing mad international money, yet its leaders are instinctively reluctant to entrust that job to unelected, unaccountable bureaucrats. . . . Perhaps, therefore, money has to become really much more mad and bad before the experience changes preferences and policies (p. 190).

ECOLOGICAL DEGRADATION

In the MCO model one of the expected outcomes is environmental degradation. That's because corporate power and the myopic view of the market combine to produce environmentally unfriendly behavior. The section below elaborates this MCO insight. Topics discussed include the ecological footprint, unsustainable use of resources, peak oil, climate change, market failure, and ecological economics.

In Susan Strange's opinion, although the short-term crisis facing the world is financial, the long-term one is ecological degradation. Human society is on a path that will lead to profound disruption of the ecological systems upon which human life depends. Our modern economic systems use or degrade more natural resources than the earth and sun make available. This deficit behavior is made possible by the existence of reserves that have been accumulated over millions of years. However, our unsustainable behavior is using up these reserves very rapidly. But instead of slowing down to avoid colliding with the wall of resource limits, we are driving faster. The incentives built into our economic systems are a major reason for our long-term destructive behavior.

One measure of our unsustainable behavior is called the **ecological footprint**. The footprint translates human resource use into one spatial measure, the acres of land and water surface required for economic activity. The economic behavior with the biggest impact on the footprint is the burning of fossil fuels for energy. The burning of fossil fuels is detrimental to humanity, directly from pollution and indirectly from the impact on global climate. The footprint measures the fossil fuel combustion impact by calculating the area of land and water required to absorb carbon dioxide emissions. The human activity with the second biggest environmental impact is the use of land and water to provide food, building materials, and other goods and services (World Wide Fund for Nature, *Living Planet Report 2004*).

The footprint of the human use of resources by our economies can be juxtaposed with measurement of the *biocapacity* that nature currently provides. Another land and water spatial measure, biocapacity includes resources such as fertile soil, fresh water, forests, and so on. By comparing the results of these two measures, it is possible to determine whether or not humans are living within the capacity that nature provides. In other words, they tell us whether or not we are living sustainably. The answer, not surprisingly, is no! Starting in the early 1980s the world's economies began to exceed their currently available natural resource capacities. That is, the world's footprint began exceeding its biocapacity. By the beginning of the twenty-first century, this continually growing gap had reached over 20 percent. In 2001 on a per capita basis (the total divided by population) the world had 4.5 acres of biocapacity available vs. a footprint usage of 5.4 acres. How is that possible? Simply stated, the answer is mining. Over millions of years nature has been storing past biocapacity. We are using these accumulated reserves. We have been using them so rapidly that their exhaustion is foreseeable. The most important and obvious examples of this rapid depletion are underground carbons—petroleum, coal, and natural gas. Other examples include soil and water, especially the large underground reservoirs of fresh water known as fossil aquifers that are not replenishable from rainfall. They are being heavily pumped all over the world, from China to the United States, mainly to support irrigated agriculture. Thousands of wells drilled into these aquifers have now run dry (World Wide Fund for Nature, *Living Planet Report 2004*).

The footprint vs. biocapacity behavior of countries can be compared by using per capita figures. For instance, the United States in 2001 used 23.5 acres per capita. That was 97 percent beyond its biocapacity of 11.61 acres and 422 percent beyond its "fair share" of the world's biocapacity (4.5 acres). "Fair share" is based on giving every human being the same amount of nature's bounty. The United States made up its ecological deficit by mining its own resource stocks as well as by importing resource stocks and biocapacity from other countries. For example, the United States imports 60 percent of its oil, and a high proportion of the forest products used in the United States comes from Canada. Obviously, any country's footprint is highly correlated with its level of economic development and consumption. In 2001 low-income countries had a per capita footprint of 2.0 acres, middle-income countries 4.7 acres, and high-income countries 15.8 acres. Because of their higher energy efficiency, Japan (10.6 acres) and Western Europe (12.6 acres) have significantly smaller footprints than the United States. China's footprint has been growing very rapidly, and its 2001 level of 3.7 acres already exceeded its biocapacity by 85 percent (World Wide Fund for Nature, *Living Planet Report 2004*).

The figures on the human overuse of natural resources are eye-opening. One crucial resource being overused is fresh water. Countries with over half of the world's population are drawing down their water resources faster than they can be replenished. Water is essential for grain crops. Four-fifths of the grain crop of China, the world's biggest producer, is dependent on irrigation. Yet its rivers are running dry, lakes are vanishing, and underground water is disappearing from overpumping. Three-fifths of India's grain is similarly dependent and vulnerable. Three other water-deficit countries, Algeria, Egypt, and Mexico, already import much of their grain. Since the production of 1 ton of grain requires 1,000 tons of water, notes Lester Brown, importing grain is the most efficient way to import water. If China's need for imported grain becomes truly desperate, its needs alone could exceed the total grain available from grain-exporting countries. As long as China has large reserves of foreign exchange, it can afford to import the grain it needs. But what happens then to all the other grain-deficit countries? In the market, the highest bidder gets the crop. Other bidders, regardless of their needs, will be left empty-handed. Actually, to some extent, the market's indifference to the consequences of unequal means is already having a global impact. Today a billion people in the world are starving—not because there isn't enough food, but because they are poor and cannot afford it (Brown, *Plan B 2.0*).

Other renewable resources that are being rapidly depleted include soils, forests, and fish. Some 75 percent of the world's fisheries are in decline, some collapsing, mostly because of overfishing. Rivalries between the fishing fleets of different countries compound the problem. The technical capacity to catch fish has far exceeded the reproductive ability of the fish. Some governments have continued to subsidize their fishing industry even after fisheries were known to be in serious trouble. Similarly, 40 percent of soils are degraded from erosion and overuse, especially from overgrazing. The loss of forest cover each year equals the size of the state of Kansas. Even though many governments, such as Brazil's, have tried to control deforestation, the illegal cutting, burning, and clearing continue. The economic incentives for overuse are just too great and law enforcement too weak. Ironically, since these resources are all potentially renewable, the problem is not with nature's bounty, but with human mismanagement (Brown, *Plan B 2.0*).

The non-renewables are also running out. Economically recoverable reserves of many minerals are getting low: lead—18 years, tin—20 years, copper—25 years, iron ore—64 years, bauxite—69 years (Brown, *Plan B 2.0*). Probably the most crucial non-renewable mineral supply problem is that of petroleum. For over 100 years the essential ingredient in economic growth has been cheap energy, and the main source of that cheap energy has been oil, appropriately nicknamed "black gold." Unfortunately, the industrial economies have been using this limited and valuable resource as if its supply were unlimited. It has been estimated that it took 422 years of sunlight to provide the fossil fuels that humans use currently during one year of energy consumption. The market is partly to blame for this wanton consumption because it prices oil on the basis of the current demand and supply, not the long-run restriction on availability. Industrial economies have been constructed around the implicit assumption that there will be cheap oil forever. The suburbs in America are a classic case, and they continue to be built with ever bigger, more energy-hungry houses. Transportation is the most salient and vulnerable part of the current oil-based economic infrastructure. But modern agriculture, or more correctly the modern food system, is also heavily dependent on petroleum-based energy. Besides transporting agricultural products long distances, petro-energy is also involved in plowing, pumping, harvesting, making fertilizers, preserving, packaging, and so forth. New discoveries of oil do not come close to matching current consumption. Consequently, many experts believe that the world will soon face *peak production* of oil. After the peak is reached, petroleum production will decrease each year, even while the demand continues to grow (Heinberg, *The Party's Over*). As a case in point, the citizens of the most populous country, China, are deciding that they would rather drive automobiles than ride bicycles. In 2006 only the citizens of the United States bought more cars than the Chinese, and the Chinese buy big cars, not little cars like the Europeans. A more expensive, bigger car "gives you more face." Beijing is already the most polluted and congested capital city in the world (Collier, in *San Francisco Chronicle*).

Perhaps the gravest challenge to the global environment and the future of industrial economies is **climate change**. Scientists agree almost unanimously that burning of fossil fuels is raising the earth's average temperature at an unprecedented rate, and thereby significantly changing the climate. Fossil fuel combustion releases greenhouse gases that trap solar heat in the atmosphere and prevent the heat from being reflected back into space. The most important greenhouse gas emitted from the burning of coal, oil, and natural gas is carbon dioxide. It is responsible for an estimated 80 percent of global warming. For the 8,000 years of human civilization up until the Industrial Revolution, carbon dioxide was stable at a level that kept the average temperature of the earth at 57°F. This level of carbon dioxide occurred naturally, and it maintained temperatures favorable to diverse life forms and human development. (With too little carbon dioxide the earth would be covered with ice; with too much the earth would be boiling. It's a fine balance.) In 1800, at the beginning of the Industrial Revolution, the concentration of carbon dioxide in the atmosphere was 280 parts per million. But as the fossil fuel–based technologies have spread around the globe, especially in the last 50 years, the carbon dioxide concentration in the atmosphere has increased to its 2007 level of 383 parts per million, the highest level in at least 400,000 years. Since carbon dioxide stays in the atmosphere for 100 years or more, the twenty-first century earth is going to be subjected to an increase in average temperature of at least 1.7°C (3°F)—even if all fossil fuel burning were to cease immediately. However, the more likely scenario is that we will at least double the carbon dioxide concentration over the next 50 years from the pre-industrial level. That would increase the earth's average temperature somewhere between 3° and 5°C (5.4°–9.0°F) during the course of the twenty-first century. The consequences of this degree of warming for human civilization and for all life will definitely be immense, possibly catastrophic (Flannery, *The Weather Makers*).

Climate is a highly complex global system. Even though it is possible for scientists to estimate an average temperature increase, it is not easy to determine how that increase will play out in specific parts of the world. We know that the poles seem to be warming twice as fast as other regions, and that the Arctic and Antarctic ice sheets are melting much faster than anyone had anticipated. There is a "positive feedback" process at work: as the ice melts, the reflection of the sun away from earth decreases significantly, since ice and snow reflect about 80–90 percent of the sun's rays, whereas water reflects only about 5–10 percent. Thus, the more ice is melted from the warmer temperatures, the more heat is absorbed, and the warmer temperatures become. One counterintuitive possibility of the Arctic ice melting was visually portrayed in former Vice President Gore's documentary film, *An Inconvenient Truth*. That involves northwestern Europe actually getting colder. That could happen if so much fresh water is melted into the North Atlantic that it severely impedes or even shuts off the Gulf Stream, which gives northwestern Europe a warmer climate than its latitude would otherwise allow. Although the likelihood of a complete Gulf Stream shutdown is fairly low, a noticeable increase in the level of the oceans is quite likely. Since the melting of all the polar ice would increase sea levels 220 feet, the possibility of a 15–30 feet increase within the twenty-first century is not remote. Many coastal areas would then be inundated, and several island countries would disappear under water. Even a sea level increase of 3 feet would displace 10 million people in Bangladesh. A similar situation would occur in the Nile Delta in Egypt. Twenty-two of the world's 50 most populous cities would be at risk of flooding. There is an even more imminent risk of salt water contamination of the fresh water aquifers upon which many of these same cities depend— cities such as Shanghai, Manila, Jakarta, Bangkok, and Mumbai (Flannery, *The Weather Makers*).

Other scenarios from climate change are also likely. Some are already happening. For instance, as the Indian Ocean warms in conjunction with other positive feedback processes, it causes drought conditions and agricultural failures in both India and the African Sahel. Desertification in Africa from drought has already meant the starvation of millions of people. Furthermore, warmer water means more intense storms, such as Hurricane Katrina, and the death of the coral reefs, which are home to one-fourth of the ocean's creatures. California is expected to lose one-half to three-fourths of its snow pack and 75 percent of its alpine forests, with devastating effects on the water supply and all economic activities dependent upon it, such as agriculture. One-third to one-half of all plant and animal species are expected to become extinct as their ecosystems are destroyed. The "evapotranspiration" system in the Amazon rainforest could break down. (This is a positive feedback system in which the trees, in effect, create their own rainfall.) Since the Amazon forest is the globe's largest container of carbon on land, its degradation would greatly magnify the processes that are already sending earth's temperatures higher. A similar feedback system could undermine the ocean's ability to serve as the world's biggest absorber of carbon dioxide emissions (Flannery, *The Weather Makers*).

Much of the scientific literature up until 2007 believed that the earth could manage an increase of 2–2.4°C (3.6–4.3°F) during the course of the twenty-first century. Even that target of average temperature increase would require a 60 percent reduction in 1990 levels of carbon dioxide emissions by 2050. However, the greatly accelerated melting of the Arctic ice in the summer of 2007 gave credence to those scientists, such as NASA's James Hansen, who argued that the temperature increases already in the earth's climate system have gone beyond the tipping point. The Arctic sea ice melt came 100 years earlier than most climate models had predicted. It was the size of California and Texas combined, or five United Kingdoms. Hansen and other scientists believe that if the earth's climate is to remain hospitable to most of its species, including humans, the level of carbon dioxide in the atmosphere must come back down to 350 ppm. Achieving that level essentially means zero burning of fossil fuels by 2050 and an expansion of natural carbon sinks such as oceans and forests. Unfortunately, the Kyoto Protocol, the first phase of the United Nations Framework Convention on Climate Change, the only international agreement to address this problem, is only targeting a 5 percent decrease from 1990 levels in industrialized countries by 2012. In addition, the first and second largest carbon dioxide–generating countries are not even participating in the greenhouse gas emissions reduction program. The United States, whose economy generates 20–25 percent of the world's total emissions, has withdrawn, claiming that reducing its emissions on a mandatory schedule would lower its economic growth. And China, as a developing country, was not required to make any reductions in the first phase. As a consequence of the non-participants and desultory efforts on the part of the ratifying countries, total global emissions increased by an average of 3 percent per year during 2000–2004. The second phase of the Convention, which is scheduled to go into effect in 2012, is currently being negotiated. All countries are supposed to participate, but China has argued that since the early industrializers have created most of the problem that we now face, they should make the biggest contributions in reductions and funding. So far the United States has resisted this argument. The culminating meeting in the negotiation process is planned to be held in 2009 in Copenhagen (Spratt and Sutton, *Climate Code Red*).

MCO proponents point out that the Bush administration argument for refusing to participate in binding carbon emission reductions demonstrates the severe limitations of the market world view. Both President Bush and Vice President Cheney have repeatedly referred to the unacceptable costs of emission reduction programs. Evidently, they are using a very restrictive market view of costs that excludes all the social and environmental costs that will be incurred from the consequences of global warming. These social and environmental costs are estimated to be much greater than the cost of installing emission-reduction technology. Yet the corporate owners of coal-burning power plants, with the support of the Bush administration, resist making this expenditure because it would lower their profits in the short run. They do not see it as a cost-effective remedy for the ecological costs that their emissions are imposing on society because the market does not charge them for these external effects. Neoclassical economists recognize this problem as a *market failure*. The market fails in this case because it does not incorporate the pollution or global warming costs in the prices that the power plants pay. Because these costs are external to the market pricing system, economists call them **externalities.** There are externalities in the market when the costs charged to private firms diverge from the actual total costs. Society has to bear the burden of the difference when the total social costs are greater, as they are in this case. An extensive study conducted by the treasury department in the United Kingdom came to the conclusion that the human and environmental costs of climate change over the next century will be a minimum of 5 percent and as high as 20 percent of global GDP, yet the cost of preventing such disastrous impacts could be limited to around 1 percent of global GDP per year (Stern, *The Economics of Climate Change*).

From the MCO perspective only the government is in a position to rectify market failure. But the adherents to the market world view are reluctant to admit serious market failures or that government intervention would be a desirable policy to follow. Gasoline prices are an interesting example, and they show how market thinking permeates U.S. society. When gas prices rose above $3.00 per gallon after the supply disruption of Hurricane Katrina, there was a hue and cry from both political parties. Most politicians and consumers were upset at these unacceptably high prices and called for ameliorative action. Some called for the suspension of gasoline taxes, even though U.S. gasoline taxes are already the lowest among the industrialized countries. Furthermore, if all the negative externalities of burning gasoline in cars were actually included in the price, a gallon of gas would cost about $10. (Negative externalities include costs of pollution, congestion, accidents, "free" parking, global warming, security, infrastructure not covered by transportation taxes, and so on.) The existing market and taxing process obviously sets the price nowhere near that full-cost level. Only by government taxation could the price of gasoline be set at its full-cost level. The tax proceeds would then be used to mitigate all the negative externalities. But, as we all know, any effort to raise gas taxes to that level would cause a political rebellion in the United States. Such a tax would be perceived as government oppression rather than an effort to create a price that would cover all associated costs. In capitalist market societies in general, but especially in the United States, the market price is perceived as the correct or natural price. Any taxation policy that attempts to internalize the externalities (true-cost pricing) clashes with the market world view, and inspires opposition from all of those individuals and companies whose market-defined short-term economic interests are negatively affected (Holtzclaw, "America's autos on welfare").

The MCO environmental criticism of the market has become quite sophisticated, especially with the rapid development of the new field of *ecological economics*. One of its founders and a mainstay of the field is **Herman Daly** (1938–), currently a professor of Public Policy at the University of Maryland. Ecological economists such as Daly have pointed out a number of serious problems with the way that the conventional market approaches environmental issues. They include the open-system error, the measurement mistake, the misidentification of nature, the misapplication of the intertemporal measure, and the misuse of free trade. Let's look at each one.

HERMAN DALY
1938–
Founder of ecological economics, the school of thought that advocates environmentally friendly revisions of neoclassical economics, for which he has been ostracized by mainstream economists. His important books are *For The Common Good* (1989) and *Beyond Growth: The Economics of Sustainable Development* (1996).

The **open-system error** relates to the presumption built into the market model that growth has no limits. The market system's viability, especially given its connection to capitalism, depends on an ever-expanding economy. Because of the constant barrage of concerned comments from both business and political spokespersons about the importance of adequate growth, the necessity for economic growth is embedded in public consciousness. The barometer of capitalism, the stock market, is strongly linked to the anticipated growth in the economy. With this commitment to growth, there is either an ignorant denial of nature's limits or a fervent belief in the ability of technology to overcome any natural limits. Daly contends that because the earth is a closed system, infinite growth is simply impossible. The no-limit open-system assumption of the market encourages the economy to travel on a path that will bring the system to inevitable collapse.

A true story involving Daly illustrates this conflict of views on the nature of the system. When Daly was working at the World Bank he was given the opportunity to review the draft of the report that the Bank was preparing on the environment and development for the 1992 Rio Summit. The report's main author was the chief economist for the World Bank, Larry Summers. Right there in the draft text was a diagram of the market model, similar to the one in this text. Daly pointed out to Summers that the market is a subsystem of the more comprehensive but finite natural system of the earth, and that it should be drawn as such. Summers disagreed. The disagreement was over the question of whether the economy is an open or a closed system. Summers's solution to their conflicting views was simply to remove the diagram (Daly, *Beyond Growth*).

The *measurement mistake* refers to the way we do our national accounting: the Gross Domestic Product accounts. The GNP and GDP accounts were designed in the 1930s and 1940s to give decision-makers some idea of what was going on in the economy so that they could better manage it—first during the depression and later during the war. They were understood to be rough measures. But, instead of their being replaced by more sophisticated measures, they have become entrenched around the world as the accepted measures of economic progress. Both the United Nations and the World Bank have played a role in their dissemination. As noted in the Chapter 3, the GDP accounting system is based on the market model. By and large, it includes only items for which a market price is available. All contributions to the society that are not bought and sold are excluded. The most important positive omission is unpaid household contributions, such as raising children, most of which is done by women. If all this activity were measured and included, it would add significantly to the total output of the economy, somewhere between 25 to 35 percent. On the other hand, there is an even larger amount of negative activity that should be deducted, but it is not counted either. That would include the loss of ecosystems; the depletion of natural resources; the toxic degradation of soil, water, and air; human health deterioration from pollution; displacement and suffering from human-made disasters such as wars; and more. None of these costs are deducted in the current GDP accounting system. In fact, not only are these deprivations not deducted from the output of the economy, but dealing with these problems actually adds to GDP. The clean-up costs of a major oil spill or the health costs from air pollution are actually recorded as positive inputs in the conventional GDP accounts. The more things that are made, used, and put in landfills; the more fossil fuels we burn; the more natural resources we use without regard to ecological consequences; the sicker people get from exposure to toxins—the better off the economy looks according to the GDP. As one

MCO author states, "GDP is best understood as a measure of the rate at which we are turning resources into garbage" (Korten, *When Corporations Rule the World*).

The *misidentification of nature* refers to the mistake that the market makes in treating products of nature as consumption commodities. It's similar to Polanyi's belief, discussed in Chapter 4, that the market turns nature into a "fictional commodity." This approach encourages the over-consumption, even the destruction, of natural resources because market pricing does not incorporate the need for preserving our limited and vulnerable natural resource base. Looking at the products of nature as commodities leads to overfishing, the overuse of fresh water, the destruction of soil, excessive deforestation, and so on. When a logging company looks at a forest, it sees lumber, not an ecosystem. The loss of nature's regenerating capacity is not conventionally recorded as a depreciating asset. In other words, nature is not looked upon as capital as, ironically, a human-made factory would be. Daly believes that nature should be conceptualized and counted in much the same way as physical capital. That means a replacement strategy should be in place. After all, without the foundation of the finite resources that nature provides, humans have nothing. All depreciation costs incurred by nature should be included in the costs of all products. The pricing of farm products, for instance, should account for soil erosion, the depletion of aquifers, the loss of forests, the use of non-renewable minerals, and so forth. This approach, however, would require a significant change in our accounting methods. It would mean a rejection of the current market pricing system. But it's the only way to recognize that we cannot have the same or better production capacity in the future if we do not replace, or allow nature to replenish, what we are taking from nature. In other words, in order to behave sustainably, we need to implement true-cost pricing. A part of that transformation in the pricing system would be counting natural resources as capital not as commodities (Daly, *Beyond Growth*).

The *misapplication of the inter-temporal measure* refers to the way in which the market prices time, or prices the present in relation to the future. As discussed in Chapter 2, in the market the interest rate serves as the link between the present and the future. That is the case because the market turns anything of value into a pile of money. Therefore, how much anything is worth over time is determined by the interest return it can accumulate, that is, how big a pile of money can be generated. Using this approach, natural resources and even human life are converted into money-making machines. If a natural resource is seemingly worth more being converted into cash—that is, the expected interest return on cash is greater that the expected return from the natural resource over time—then it makes sense from the market perspective to use up the resource in the near term and put the proceeds into an interest-bearing instrument. Daly believes that this kind of market thinking is a major philosophical error because it confuses nature with human-made commodities. Nature provides the basic life-blood for the human economy. Life depends on nature's continuing output within sustainable limits. Although the expansion of money has no limit, it also provides, in and of itself, no sustenance whatsoever (Daly and Cobb, *For The Common Good*).

This intertemporal error is further perpetuated by the use of market-based benefit–cost analysis in evaluating public projects for funding. The U.S. Congress, under the influence of the market world view, has mandated that all public programs be subjected to benefit–cost analysis before public funds are committed to their implementation. That includes programs dealing with the environment and human health. Of course, benefits that will occur in the future need to have a present value in order to compare them with current budgetary expenditures. Therefore, the same interest rate principle discussed above is applied. The expected future value has to be discounted to the present. If the expected future value in 20 years is $10,000, then at a 7 percent interest rate the present value is $2,600. That is, $2,600 earning 7 percent a year would be $10,000 in 20 years. The higher the interest rate applied, the lower the current monetary value of the benefit. The lower the interest rate utilized, the higher the benefit. Neoclassical environmental economists do not argue about the appropriateness of using the discounting approach in benefit–cost analysis. But they do argue about what the discount rate should be. When applied to a social good such as preservation of the environment with positive externalities, some argue that a lower-than-market rate, such as the 3 percent that the Environmental Protection Agency (EPA) has traditionally used, is more appropriate. Economic advisers in the Bush administration have argued that the EPA should use a higher interest rate. Daly argues that the whole discounting idea is nonsense and dangerous to the long-term viability of the environment. Nature has limits and tipping points after which restoration and even viability of ecosystems may be impossible. Climate change, as discussed above, is certainly a crucial illustration. To argue that public expenditures should not be made to save us from ecological catastrophe because they are not justified by market-based benefit–cost ratios is utter irrationality to MCO'ers. Yet that is exactly what some of the market-oriented political and business communities in the United States believe, and they have been supported by the Bush administration (Ackerman and Heinzerling, *Priceless*).

Next let us consider the *misuse of free trade*. Daly contends that the practice of "free trade" promotes ecological degradation and the transfer of environmental costs from the rich to the poor. The globalization of production means that supply chains reach around the world. Transporting parts and products thousands of miles consumes immense amounts of fossil fuels—depleting a non-renewable scarce resource, creating pollution, and magnifying the global warming problem. Daly argues that if all the ecological costs generated by the production and transportation processes were included in the prices of traded goods, at least two-thirds of trade would be uneconomic. The prices of traded goods, especially from developing countries, do not incorporate negative environmental externality costs. For instance, the levels of air and water pollution in China are recognized as horrendous. Even the pro-market World Bank estimates that the annual cost of dealing with environmental degradation in China may equal or exceed the percentage by which its overheated economy is reputed to be growing yearly, somewhere in the range of 10 percent. Yet all efforts to incorporate environmental costs in the rules of the World Trade Organization have failed. Opponents claim that doing so would "interfere with free trade." Some developing countries go so far as to argue that their lower prices, which are partly due to their not incorporating environmental costs, are a part of their comparative advantage. Market thinking certainly supports that contention.

When Larry Summers was chief economist of the World Bank, he circulated an infamous memorandum that made this case:

> Just between you and me, shouldn't the World Bank be encouraging more migration of the dirty industries to the LDCs? I can think of three reasons:
>
> 1   The measurement of the costs of health-impairing pollution depends on the foregone earnings from increased morbidity and mortality. From this point of view a given amount of health-impairing pollution should be done in the country with the lowest cost, which will be the country with the lowest wages . . .
>
> 2   The costs of pollution are likely to be non-linear as the initial increments of pollution probably have very low cost. I've always thought that under-populated countries in Africa are vastly under-polluted . . .
>
> 3   The concern over an agent that causes a one-in-a-million change in the odds of prostate cancer is obviously going to be much higher in a country where people survive to get prostate cancer than in a country where under-5 mortality is 200 per thousand . . .
> (Summers, in *The Economist*).

Summers claimed that the point of the memo was to show how some neoclassical economists got carried away with pure market reasoning. He certainly succeeded at that objective. Daly observes that countries that swallow their environmental costs do give themselves a temporary pricing advantage, but the long-term consequences are troubling. Exporting countries will pay the cost eventually, and the importing countries facilitate the absorption of the ecological costs in somebody else's backyard. Trade becomes the vehicle for the transfer of ecological costs, undoubtedly to less affluent countries, in exactly the manner that Summers describes.

CORPORATE COLONIALISM

The MCO model, or world view, focuses on the decision-making roles of the big power players. Though the model recognizes the power possessed by nation-states, it contends that decisions in the current political economy are predominantly influenced by the interests of corporations. Even in international organizations such as the International Monetary Fund in which the members are ostensibly nation-states, the economically powerful members, such as the United States, support the corporate agenda. However, it should be noted that U.S.-based corporations no longer overwhelmingly dominate the global corporate landscape as was the case just a few decades ago. Among the world's 100 largest corporations as determined by their 2005 revenues, almost one-third, or 31, are still based in the United States, but 14 are based in Germany, 11 in France, ten in the United Kingdom, nine in Japan, five in the Netherlands, four in Switzerland, three each in China, Italy, and South Korea, two in Spain, and one each in Belgium, Brazil, Mexico, Norway, and Venezuela ("World's 500 largest corporations," *Fortune*, July 24, 2006). As transnational corporate power becomes more widely dispersed around the globe, it reduces U.S. hegemony. Susan Strange felt ambiguous about this development because the contraction of the hegemon means an increase in global corporate power, a reduction in nation-state authority, and more instability.

MCO institutionalists argue that corporations are the front-line imposers of the Western economic system throughout the world, just as the mercantile trading companies, such as the East India Company, were the front line in the early days of colonialism. That's why one of these institutionalist authors, David Korten, contends that the process of globalization is really "**corporate colonialism.**"

> Traditional colonialism came to an end after World War II, and the new corporate colonialism—advanced through foreign aid, investment and trade—stepped into the breach ... It was more subtle, more sophisticated, and more appealing than the old colonialism, but the consequence was much the same—ever greater dependence on the money economy and thus on institutions of money that could be controlled by the few (Korten, *When Corporations Rule the World*, pp. 252–253).

Korten argues that corporate objectives are facilitated by the corporate-dominated political process, the corporate-controlled media, the global casino, the programs of the Bretton Woods organizations, international and regional trade agreements, and the spread of consumerism. The consequences of the corporate-run world, according to Korten, are exactly what one would expect from an MCO scenario—less democracy, greater inequality, environmental deterioration, greater financial volatility, and the decline of community. This section looks at some of the corporate colonial strategies that he mentions as well as the resistance to them.

The ultimate vehicle for global corporate domination is the **transnational corporation. TNCs** are characterized by having business activities in many countries with no clear identification with any particular national base. In reality, very few globally active corporations are truly unconnected to any nation-state even though they are all loosely called TNCs. In most cases the previously prevailing term, "multi-national corporation," is probably the best descriptive term. A 2001 UNCTAD study of corporate transnationality supports this observation. It uses the TNI index, which averages the foreign proportions of assets, sales, and employment for major corporations. The average TNI score was 52.6. Only 16 of the top 100 TNI corporations had scores over 75, and none of them were based in the United States or Germany. ExxonMobil had a TNI score of 68, whereas Wal-Mart's was only 25.8 (Dicken, *Global Shift*).

In *Big Business: Poor Peoples*, John Madeley summarizes the economic dominance of the 500 biggest TNCs, the megacorporations, by noting that they control about 70 percent of international trade, 80 percent of international investment, and about 30 percent of global GDP (p. 4). Even Nike, the five hundredth corporation on *Fortune*'s 2005 list, had annual revenues of $13.7 billion. That amount exceeds the total annual production (GDP) of most of the small and poor countries of the world. In fact, one commonly used measure to determine the "economic clout" of TNCs is to compare their annual revenues with country GDPs. One widely quoted study by the Institute of Policy Studies compared 1999 corporate revenues with country GDPs and came to the conclusion that, of the 100 largest economies, 51 are corporations. The top 22 economies in their rank-order listing were countries. At number 23 General Motors was the top-ranking corporation (Anderson and Cavanagh, *Top 200*). Charles Gray took a different view in an article that appeared in the *Multinational Monitor*, arguing that using GDP to measure economic clout exaggerated the position of countries. In his opinion, the more appropriate figure to use is government budget revenues. Using that approach, Gray came to the conclusion that, out of the top 100 economic entities, only 34 are national governments, while 66 are corporations. In his listing, the top corporation ranked number 7. Christopher May disagreed with the ranking methods used by both Anderson and Cavanagh and Gray. He argued that since

GDP accounted only for final values, whereas corporate revenues included all intermediate values, corporate revenues should be discounted by at least two-thirds. He did not, however, provide a ranking of his own (May, *Global Corporate Power*).

No single list can do any more than give a sense of relative economic power, since whatever approach is taken will have some methodological weaknesses. The list of the top 100 countries and corporations provided in Table 5.1 builds the rank ordering differently from any of those discussed above. Corporate revenues continue as the measure of relative economic clout for TNCs. However, for countries a different measure is used: gross national income as calculated by purchasing power parity (PPP). As discussed in Chapter 3, the PPP approach attempts to overcome the distortion that foreign exchange ratios and other price anomalies build into the country-comparison system. For instance, for the last several years many financial observers have contended that China is controlling its currency value on the downside, that is, keeping it undervalued, so that its exports will be cheaper. From the World Bank's database we learn that China's 2004 GDP figure in U.S. dollars, using its set foreign exchange relationship with the U.S. dollar, is $1,860 billion, whereas the PPP figure is $7,386, a difference that seems much bigger than can be explained by an estimated 25 percent currency undervaluation. By using the higher PPP number, China, as the second largest economy in the world, probably receives a better indicator of its economic clout. The PPP approach gives most Third World countries a significantly higher economic production value than GDP at nominal foreign exchange values, whereas a few of the richer countries, presumably because of overvalued currencies in purchasing power terms, actually end up with lower numbers. Two examples of the latter would be the United States and Switzerland. Methodologically, the PPP estimates probably suffer from more problems than GDP numbers. That's because the PPP estimates rely on GDP base data and problematic price surveys. In fact, China has never officially provided any price survey data, so some scholars wonder how the World Bank arrives at its PPP estimates for China. Nevertheless, the rank-order results are not that different from the GDP approach with the highest-ranking corporation, ExxonMobil, coming in at rank-number 24; and corporations still fill 45 of the top 100 positions (Moran, "'Wealth Doesn't Matter' and Other Reassurances to the World's Poor").

Another complication in the estimation of relative power in the global political economy is *corporate alliances*. Countries have alliances, such as in the European Union, but so do corporations. We are all familiar with airline alliances, but there are strategic alliances in all fields, even among rivals. Peter Dicken calls them "constellations of economic power" (*Global Shift*, p. 259). They are very widespread in the computer industry. They are also prevalent in pharmaceuticals, chemicals, automobiles, telecommunications, financial services, and other sectors. For example, in 1998 one global semiconductor consortium included Lucent (US), Philips (Netherlands), Hyundai (South Korea), LG Semicon (South Korea), Siemens (Germany), AMD (US), Texas Instruments (US), Intel (US), Motorola (US), IBM (US), STM (Italy/France), Samsung (South Korea), and TSMC (Taiwan). Yet there is no transnational anti-trust body to investigate whether these alliances create monopoly-like controls over global markets. The only transnational regulatory body that seems to raise questions about the anti-competitive implications of these alliances is the Competition Ministry of the European Union. Governments sometimes also get in the act of trying to set up monopoly controls over a segment of the global market. These governmental alliances are known as *cartels*, and the best-known example is OPEC, the Organization of Petroleum Exporting Countries (Dicken).

Corporations pursue their objectives by using their economic power in the political arena. In recent U.S. election campaigns corporations outspent labor unions by a ratio of 15 to 1. Most of the 17,000 lobbyists who work in Washington, D.C., represent corporations. The top spender on lobbying in the 1998–2004 period was the U.S. Chamber of Commerce ($205 million). In that same period, almost $13 billion was spent lobbying Congress and federal officials. The situation is not much different in Brussels, where 15,000 lobbyists try to influence the decisions of the European Union. Their efforts seem to have been quite successful. For instance, in the United States the proportion of federal taxes paid by corporations dropped from 21 percent in 1962 to 7 percent in 2003. The corporate taxation situation is about the same in all 30 OECD countries (Eagleton, *Under the Influence*). Moreover, according to the *Financial Times* (July 21/22, 2004), through their complex and manipulative bookkeeping, corporations are able to use techniques such as "transfer pricing" between countries to lower their taxes, despite the best efforts of tax authorities. Transfer-pricing accounting involves showing high costs and low profits in relatively high tax jurisdictions such as the United Kingdom, while shifting profits to low-tax jurisdictions such as Ireland or Luxembourg.

MCO analysts see the Uruguay Round of international trade negotiations, which culminated in the establishment of the World Trade Organization (WTO) in 1995, as another example of effective corporate lobbying. The most salient manifestation of corporate power was the inclusion of Trade Related Intellectual Property Rights (TRIPs) in the WTO agreement. Over 90 percent of the patents protected by this agreement are held by corporations based in the "Golden Triad," that is, North America, Western Europe, and Japan. Evidently, the TRIPs draft language was provided by three of the world's biggest corporations: Pfizer (pharmaceuticals), IBM (information technology), and DuPont (chemicals). During the most recent trade negotiations, at the urgent demand of less developed countries, a health emergency exception to TRIPs

Table 5.1 Top 100 rankings of countries (by GNI-PPP*) and corporations (by revenues), 2004–2005

	Country/Corporation	Based in	GNI or revenues (in million $)		Country/Corporation	Based in	GNI or revenues (in million $)
1	United States		11,655,000	51	Denmark		170,000
2	China		7,386,000	52	Chile		168,000
3	Japan		3,838,000	53	ConocoPhillips	USA	166,683
4	India		3,347,000	54	Israel		160,000
5	Germany		2,310,000	55	General Electric	USA	157,153
6	United Kingdom		1,897,000	56	Hungary		157,000
7	France		1,759,000	57	Finland		154,000
8	Italy		1,604,000	58	Total	France	152,361
9	Brazil		1,433,000	59	Venezuela		150,000
10	Russia		1,374,000	60	Peru		148,000
11	Spain		1,035,000	61	ING Group	Netherlands	138,235
12	Mexico		995,000	62	Ireland		133,000
13	South Korea		982,000	63	Citigroup	USA	131,045
14	Canada		978,000	64	Nigeria		130,000
15	Indonesia		753,000	65	Axa	France	129,829
16	Australia		588,000	66	Morocco		125,000
17	Turkey		557,000	67	Allianz	Germany	121,406
18	Netherlands		507,000	68	Volkswagen	Germany	118,377
19	Iran		505,000	69	Singapore		115,000
20	South Africa		500,000	70	Fortis	Belgium/NL	112,351
	Thailand		500,000	71	Crédit Agricole	France	110,765
21	Poland		482,000	72	American Int'l Group	USA	108,905
22	Argentina		476,000	73	Kazakhstan		104,000
23	Philippines		406,000	74	Assicurazioni Generali	Italy	101,404

	Name	Country	GNI-PPP / Revenue
24	ExxonMobil	USA	339,938
25	Pakistan		328,000
26	Belgium		326,000
27	Saudi Arabia		325,000
28	Wal-Mart	USA	315,654
29	Colombia		309,000
30	Royal Dutch Shell	Netherlands	306,731
31	Ukraine		300,000
32	Egypt		283,000
33	Bangladesh		278,000
34	British Petroleum	UK	267,600
35	Sweden		267,000
36	Switzerland		261,000
37	Austria		258,000
38	Greece		244,000
39	Malaysia		243,000
40	Vietnam		222,000
41	Algeria		203,000
42	Portugal		201,000
43	General Motors	USA	192,604
44	Chevron	USA	189,481
45	Czech Republic		187,000
46	Daimler-Chrysler	Germany	186,106
47	Toyota	Japan	185,805
48	Romania		179,000
49	Ford	USA	177,210
50	Norway		177,000
75	Siemens	Germany	100,099
76	Sinopec	China	98,785
77	Nippon T&T	Japan	94,869
78	Carrefour	France	94,455
79	HSBC Holdings	UK	93,494
80	ENI	Italy	92,603
81	Aviva	UK	92,579
82	IBM	USA	91,134
83	New Zealand		90,000
84	McKesson	USA	88,050
85	Honda	Japan	87,511
86	State Grid	China	86,984
87	Hewlett-Packard	USA	86,696
88	BNP Paribas	France	85,687
89	PDYSA	Venezuela	85,618
90	UBS	Switzerland	84,708
91	Bank of America	USA	83,980
92	Hitachi	Japan	83,596
93	China Nat'l Petroleum	China	83,557
94	Pemex	Mexico	83,382
95	Nissan	Japan	83,274
96	Berkshire Hathaway	USA	81,663
97	Home Depot	USA	81,511
98	Valero Energy	USA	81,362
99	JP Morgan Chase	USA	79,902
100	Samsung Electronics	South Korea	78,717

Sources: World Bank, *World Development Report, 2006*, and "World's 500 Largest Corporations," *Fortune*, July 24, 2006.
* GNI-PPP = Gross National Income by purchasing power parity.

was made to allow for the production and exporting of patented drugs by generic makers in relatively poor countries, such as Brazil, India, and South Africa. The demand was primarily driven by the high cost of AIDS drugs from the pharmaceutical-manufacturing TNCs. Though language ostensibly supporting the medical emergency exception was approved in 2003, the required process of compulsory licensing was made so complex ("the Pfizer proposal") that it took four years for the first developing country to receive an import license (Eagleton, *Under the Influence*).

Another controversial aspect of TRIPs is its coverage of animal and plant materials. Critics claim that TNCs engage in "biopiracy," that is, taking seeds and medicinal plants from old cultures and then engineering laboratory equivalents that are submitted for patent protection. The perverse result is that poor people in Third World countries are forced to pay for products that they have developed over centuries (Shiva, in *Alternatives to Economic Globalization*). A related issue is genetically modified (GM) crops. The World Bank, with funding from the Global Environmental Facility, is pursuing the introduction of GM crops into the farmer seed systems of five countries in West Africa and five countries in Latin America. The projects are being promoted by corporate agribusinesses and the U.S. government. They speak of "biosafety harmonization," whereas local farmers' organizations see the effort as a "deliberate GM contamination of farmer seed systems" (ETC Group, website).

Other new, corporate-friendly provisions of the WTO include Trade Related Investment Measures (TRIMs) and the General Agreement on Services (GATS). TRIMs prohibit governments from giving any special treatment to local businesses over foreign businesses, the "national treatment" provision that was mentioned in Chapter 3. GATS is intended to reduce the protection of locally offered services so that TNCs can offer not only commercial services but also public services such as health and water. The efforts to implement the provisions of GATS have run into widespread resistance; thus, in contrast to TRIPs, their impact so far is as more of a "foot in the door" than a fully actualized policy. Corporations would like the WTO to look more like the North American Free Trade Agreement (NAFTA), which has many sections that provide protection for the investments of foreign corporations. One of the most controversial is Chapter 11. It gives corporations the right to sue governments in secret tribunals for losses allegedly incurred when business opportunities are inhibited by local laws and regulations. So far the restrictions that have been challenged in cases filed under Chapter 11 have been mostly environmental. For example, the Canadian maker of MTBE, a gasoline additive and alleged carcinogen, sued the United States and California for its lost revenues after the use of MTBE was prohibited when it was discovered to be leaching into ground water. Under NAFTA Mexico agreed to open its financial services industry to foreign ownership and investment. As a consequence

Mexico has virtually no locally owned banks (Barlow, *The Free Trade Area of the Americas*).

The Golden Triad governments make no secret of their reliance on major corporations in formulating trade policy. For instance, the Office of the U.S. Trade Representative is required by law to consult with a group of advisory committees whose membership is supposed to be "balanced." However, 93 percent of the nearly 750 individuals on the 26 advisory committees represent corporations or business associations. When the Bush administration came to power, it proceeded to start removing the small minority of representatives from labor, environmental, and consumer organizations. The remaining non-business representatives serve mostly on one committee, the Labor Advisory Committee. The situation in Europe is quite similar. Business association representatives are known to work closely with the 133 Committee, the central and secretive trade policy committee of the European Commission. In Japan the most influential corporate group is Keidanren, the Japanese Federation of Economic Organizations. In the Doha Round negotiations, a group of 20 countries led by the BRIC nations (Brazil, Russia, India, and China) has challenged the leadership of the Golden Triad, but the same global corporations are lurking in the background. In Brazil, for instance, government trade negotiators listen to the Institute for the Study of Trade and International Negotiations (ICONE). Most of the Institute's funding comes from those ubiquitous, well-known corporate agribusinesses Cargill, Archer Daniels Midland (ADM), and Bunge (Eagleton, *Under the Influence*).

In this corporate-controlled drama, the MCO critics see the World Bank and the International Monetary Fund as supporting players. The structural adjustment programs of both organizations in the 1980s and 1990s were the means of imposing the so-called liberalization principles of the Washington Consensus. In essence, countries indebted to the Bank and the IMF were coerced into opening up their economies to TNC trade and investment. As a result, many poor countries in Africa lost 30 to 50 percent of their local manufacturing capacity to cheaper imports. Even big countries such as India have been affected; its small-unit silk-weaving industry has been devastated by cheap imports (Eagleton).

Several MCO authors point out that one of the most egregious demonstrations of global corporate dominance was the demise of the U.N. Center on Transnational Corporations. The Center was established in 1974 through a resolution of the U.N. Economic and Social Council (ECOSOC), with the purpose of assisting Third World countries in their dealings with TNCs. The Center's lawyers began to develop the U.N. Code of Conduct for Transnational Corporations with the intent of regulating corporate practices that weak Third World countries considered exploitation. But agreement on a code could not be reached, and the complaints about the very existence of the Center and its mission from corporations and countries friendly to them reached a crescendo in 1992. The U.N. Secretary-General, following a recommendation from his deputy secretary for administration (a former U.S. attorney general) abolished the Center. Its fact-gathering function was shifted to UNCTAD, the United Nations Conference on Trade and Development, located in Geneva, home of the WTO. More recently, in 2000, Secretary-General Kofi Annan initiated the Global Compact of best practices to which corporations are asked to voluntarily agree. However, there is no monitoring or enforcement of actual behavior, so the program's critics call it "blue washing" (Patomaki and Teivainen, *A Possible World*). (See also Chapter 7.)

In addition to influencing international organizations and governments to pursue corporate-friendly policies, TNCs also seek to influence the general population. TNCs promote a global consumer culture. Through advertising they sell the idea that the "good life" is about consumption. The MCO model highlights the importance of advertising to the system. Advertisers sell not only their products but also the virtues and pleasures of materialism. In 2005, $570 billion was spent around the world on advertising. That's about seven times more than the total that was distributed in official development assistance to less developed countries. In 2004 the corporation that spent the most on advertising was U.S.-based Procter & Gamble, at almost $8 billion. The other TNCs in the 2004 list of top-ten advertisers include General Motors (US), Unilever (UK/Netherlands), Ford (US), L'Oreal (France), Toyota (Japan), Time Warner (US), Daimler Chrysler (Germany), Johnson & Johnson (US), and Nestlé (Switzerland). Disney, Coca-Cola, and McDonald's are in the next ten. Corporations also use advertising to promote positive and benign images of themselves. We are all familiar with the ads of major oil and gas corporations trying to convince us how "green" and environmentally friendly they are, while making huge profits from selling products that are the major contributors to global warming. Though Internet advertising is growing rapidly, television advertising still reaches more people around the world. In the United States, the most advertising-inundated country in the world, the average citizen sees 28,000 commercials a year (Godrej, in *New Internationalist*).

Besides marketing products in commercials, advertising also influences the content of the programs it supports, including the news. "Infotainment" favors corporate interests and those governments that are friendly to them. Over 70 percent of global media are controlled by only eight TNCs: Time Warner, Disney, News Corporation (Fox), Viacom, Seagram, General Electric, Sony, and Bertelsmann. They are all multi-pronged, global conglomerates. News Corporation is an interesting example. It was started in Australia by Rupert Murdoch. Its best-known component is probably Fox television. In addition, the corporation owns the Fox networks and over 30 local stations in major markets. News Corporation also owns satellite broadcasting companies in many parts of the world, including Asia, Latin America, and North America. It has many portals on the Internet, including MySpace. It publishes many magazines and over 175 newspapers around the world; among them are *The Times* (London) and *The Wall Street Journal*. It also owns some publishing and music companies. Finally, News Corporation includes the Twentieth Century Fox movie production group, probably the original source of the "Fox" moniker ("The national entertainment state," *The Nation*, July 3, 2006; Cavanagh and Mander, *Alternatives to Economic Globalization*).

Political scientist Benjamin Barber calls this globalization of consumerism "McWorld." He reinforces the point with a clever aphorism that parodies Marx: "Consumers of the world unite! We have everything you need in our chains!" (Barber, *Jihad vs. McWorld*, p. 78). Following in the footsteps of Polanyi's analysis, Barber sees corporate globalization as generating a powerful resistance movement that he characterizes as "Jihad." This dialectical dynamic is the analytical core of his well-known 1995 book, *Jihad vs. McWorld*. He argues that unaccountable corporate elites are trying to impose a universal culture of materialism that turns everyone into individual consumers with little interest in community ties or public responsibilities. In Barber's view the major resistance to this secular modernization comes from religious fundamentalism. Though Barber names the resistance movement "Jihad," highlighting the membership of Islamic fundamentalism in it, he includes all religious fundamentalists. The "Jihadists" are all characterized by adherence to "absolute truth," dictatorial religious authority, group identity in opposition to the "infidels," and reliance on sacred texts rather than science. In many respects, these movements advocate pre-modern or anti-modern ideas. Ironically, however, the anti-modernists and the modernists use each other to further their own objectives. On the one hand, the perceived presence of moral decadence in materialist societies gives the fundamentalists a rallying cry. On the other hand, the anti-modernists are not reluctant to use the high-tech products of modernism, such as the Internet, to advance their causes. TNC products are actually tailored for particular ethnic and religious groups, regardless of their political orientation. Therefore, Barber notes that paradoxically the "Jihadists" and the "McWorld'ers" have a symbiotic relationship. His major concern is that both of these global movements, corporate materialism and religious fundamentalism, are authoritarian in nature. If either or both of them prevail, it will be at the cost of democratic decision-making in the local, national, and international communities. Thus, in order to prevent the undermining of true democracy, the people and nations of the world need to gain the upper hand over both of these authoritarian movements (Barber, *Jihad vs. McWorld*).

THE MCO REFORM AGENDA

Democracy

Members of the MCO school of thought are reformers, not revolutionaries. They believe that the problems of the current system can be rectified with appropriate modifications. They have faith in democratic processes and the ability of democratically controlled governments to act on behalf of the public interest. Their approach is captured by the theme of the 2004 World Social Forum held in India, "Another World is Possible" (Patomaki and Teivainen, *A Possible World*).

When MCO reformers talk about **democracy**, they are not just talking about elections. In fact, just focusing on elections can be counterproductive. If a strong rule of law with a protection of minorities is not yet in place, elections can be used as a means of oppressing ethnic and other minorities. Real liberal democracies require a whole set of embedded institutions that start with the rule of law and the effective protection of human rights. It takes many hundreds of years for these institutions to become truly embedded in the political culture, and even then they are fragile. The reformers also recognize that in order for democracy to be truly successful, a number of institutions need to be sufficiently in place: an honest and competent executive branch; a rational, deliberative legislature that responds to the wishes of the public; and a truly independent judiciary. Furthermore, the government structure requires effective checks and balances, the protection of minorities from the "tyranny of the majority," and a separation of religion and state. Basic freedoms need to be in place, such as freedom of speech, freedom of association, freedom for equality of opportunity, and freedom from personal insecurity. All of these democratic standards are more easily articulated than achieved. Even "old" democracies such as the United States have difficulties living up to them. Many countries of the world that claim to be democracies are far from achieving these standards. Fareed Zakaria calls them "illiberal democracies" (Zakaria, *The Future of Freedom*).

Pointing out what is meant by democracy in the minds of the reformers is an important preliminary step, because not only is enhancing democracy an important objective in and of itself, but also the presence of an effective democratic government is the crucial requirement for the success of the reform agenda. It doesn't make much sense to expect governments to act on behalf of the public if the governments are controlled by small elite groups whose interests are opposed to the interests of the broader public. As noted earlier, John Kenneth Galbraith recognized with considerable dismay that his earlier expectations of the 1950s and 1960s that the U.S. government would provide a "countervailing" or at least a "balancing" force to corporations were disappointed as corporate interests, especially after the 1980s presidency of Ronald Reagan, gained pervasive dominance over governmental decision-making processes.

The MCO reliance on the balancing and reforming role of democratic governments contrasts with the belief of free market adherents that government is the problem rather than the solution. From the perspective of free market advocates, the more limited the role of governments, the better. However, they strongly believe in democracy, as it is the form of governance most compatible with an individualistic economic system. Maybe because free market supporters see corporations as individual persons, they don't seem to share the MCO view that excessive power in corporations is just as bad as excessive power in governments.

Most of the reforms suggested for the international arena by MCO proponents require a significant move away from narrow nationalism and corporate authoritarianism and toward democratic global governance. Ironically, the strongest opposition to moving in that direction comes from the country that claims its foreign policy is based on spreading democracy around the world, the United States. Instead, the behavior of the United States is quite consistent with the selfish exercise of "sovereign" national power predicted by the theories of realism and neomercantilism. The proponents of those theories are not surprised that the country that controls the levers of power is resistant to giving them up, even though this seems to contradict its rhetoric of democracy.

If one were really serious about building a world system with effective democratic governance, where would one start? International organizations that do have the potential to evolve into global democratic bodies with real authority include the United Nations, the Bretton Woods organizations (the IMF and World Bank) and the WTO. The only body of the United Nations that has any enforcement power is the Security Council. However, in the Security Council the United States has a veto, as do the four other permanent members (China, France, the United Kingdom, and Russia). The "Big Five" acquired this non-democratic power because they were the winners of World War II. Naturally, with the change in circumstances many suggestions have been made over the past few decades to expand the permanent membership of the Security Council or to turn the General Assembly into a genuine world parliament, maybe with voting based on population rather than the "one country, one vote" principle. But so far the "Big Five" have shown little eagerness to give up their privileged positions.

As discussed earlier, the **Bretton Woods organizations** have enforcement power through their ability to impose conditions on the loans that they provide. Because of the weighted voting system in these organizations, the United States is the only country with effective veto power. Recently, there has been a move toward slightly modifying the weighted voting percentages so that the voting strength of Asian countries corresponds a little better to their increased economic strength. But doing that will not change much. The corporate and market world view will still dominate not only among the representatives of the member countries to the IMF and World Bank but also among their professional staffs, most of whom are neoclassical economists. The democratic reformers have the most hope for the *World Trade Organization* because its decision-making system formally requires consensus among all of its nation-state members, each of whom have one vote. Nevertheless, in the past the United States and other developed countries have been able to dominate this process as well through economic intimidation and superior staff work. Recent negotiations in the Doha Round demonstrate that other countries are now beginning to effectively resist impositions, however. This development provides some hope for more open and democratic decision-making. The downside is that consensus decision-making gives any major trading country or group of countries an effective veto, making it exceptionally difficult to reach any agreement. Thus all of the international organizations that have the potential for evolving into part of a global democratic governance system require substantial modification to their decision-making systems before they are suitable vehicles (Patomaki and Teivainen, *A Possible World*).

Specific reform proposals

Presuming that enough democratic governance is achieved, what would be some of the components of an MCO reform agenda? Definitely, one of the top priorities would be fair trade. In order to achieve **fair trade** within the WTO system, reformers are proposing that the *emphasis shift from "non-discrimination" to "special and differential treatment."* The problems of the less developed countries should be given special attention with the adoption of a more fair trading system. Achieving the Millennium Goals of the United Nations (sustainable development and the reduction of poverty) should be the overriding objective, not "free trade." Therefore, poorer countries should be given the right to protect their infant industries from the premature lowering of tariffs and protected from liberalization strong-arming by the Bretton Woods organizations and powerful transnational corporations (TNCs). As noted earlier, doing away with reasonable tariffs in a premature rush to liberalize undermines government budgets in less developed countries, as tariffs are a major source of revenue. Fair trade means that rich countries give up their agricultural subsidies and stop dumping subsidized agricultural crops into international markets. In the Uruguay Round the rich countries supposedly agreed to do exactly that by 2005, but they have been dragging their feet. The U.S. subsidy of 25,000 cotton farmers is an especially poignant case. Because of the $3 to $4 billion it pays in annual subsidies, the United States is the world's largest cotton exporter, and it undercuts 10 million small cotton farmers around the world. Farmers in very poor countries such as Burkina Faso, Mali, and Benin are severely affected. These countries have lost twice as much from the collapse of their cotton export markets as they have received in foreign aid (Cavanagh and Mander, *Alternatives to Economic Globalization*; Stiglitz, *Making Globalization Work*).

Another reform would be *removing the TRIPs provision* from the WTO. The responsibility for protecting patents, copyrights, trademarks, and similar should be returned to the World Intellectual Property Organization (WIPO) where it belongs. Indigenous knowledge and plants should be freed from patentability and "biopiracy." The inclusion of TRIPs in the WTO is a highly salient example of how corporate operatives with the collusion of their state partners can hijack the concepts of "free trade" and "free markets" in order to achieve monopoly objectives. Joseph Stiglitz notes that TRIPs have been called the "enclosure of the intellectual commons" (Stiglitz, *Making Globalization Work*, p. 109). He observes that U.S. and European pharmaceutical corporations, the biggest proponents of TRIPs, spend much more on advertising than on research. Yet the supposed justification for TRIPs was the need for monopoly profits that would support more research for a continuous flow of improved products. The MCO model directs attention to this kind of deceitful, power-wielding, profit-seeking behavior, so that reformers can pursue corrective action (Stiglitz, *Making Globalization Work*).

In an effort to counter the distorting effects of "free trade" and "free capital mobility," MCO adherents suggest a number of additional reforms. For instance, they recommend changing the trade rules so that **compensatory tariffs** could be imposed in order to counter the "race to the bottom" in the exploitation of labor (Ravi Batra) and the environment (Herman Daly). The current global dynamics of labor exploitation, which are facilitated by the trade agreements, undermine the possibility of labor acquiring a countervailing power to corporations. Therefore, in the struggle for distribution of income, labor is the loser. One way to counter that outcome would be for governments favoring a more fair and balanced distribution to implement compensatory tariffs against goods and services coming from countries that facilitate labor exploitation. Such tariffs would inhibit the importation of products from countries that actually seek foreign investment by promising to restrict any mobilization of labor power through unionization or other means. The same sort of compensatory tariff could be used against countries that do not include environmental costs in the prices of their products. Stating the purpose of these compensatory tariffs is easy. However, calculating what the appropriate tariff percentage should be on various products is complicated and contentious. That is the reason why the world needs a global monitoring organization to oversee this complex process. A reconstituted WTO with appropriate enforcement authority and democratic legitimacy could play that role. Batra and others have estimated that under such a socially oriented protective tariff regime, the magnitude of current international trade would be cut by at least one-half as production would relocate back to communities that have sensible labor and environmental practices. A further benefit would be a significant reduction in the environmental costs associated with transportation. A complication foreseen by Batra is the potential for oligopolistic corporations to engage in non-competitive behavior behind the protective tariff barriers. Therefore, he urges an aggressive break up of oligopolies into smaller, competitive units. He argues that both productive efficiency and sustainable practices could be enhanced by this localized, smaller-scale approach to the economy (Batra, *The Myth of Free Trade*).

Trade and debt are related, since export revenues provide the means for servicing debt. Export revenues also pay for importing food and capital products. Consequently, pressure to export is strong, sometimes leading to the destruction of subsistence agriculture as land is converted to growing cash crops for export. The late president of Tanzania, Julius Nyerere, plaintively asked, "Must we starve our children in order to pay our debts?" Before the debt relief campaign of Jubilee 2000, the answer was unequivocably "Yes." Now, partly because of public pressure and the recognition that dozens of poor countries have debts beyond their abilities to repay, the G-8 (United States, United Kingdom, Japan, France, Germany, Italy, Canada, and Russia) and the Bretton Woods organizations (the World Bank and the IMF) have started *debt relief programs*. The World Bank and IMF program began in 1996 under the title Heavily Indebted Poor Countries, or HIPC. Without **debt relief**, economic modernization is nearly impossible and poverty will continue to prevail. Despite this belated recognition, debt relief programs have been implemented very slowly, and MCO critics argue for more relief and at a faster pace. They direct attention to the fact that, because of debt servicing, poor countries in the 1980s and 1990s were actually sending more capital to rich countries than rich countries were providing to them. That is the height of inequity. One proposed institutional innovation that would help countries get out from under impossible debt burdens is the establishment of an *International Insolvency Court*. In effect, this organization would provide a regularized bankruptcy process for countries, something that does not exist now. Currently, whenever a country gets into difficulty in paying its debt obligations, an ad hoc legal and negotiating process occurs with uncertain outcomes for both the country and the creditors involved (Stiglitz, *Making Globalization Work*).

Besides debt servicing there is another way in which relatively poor countries may end up transferring wealth to the already rich. That is through the recycling of surplus foreign exchange reserves. As mentioned earlier, the most prominent example of this paradoxical phenomenon in the early twenty-first century is China's financial support of the United States. Because of China's large trade surplus with the United States (over $256 billion in 2007), it acquires large amounts of dollars. China recirculates those dollars back to the United States, mostly by purchasing instruments of U.S. government debt—U.S. Treasury bills and bonds. The citizens of China, therefore, are financing U.S. deficit spending. As depicted in Figure 3.4 on global macroeconomic connections, the Chinese are transferring some of their saving to the United States. Besides the issue of questionable equity in this transfer, the substantial imbalances involved have the potential to create serious instability in the global economy. In order to address such a problem, Keynes argued that there should be an *International Clearing Union* that would have the means to prevent these types of global imbalances from persisting. Penalties would be imposed on governments that continued to generate excessive surpluses or deficits in their international accounts in order to encourage them to get their monetary and fiscal houses in order. Much to Keynes's disappointment, his proposal was vetoed by the United States. MCO reformers would like to resuscitate it. A reconstituted IMF could be the institutional vehicle for implementing this global balancing responsibility (Stiglitz, *Globalization and Its Discontents*).

One of the reasons the United States is able to easily borrow from other countries—which enables it to run a persistent deficit in its current account—is the role of the dollar as the major foreign exchange reserve currency. As long as countries are prepared to keep using the dollar in this role, instead of euros, yen, or even Chinese yuan (renminbi), the United States can continue to spend beyond its means. To avoid privileging any particular national currency, Keynes proposed a truly *global reserve currency*, which he called the "bancor." This proposal was also vetoed by the United States, preferring instead the U.S. dollar/gold exchange reserve currency that lasted from 1945 to 1971, when President Nixon severed the dollar's relationship to gold. Since then, as discussed earlier, the world economy has been functioning with a mix of floating and fixed national currencies, but with the U.S. dollar retaining its role as the major reserve currency. As explained in Chapter 3, since 1960 the IMF has issued small amounts of a reserve asset that is not nationally based, namely SDRs, or Special Drawing Rights. To deal with this lack of a truly global currency, Stiglitz has proposed a new international reserve currency that he calls "global greenbacks." Countries' central banks would get global greenbacks in return for their own currency, but the basis of distribution would be countries' commitments to enhancing global public goods, serving social and development needs, and assisting environmental preservation. Every year in order to maintain stable price levels, an additional issuance of global greenbacks would occur based on the ratio of trade value to total economic production value. In 2006 that would have created $200 to $400 billion per year. It would supplement, but not replace, the use of hard currencies for foreign exchange purposes. Richard Douthwaite has made an even more radical proposal. In agreement with Keynes, he contends that the creation of a whole new international reserve currency is the only effective way to deal with both the unstable and skewed global financial situation as well as the inadequate effort to address environmental degradation. Countries' allocation share of the new reserve currency would be based on their performance in the reduction of greenhouse gas emissions. Therefore, he calls the new currency *special emission rights* (Stiglitz, *Making Globalization Work*; Douthwaite, *The Ecology of Money*).

These reserve currency suggestions are intended to address inherent problems in the current global financial structure. After the financial crises of the late 1990s in Asia, Latin America, and Russia, it became evident that unregulated short-term capital mobility (hot money) was destabilizing, even in countries with sound economies. Therefore, MCO analysts support national controls over these financial capital movements, but it's important that national programs be globally monitored for balance and fairness by some type of global financial authority, possibly a reconstituted IMF. Capital movements should occur primarily for sound economic reasons, and not be spurred by the speculation that currently dominates global financial markets. A more targeted proposal to deal with this excess speculation problem is the **Tobin tax**, a small tax (one-quarter of 1 percent) on all foreign exchange transactions. It is intended to discourage speculative trading that takes advantage of small differences in exchange ratios, interest rates, present and future values, and so on. Since the foreign exchange market amounts to $2 trillion a day, even this small percentage would raise a large sum. The issues of concern are how to ensure the effective application of the tax around the world and how to distribute the collected funds. As with most MCO proposals, its effective implementation would require some kind of international governance authority with enforcement powers and democratic legitimacy. Associated reforms that would increase the effectiveness of the Tobin tax would be comparable regulations, transparency, and tax policies in the banking and financial services sectors of all countries. They would counter the practices of some small countries that currently specialize in secret banking and low-tax policies that facilitate tax evasion by corporations, money laundering by organized crime, and corruption by government officials. The sixth largest financial center in the world is the Cayman Islands, a small island state in the Caribbean. Susan Strange was astonished that governments could not find the political will to tackle this problem (Strange, *Mad Money*).

As discussed earlier, another problematic aspect of the global casino is the financial power given to banks and bank-related financial services by the credit-money system. The MCO criticism of the IMF bailouts in

Asia in the late 1990s was that their main beneficiaries were the Western banks that had made the loans, not the economies of the countries that were suffering from the financial crises. Since the essence of the credit-money system that created the problem is the privately based but publicly approved fractional reserve banking system, why keep this system? Korten calls for *100 percent reserves* in the banking system, a change that would eliminate the ability of banks to create credit-money beyond their deposits. Douthwaite points out that fractional reserve bank money is based on the creation of interest-bearing debt. But the ability to make interest payments requires continuous economic growth, and continuous growth puts an unsustainable burden on the natural environment. The only cure for this cause of downward spiraling environmental degradation is the elimination of the source—the fractional reserve banking system. The responsibility for creating the right amount of money would then shift from private-sector banks to governments. Under optimum democratic circumstances, allocation priorities should then shift toward public goods and labor, and away from large holders of wealth. In Douthwaite's proposal, the amount of currency created domestically would be related to the energy efficiency required to meet greenhouse gas emission limits, not the private credit needs of corporations and hedge funds. His system would have a contraction/convergence dimension. That is, the monetary limits imposed would lead to the contraction of total greenhouse gas emissions, while the amount allowed per capita would converge so that some countries, like the United States, would eventually lose the ability to use much higher amounts of fossil fuels per capita that they have enjoyed over the last hundred years or so. In fact, the United States would have to decrease its emissions from burning fossil fuels by 95 percent. On the other hand, poor countries would be allowed to increase their per capita emissions, consistent with their development needs and overall environmental sustainability (Douthwaite, *The Ecology of Money*).

Despite recognizing the creative, environmental, and equity-related virtues of Douthwaite's proposal, other MCO reformers are doubtful about its political feasibility. Consequently, to address the greenhouse problem, they make presumably a more modest proposal, a universal *carbon tax*. It would facilitate the objective of limiting carbon emissions, thereby reducing the potential impacts of global warming. A carbon tax is consistent with the ecological taxing principle that taxes should be imposed on undesirable activities, such as polluting, not desirable ones, such as working. Stiglitz likes this idea better than the carbon emissions trading system that is preferred under the Kyoto Protocol of the Framework Convention on Climate Change. He believes that setting emission caps, the necessary first step in creating a carbon market, is open to political manipulation and corruption, as it involves allocating private property rights with monetary value. Even the European Union's emissions trading system did not achieve much initially because it set the caps too high. Stiglitz argues that a carbon tax would be more successful in avoiding these problems. Taxes are straightforward and less subject to manipulation. Carbon taxes are imposed on carbon inputs rather than greenhouse gas emission outputs. They would be applied to gallons of gasoline, diesel, or jet fuel, cubic feet of natural gas, and tons of coal. They are intended to compensate for the negative global warming externalities of burning carbon-based fuels. They would help make renewable energy options, such as wind, solar, and biofuel, cost-effective. However, how much this ecological tax approach benefits the public good will depend upon the political process in each country. The revenues need to be spent on reinventing the whole infrastructure of the economy (Stiglitz, *Making Globalization Work*). Furthermore, the taxes required to effectively address what some scientists believe is a climate emergency are only politically conceivable if the public accepts the situation as comparable to the crisis of an all-out war (Spratt and Sutton, *Climate Code Red*).

The issue of *political feasibility* permeates the whole reform discussion. As long as corporations or corporate–government associations dominate the political process, any reforms that threaten their hegemony will be rejected. Polanyi derived some hope from the historical process of capitalism, which he believed was characterized by progressive cycles. Market capitalists, in cahoots with the government, would push for uncontrolled business dominance until the resulting exploitation became intolerable to the general public. In response to public protests, there would then be intervention by government to control some of the worst abuses. Businesses would chafe under these controls and push for their removal. They would eventually receive some deregulation relief, but then the exploitation and unequal distribution would grow again until the public reaction forced the government to reintroduce controls. Optimists like Korten believe that after each crisis of business excess the resulting government reform intervention will improve the condition of the general public. Therefore, imagining and promoting reforms will assist the process of making a better world. To help the process along, Korten argues for controls over corporate participation in politics and the public financing of campaigns. In agreement with Batra, he also believes in breaking up oligopolies both within countries and globally. Politics and production should be more community-based, but that can only work within the context of a truly democratic global governance system. That's why he and others favor the revival of the effort to construct a global code of conduct for corporations, and the establishment of a Global Corporate Accountability Board to enforce the code. The content of the code has already been articulated, in some cases in already existing but unenforceable international agreements, such as the working conditions standards stipulated by the International Labor Organization (Korten, *When Corporations Rule the World*; Polanyi, *The Great Transformation*).

Improving global environmental behavior involves actually implementing some basic principles that were enunciated in the consensus documents that came out of the World Conference on Environment and Development (the Rio Summit) held in 1992. They are known as sustainability, common heritage, the precautionary principle, and "polluter pays."

1 *Sustainability* presumes a moral commitment to future generations, namely, that the current generation leaves an earth that has the same productive capacity in the future that exists in the present. In order to achieve that result, at least three conditions must be met. First, renewable resources, such as fish, trees, water, and soil, should not be consumed and/or destroyed faster than they can replenish themselves. Second, non-renewable resources, such as fossil fuel deposits, should not be utilized at a rate faster than appropriate substitutes can be developed. Third, wastes, such as toxic chemicals, should not be dumped into the environment in amounts greater than the capacity of nature to process them and render them harmless. Currently all three of these conditions are being violated, so that collectively we are living unsustainably.

2 *Common heritage* means in essence that the earth's resources belong to everyone and that everyone shares the responsibility to behave sustainably. No country, corporation, or other entity has the moral or legal right to claim more than its fair share of the earth's resources. Clearly, the great inequalities in today's world do not reflect or honor this principle.

3 The *precautionary principle* holds that when scientists discover a human practice that could have potentially devastating and irreversible consequences, that practice should be halted as soon as possible rather than waiting for incontrovertible evidence. The most pertinent current example of a problem that should be addressed under this principle is global warming. The worst-case climate change scenario involves the small chance that continued and uncontrolled expansion of greenhouse gas emissions during the twenty-first century could put a spiraling feedback process into motion that would make the entire earth too hot for human habitation. Some scientists believe that the chances for a catastrophic outcome from "business as usual" are as high as 15 percent, which is not so small anyway. Scientists have called this worst-case possibility the Venus Effect. To not take it seriously would be the height of irresponsibility.

4 The *polluter-pays principle* simply proclaims that any organization or person responsible for emitting pollution or causing environmental destruction of any kind should pay for the cost of their actions. No business, government or person should gain by avoiding the environmental costs that they are imposing on society. Yet avoiding paying for these external costs is exactly what the market allows. Only government intervention can assure that this market failure is addressed (Korten, *When Corporations Rule the World*).

Earlier the views of the ecological economist Herman Daly were discussed. He proposes four reforms: (1) count nature as depreciable capital rather than as a consumption commodity, (2) replace the GDP with a more accurate national accounting system, (3) consider the earth a closed system with natural limits, and (4) locate nearly all economic and environmental responsibility at the community level.

The first two reforms require changes in conventional accounting systems. The Environmental Section of the World Bank has been working on creating a system of **natural capital** valuation. It's a start, but no country has yet to fully incorporate this approach in its decision-making processes. Central government officials in China expressed an interest in using natural capital accounting, but so far nothing has been implemented. Daly and Cobb devised a new national accounting system that they call the **Index of Sustainable Economic Welfare (ISEW)**. It incorporates both the positive contributions (e.g., child-rearing) and the negative activity (e.g., pollution) that the GDP either omits or counts incorrectly. Using the ISEW, Daly and Cobb calculated that between 1967 and 1987 the actual increase in real welfare for the United States had been only 6 percent, in contrast to the 46 percent increase that the GDP recorded (constant dollars). Other MCO analysts have continued to improve on this accounting method, which they now call the *Genuine Progress Indicator* (GPI). In contrast to the growth record of the GDP, the GPI records a decline in overall welfare since 1980. The difference in the welfare assessments are quite striking. For instance, in 2002 U.S. per capita GDP was $34,938 while per capita GPI was only $10,083. Despite the erroneous messages that the GDP measure is sending about how our economies and the environment are doing, there are no serious moves to officially replace it (Daly and Cobb, *For the Common Good*; Venetoulis and Cobb, *The GPI 1950–2002*).

Daly's third and fourth reform proposals directly challenge the major thrusts of globalization—growth as panacea and the worldwide consumer society. Daly and his fellow MCO'ers are trying to awaken the public to the realistic limits of planet earth. If we continue to grow, ecological catastrophe is the inevitable outcome. Human survival would then be an open question. **Sustainable development** should mean running our economies within the limits of nature's carrying capacity. However, if the term "development" is just a substitute for growth, then the phrase "sustainable development" is an oxymoron. Daly also believes that each community should take responsibility for its own economic welfare and not rely on the exploitation of others' resources for high levels of consumption. In fact, consumption should not be the overriding objective, but improving the quality of life. That can best be done at the community level. Daly's position was reflected in the final statement from the 1992 Rio Summit that embraced the democratic principle of *subsidiarity*. Subsidiarity calls for political-economic decision-making to be made at the lowest possible level. An extensive list of social and environmental responsibilities that local communities should undertake was spelled out in another Summit document, *Agenda 21*.

Fully implementing this reversal of economic globalization would significantly cut back on global trade and capital flows, probably by about two-thirds. An important consequence would be a great reduction in the transfer of some countries' environmental resources to other countries whose usage far exceeds their natural resource base and their fair share. Though the United States is not the only country incurring an ecological debt from this type of transfer, it is probably running the biggest deficit, using approximately 25 percent of the world's natural resources for less than 5 percent of the world's population. Realistically, of course, as long as the United States has the power (and the world's ecosystems don't collapse), it will not give up its privileged position. In fact, at the Rio Summit, President George H. W. Bush said quite adamantly, "The standard of living of the United States is non-negotiable." However, MCO proponents know that this is an untenable position in the long run (Daly, *Beyond Growth*).

Moving toward even partial implementation of some of these MCO environmental reforms would require more international agreements and a global enforcement body. There actually are some international environmental agreements already in place. One of the most successful is the 1987 Montreal Protocol, in which countries agreed to restrict their use of CFCs, the gas that was discovered to be responsible for destroying the ozone layer, which protects humans and all life from excess exposure to ultraviolet rays. As a group these agreements are known as **MEAs**, for **multilateral environmental agreements**. Not only has the United States resisted ratifying most of the major environmental agreements, such as the Framework Convention on Climate Change, but also, at the 2002 Johannesburg Summit on Sustainable Development, the United States attempted to insert in the final statement a provision that all MEAs would be given lower status in international law than WTO agreements. The attempt did not succeed. Among existing international organizations, two could conceivably serve as the basis of a new global enforcement body for environmental agreements, most importantly the forthcoming

Copenhagen Protocol on Climate Change. They are the United Nations Environmental Program (UNEP) and the Global Environmental Facility (GEF). However, though the Nairobi-based UNEP has been responsible for some important initiatives, it has little money or power. The GEF has some money, but it tends to follow the leadership of its most powerful constituent, the World Bank.

Thus, in order for most of the reforms suggested above to be effectively implemented to the expectation level of most MCO advocates, a new international governance structure with an MCO perspective would need to be adopted. Summarizing the discussion above, the institutions in that structure would include:

1   A more democratic United Nations that would serve as the oversight body for all the specialized organizations listed below.

2   A Global Corporate Accountability Board that would monitor and enforce a global corporate code of conduct.

3   A more democratic World Bank that would focus on assisting poor countries in achieving sustainable development.

4   A more democratic International Monetary Fund that would serve as the issuer of the global foreign exchange reserve currency and monitor trade and capital flows in the promotion of balance.

5   A more effectively democratic World Trade Organization that would facilitate fair trade, including the allowing and monitoring of compensatory tariffs in support of local development, labor protection, and environmental preservation.

6   A Global Insolvency Court that would facilitate debt relief as well as fairness to creditors.

7   A newly constituted global environmental body that would monitor and enforce international environmental agreements, especially the next phase of the Framework Convention on Climate Change.

The presentation of the MCO reform agenda is intended to demonstrate that MCO proponents are not just putting forth criticisms of the market world view–oriented system; they also propose many substantive reforms to the current system. However, it's not clear what paths to follow or strategies to implement in bringing about the realization of these reforms. The problem of feasibility looms large. Serious crises may have to occur before most of the reforms that have been proposed are seriously considered. From the perspective of classical Marxism, reforming capitalism is an illusory pursuit. Only after capitalism is replaced by a socialist system will most of these reforms have any chance of being adopted. The next chapter presents the model and world view of classical Marxism.

REVIEW QUESTIONS

1 Multi-centric organizational (MCO) analysts have identified six problematic consequences from the use of the "free trade" policy that is supported by the market world view. These problems are discussed under the headings of static vs. dynamic, terms of trade, capital confusion, conditions contravention, deindustrialization, and benefits vs. losses. Explain the meaning of each heading and why MCO analysts consider each of them to be a problem.

2 Explain how the MCO sense of "moneyness" is different from that of the market view of money, both in form and societal role.

3 Explain what is meant by the phrase "global casino," and how it contributed to the global financial crises of the late 1990s.

4 Discuss the ups and downs of the financial sector in the twentieth century and why MCO critics are concerned about the situation at the beginning of the twenty-first century.

5 What is the connection between market failure and ecological degradation?

6 Explain what the following three measures tell us that the market does not: ecological footprint, peak production, and the ISEW.

7 Discuss the characteristics and causes of climate change and why MCO proponents believe that the market is not only part of the problem but also an obstacle to its mitigation.

8 Ecological economist Herman Daly has identified a number of problems with the way that conventional market economics deals with environmental issues. They are discussed under the headings of the open-system error, the measurement mistake, the misidentification of nature, the misapplication of the intertemporal measure, and the misuse of free trade. Explain each one.

9 Discuss from an MCO perspective how transnational corporations have used the World Bank, the International Monetary Fund (IMF), and the World Trade Organization (WTO) to further their ends.

10 Present the political scientist Benjamin Barber's perspective on globalization, which he characterizes as "Jihad vs. McWorld."

11 Why does the MCO reform agenda discussion start with democracy? What is the difference between a liberal and illiberal democracy? How does democracy relate to the Global Corporate Accountability Board?

12 Explain how some of the other reform suggestions, including fair trade, debt relief, a global reserve currency, and sustainable development, are expected to improve social and economic conditions. Do they make sense to you? Are they feasible?

13 Other suggested reforms are compensatory tariffs, the Tobin tax, a carbon tax, special emission rights, 100 percent bank reserves, and the use of the precautionary principle. Explain how these reforms are supposed to work and what they are intended to achieve.

14 How would existing international organizations such as the World Bank, the IMF, and the WTO have to change in order for this array of reforms to become effective?

BIBLIOGRAPHY

Ackerman, Frank and Lisa Heinzerling, *Priceless: On Knowing the Price of Everything and the Value of Nothing* (New Press: New York) 2004.

Anderson, Sarah and John Cavanagh, *Top 200: The Rise of Corporate Global Power* (Institute for Policy Studies: Washington, D.C.) 2000.

Barber, Benjamin, *Jihad vs. McWorld* (Ballantine Books: New York) 1995.

Barlow, Maude, *The Free Trade Area of the Americas* (International Forum on Globalization: San Francisco) 2001.

Batra, Ravi, *The Myth of Free Trade: A Plan for America's Economic Revival* (Charles Scribner's Sons: New York) 1993.

Bello, Walden, Nicola Bullard, and Kamal Malhotra, *Global Finance: New Thinking on Regulating Speculative Capital Markets* (Zed Books: London) 2000.

Brown, Lester, *Plan B 2.0: Rescuing a Planet Under Stress and a Civilization in Trouble* (W. W. Norton and Company: New York) 2006.

Cavanagh, John and Jerry Mander (eds.), *Alternatives to Economic Globalization: A Better World is Possible* (Berrett-Koehler Publishers: San Francisco) 2004.

Collier, Robert, "Upwardly mobile Chinese in love with big cars," *San Francisco Chronicle*, August 18, 2007, pp. 1 and 9.

Daly, Herman, *Beyond Growth: The Economics of Sustainable Development* (Beacon Press: Boston) 1996.

Daly, Herman E. and John B. Cobb, Jr., *For the Common Good: Redirecting the Economy toward Community, the Environment, and a Sustainable Future* (Beacon Press: Boston) 1989.

Dicken, Peter, *Global Shift: Reshaping the Global Economic Map in the 21st Century* (Guilford Press: New York) 2003.

Douthwaite, Richard, *The Ecology of Money* (Green Books: Totnes, United Kingdom) 1999.

Dunkley, Graham, *Free Trade: Myth, Reality and Alternatives* (Zed Books: London) 2004.

Eagleton, Dominic, *Under the Influence: Exposing Undue Corporate Influence over Policy-Making at the World Trade Organization* (Action Aid: London) 2006.

Eatwell, John and Lance Taylor, *Global Finance at Risk: The Case for International Regulation* (New Press: New York) 2000.

Edwards, Chris, *The Fragmented World: Competing Perspectives on Trade, Money and Crisis* (Methuen: London) 1985.

ETC Group, "Groups in Africa and Latin America condemn World Bank biosafety projects," 2006. Available at www.etcgroup.org.

Flannery, Tim, *The Weather Makers: How Man Is Changing the Climate and What It Means for Life on Earth* (Atlantic Monthly Press: New York) 2005.

Galbraith, John Kenneth, *American Capitalism: The Concept of Countervailing Power* (Riverside Press: Cambridge, Massachusetts) 1952.

Galbraith, John Kenneth, *Money: Whence It Came, Where It Went* (Houghton Mifflin: Boston) 1975; revised edition 1995.

Gray, Charles, "Corporate goliaths," *Multinational Monitor*, June, 1999, pp. 26–27.

Godrej, Dinyar, "Advertising overload," *New Internationalist*, September, 2006, pp. 2–5.

Heilbroner, Robert, *The Making of Economic Society* (Prentice-Hall: Englewood Cliffs, New Jersey) 1986 (first published in 1962).

Heinberg, Richard, *The Party's Over: Oil, War and the Fate of Industrial Societies* (New Society Publishers: Gabriola Island, Canada) 2003.

Holtzclaw, John, "America's autos on welfare: Summary of subsidies," Sierra Club website, October, 1996. Available at www.sierraclub.org/sprawl/articles/subsidies.asp.

Hutchinson, Frances, Mary Mellor, and Wendy Olsen, *The Politics of Money: Towards Sustainability and Economic Democracy* (Pluto Press: London) 2002.

Ingham, Geoffrey, *The Nature of Money* (Polity Press: Cambridge, United Kingdom) 2004.

Kaplinsky, Raphael, *Globalization, Poverty and Inequality: Between a Rock and a Hard Place* (Polity Press: Cambridge, United Kingdom) 2005.

Korten, David C., *When Corporations Rule the World*, 2nd edn. (Berrett-Koehler Publishers: San Francisco) 2001.

Lawton, Thomas C., James N. Rosenau, and Amy C. Verdun, *Strange Power: Shaping the Parameters of International Relations and International Political Economy* (Ashgate: Aldershot, United Kingdom) 2000.

Madeley, John, *Big Business, Poor Peoples: The Impact of Transnational Corporations on the World's Poor* (Zed Books: London) 1999.

May, Christopher, *Global Corporate Power* (Lynne Rienner Publishers: Boulder, Colorado) 2006.

Moran, Timothy Patrick, "'Wealth doesn't matter' and other reassurances to the world's poor," paper presented at the International Studies Association Conference, Chicago, Illinois, February 2007.

"The national entertainment state," *The Nation*, July 3, 2006, pp. 13–30.

Patomaki, Heikki and Teivo Teivainen, *A Possible World: Democratic Transformations of Global Institutions* (Zed Books: London) 2004.

Polanyi, Karl, *The Great Transformation: The Political and Economic Origins of Our Time* (Rinehart: New York) 1944.

Shiva, Vandana, "From commons to corporate patents on life," in J. Cavanagh and J. Mander (eds.), *Alternatives to Economic Globalization* (Berrett-Koehler Publishers: San Francisco) 2004, pp. 115–117.

Spratt, David and Philip Sutton, *Climate Code Red: The Case for a Sustainability Emergency* (Fitzroy, Australia: Friends of the Earth) 2008.

Stern, Nicholas, *The Economics of Climate Change* (HM Treasury: London) 2006.

Stiglitz, Joseph, *Globalization and Its Discontents* (W. W. Norton: New York) 2002.

Stiglitz, Joseph, *Making Globalization Work* (W. W. Norton and Company: New York) 2006.

Strange, Susan, *Casino Capitalism* (Manchester University Press: Manchester, United Kingdom) 1986.

Strange, Susan, *States and Markets* (Pinter: London) 1988; 2nd edition, 1994.

Strange, Susan, *Mad Money: When Markets Outgrow Governments* (University of Michigan Press: Ann Arbor) 1998.

Summers, Lawrence, "World Bank memo," *The Economist*, February 8, 1992, p. 66.

Venetoulis, Jason and Cliff Cobb, *The GPI 1950–2002* (Redefining Progress: Oakland, California) 2004.

Wise, Timothy and Kevin Gallagher, "Doha Round and developing countries: Will the Doha deal do more harm than good?" RIS Policy Briefs (Global Development and Environment Institute, Tufts University: Boston) April 2006.

World Wide Fund for Nature, *Living Planet Report 2004* (World Wide Fund for Nature: Gland, Switzerland) 2004.

"World's 500 largest corporations," *Fortune*, July 24, 2006, pp. 95–126.

Zakaria, Fareed, *The Future of Freedom: Illiberal Democracy at Home and Abroad* (W. W. Norton and Company: New York) 2003.

CHAPTER 6

The Classical Marxist Model and World View

This chapter presents the basic model for understanding human societies articulated by **Karl Marx** (1818–1883) in his extensive scholarly writings. The discussion begins by making an argument for the continuing relevance of Marx's analytical framework. It then spells out the philosophical premises of his system, which taken together have come to be known as *dialectical materialism*. Moving on to the interactions, the discussion covers the basic analytical tool used by Marx: mode of production. *Historical materialism* refers to the application of Marx's mode of production analysis to human history. Attention is then directed to the capitalist mode of production, its interactions, and its outcomes, with the most interesting feature being the process by which Marx thought that capitalism would destroy itself. Finally, we look briefly at Marx's vision of the ultimate future.

Many pundits have questioned whether the works of Karl Marx have relevance anymore after the 1990 collapse of the Soviet Union and its state-run central-planning system. After all, the system was called **communism**, and its ideological heroes were Karl Marx and Vladimir Lenin. However, the designer of the Soviet system was neither Marx nor Lenin. It was Joseph Stalin. As leader of the Communist Party, Stalin was the dictator of the Soviet Union from 1928 to 1953. The system he established has been called **Stalinism**. It began to unravel after his death, but it did not fully collapse until the disintegration of the Soviet Union in 1990. Nowhere in Marx's writings is there a blueprint for a future totalitarian state such as the one that Stalin imposed. In fact, Marx's vision for the future socialist/communist society was the opposite of Stalin's. Marx imagined the future, post-capitalist society as one that was based on participatory democracy and that promoted individual freedom. Unfortunately for Marx's reputation, the Soviet Union, China, and other self-identified communist countries have claimed descent from Marx. However, it is almost certain that their centralized, totalitarian systems would not have received his blessing.

What Marx wrote mostly about was capitalism. It's his extensive analysis of capitalism that makes Marx highly relevant today. Marx's major work was a three-volume treatise on capitalism, simply titled *Capital*. Marx wanted people to understand the nature of capitalism, where it came from, how it worked, what was wrong with it, why it was a temporary phase of human history, and what one needed to do in order to speed up its demise because reform was not feasible. Many scholars have observed that no one has written more insightfully about these subjects than Karl Marx. For instance, Robert Heilbroner, another institutionalist like Galbraith, stated that "Marx's combination of insight and method permanently altered the manner in which reality would thereafter be perceived" (*Marxism*, p. 17). Therefore, if it is true that one of the major transformations under way in the world today is economic globalization, and if globalization really is just another term for the spread of capitalism around the world, then it makes sense to at least consider the analyses of Karl Marx. He has probably been more influential than any other scholar on how people think about capitalism. In fact, when people across the political spectrum discuss the capitalism system, they are very likely using some aspect of Marx's analysis, even though they may not be aware of it.

Karl Marx (see box on p.13) was the last great classical political economist. He was born in 1818 in Trier, a small town on the Mosel River in western Germany. In 1841 he received his doctoral degree in philosophy from the University of Jena. Marx and his fellow students were strongly influenced by the views of Professor G. W. F. Hegel, arguably the pre-eminent German philosopher of the early nineteenth century. After graduating Marx tried his hand at writing for small periodicals in Berlin, Paris, Cologne, and Brussels. But the views expressed by Marx and his fellow authors were too politically radical for the German authorities, who applied pressure to have the periodicals shut down. In the mid-1840s during one of those journalistic stints, Marx met Friedrich Engels, a member of a German textile family, with whom he collaborated throughout the rest of his life. In 1848 Engels and Marx co-wrote and published *The Communist Manifesto*. A year later Marx moved permanently to London, the place that had the greatest intellectual freedom in Europe at that time. Engels also was based in England, where he managed his family's textile mills in Manchester. After Marx died in 1883, Engels put together and published volumes 2 and 3 of *Capital: A Critique of Political Economy* from Marx's notes and manuscripts. Engels died in 1895 (Heilbroner, *The Worldly Philosophers*).

Marx's lifetime spanned the height of the Industrial Revolution in England. He observed and wrote about the harsh conditions in the factory cities. He was a witness to the oppressive working conditions in the textile and steel mills. Women and children worked long and arduous hours in the factories for very low wages with no social or legal protections against abuse. Workers lived in grimy, unsafe, and unclean slum environments that surrounded the pollution-spewing factories. Marx shared with many other intellectuals and social activists an abhorrence of these terrible conditions of industrial capitalism. What he did not share was Adam Smith's optimism about how market capitalism would eventually benefit all members of the society. But it should be noted that Adam Smith had died in 1790, 28 years before Marx was born and well before the massive transformation of English towns into the ugly factory cities that made England the industrial workplace of the world.

Karl Marx did share with Adam Smith as well as other great classical political economists, such as David Ricardo and Thomas Malthus, the fundamental concept of the **labor theory of value**. Essentially they all believed that the crucial component in determining the relative values of all exchanged commodities was the amount of labor time involved. However, there were differences in how they calculated labor time and in how they understood underlying values to be related to actual prices. Marx's belief that the exploitation of labor is built in to capitalism is dependent on his version of the labor theory of value, which will be described more fully later in this chapter. As mentioned in earlier chapters, one of the fundamental differences among the world views of International Political Economy is their theories of value. Both the free market and MCO schools of thought reject the labor theory of value. The classical Marxists continue to contend that Marx and the other classical political economists had it right in the first place.

The modifier "classical" in this chapter's title refers to the original ideas of Marx himself. Even before Marx had died, a number of his followers had begun creating their own variations on his analytical themes. The process continues today. Some of these self-proclaimed Marxists have adopted views that have little relation to some of Marx's core ideas. For instance, some neo-Marxists have rejected the labor theory of value, which was a fundamental building block in Marx's analysis of capitalism. Marx was not happy with several of the interpretations of his work with which he was familiar during his lifetime. He actually exclaimed at one point, "I am not a Marxist!" (Heilbroner, *The Worldly Philosophers*, p. 151). Undoubtedly, he would be even more annoyed with some of the schools of "Marxist" thought and practice that have appeared since his death. The presentation of Marx's ideas in this chapter is intended to reflect the original positions of Marx, though the arrangement and presentation will contain some modifications to make Marx's views clearer and easier to comprehend. Whether or not Marx would approve is an open question.

Karl Marx was a holistic thinker. He was primarily a philosopher, though his major field of interest was clearly political economy. The scope of his work went far beyond the boundaries of today's specialized academic disciplines. Marx's transcendent analyses and theoretical frameworks are applicable to many fields, certainly to all of the social sciences, but even to the arts and sciences. Karl Marx was truly a "Worldly Philosopher," to use the epithet in the title of Robert Heilbroner's well-known book. As a philosopher Marx knew that in order to persuade others that his view of human history was credible, he had to create a comprehensive system of analysis that was internally consistent. Therefore, he had to be transparent about the assumptions and method upon which the structure of his analysis was to be built.

The fundamental philosophical premises of the Marxian system of thought have been called **dialectical materialism**, though this is a phrase that Marx himself never used. Evidently, the first person to use this term in print was another German author and political activist who lived about the same time as Marx, by the name of Joseph Dietzgen (Burns, in *Science and Society*). The term has become widely used because it serves as convenient shorthand for Marx's approach. *Dialectical* refers to a logic-of-process that Marx borrowed from Professor Hegel. *Materialism* refers to the importance of actual physical experience in the determination of reality. Ludwig Feuerbach, yet another German philosopher, was influential in Marx's thinking on this subject. He is supposed to have exclaimed in disagreement with Hegel, "Armies live on their stomachs, not their ideas." We will see below not only the philosophical assumptions of dialectical materialism but also how Marx used them to inform his analysis of capitalism.

Philosophers tend to start the presentation of any explanatory system by spelling out their ontology and epistemology. **Ontology** refers to the nature and relations of being (the theory of reality); **epistemology** refers to how we think we know what we know (the theory of knowledge). These philosophical concepts, and the premises section that follows, will seem very abstract at first. However, the abstractions will be converted to solid historical examples as the discussion progresses.

PREMISES OF THE CLASSICAL MARXIST MODEL

The ontological premises of the **dialectic** are:

1 *All phenomena are interrelated and interdependent.* The relations between phenomena are more important than the phenomena in and

of themselves. The whole is always greater than the sum of its parts (holism). This assumption differs from the basic analytical approach of conventional science (including neoclassical economics), which focuses on the parts themselves. For example, the market looks at the profitability of a single crop, not the overall ecological impact of producing it. Because the conventional approach reduces larger entities into smaller, presumably more manageable parts, it is known, especially among its critics, as **reductionism.**

2 *All things are always in flux, always changing, always moving.* Nothing is ever the same. Nothing is constant. History is a moving stage, and it does not repeat itself. The dominant Greek philosophical tradition held the contrary, namely that the underlying, essential reality was a fixed state. The equilibrium approach of neoclassical economics follows in this tradition, as the equilibrating outcome of the market is a balanced, at-rest state. Although actors may seek their proper position, the stage itself is stationary.

3 *"Quantitative" changes are continuously occurring, which sometimes generates major or "qualitative" changes.* Qualitative transformations occur when an accumulation of quantitative changes makes the original form unrecognizable or impossible. Qualitative changes can be characterized metaphorically as metamorphoses in nature, like the change from larva into butterfly. In societies, qualitative changes are revolutions, such as the agricultural revolution, which emerged from the accumulation of many small, quantitative changes in technology and social arrangements over centuries. By contrast, neoclassical economics sees all movement as quantitative, that is, as shifting price arrangements. Revolutions or major social transformations are not part of the neoclassical world view, as it takes an ahistorical stance.

4 *Change is evolutionary.* However, the forward movement does not necessarily follow a simple linear path. There can even be setbacks. Revolutions occur along the way. No pre-determined historical path can be precisely identified; nor can any time frame be pre-established. However, the general trend is progressive from simple to complex, and an overall outcome can be predicted. That is, there is an end-in-view. Therefore, the evolutionary process is **teleological.** The eventual outcome can be broadly described, even though it is a moving state, as quantitative changes never end. On the contrary, since neoclassical economics does not incorporate history within its basic model, any discussion of evolution is irrelevant to it.

5 *Change is driven by tensions, the internal oppositions within all things.* Marx agreed with Hegel that the dynamic of the unity of opposites characterizes all phenomena, from the atomic coherence of negative

and positive charges to the societal complementarity of conflicting classes. Some Marxists call these oppositions "contradictions," which they see as natural, creative, and logically sensible within a Hegelian-type dialectical system. The opposing philosophical position, which was held by Aristotle, regards oppositions and conflict to be unnatural and destructive. Contradictions are illogical. Internally consistent order is the desired state. The market model of neoclassical economics takes this approach. Supply–demand equilibria are harmonious, not conflictual, relationships. Therefore, free market proponents see the economic dimension of a market society as essentially harmonious.

The ontological premises of **materialism** are:

1 *The fundamental level of reality consists of material—that is, physical—phenomena.* Thus for human beings the basic reality is acquiring food, eating, drinking, dealing with storms, struggling with disease, joining with others, fighting with others, and so on. This assumption contrasts with those who see ideas or symbolic pictures as more defining of reality. In their view, experience is mediated through the shared concepts that people use to make sense of things. In fact, these human-created cognitive structures actually define what is real. Hegel took this position; Marx thought about it, but eventually rejected it as secondary to the material base of life.

2 *Material phenomena have an independent, objective reality*; that is, their existence is not dependent on human perception or human conceptualization of them. Hurricanes happen whether or not humans are around to experience them.

3 *Material conditions are the primary determinant of the character and qualities of all other dimensions.* In other words, the surrounding material or physical conditions that people experience are more important in influencing how people think and behave than any other influence. By attributing primary causal power to material conditions, Marx continued his disagreement with Hegel, who gave thinking primary causal power. However, Marx did not believe that the causal relationship was a simple one-way street. He understood that how people thought did affect the way they experienced a particular material condition. Therefore, he saw the relationship between material and cognition as interactive. Nevertheless, he still maintained that material conditions dominated the interaction. If one were looking for a simple statement about why something happened the way it did in a Marxian system, one could glibly attribute it to the "material conditions." The comparably simple catch-all explanation for the free market approach

would be "supply and demand." For the MCO perspective, it would be "power negotiations."

The epistemological premises of **dialectical materialism** are:

1   *The relationships among material phenomena are regular and law-like.*

2   *Generalizations (laws) about these relationships are discoverable through an empirical process, that is, a scientific method.*

3   *This scientific method, however, as mentioned above, must be holistic, not reductionist.* It must look at systemic relationships rather than discrete, unconnected, or incomplete parts.

4   *Important relationships, that is, underlying oppositions, are often not revealed by superficial observations, but must be inferred from relational dynamics.* The dialectical method involves looking for the real, underlying power dynamics, the "hidden agenda." People seldom will publicly share, or in some cases even know, the real interests that are driving their behavior.

By contrast, according to Marxists, conventional science (positivism) limits itself to superficial observation, thereby guaranteeing that, especially when applied to human activities, it will be an endeavor focused mostly on trivialities. For instance, questionnaire or survey results almost never provide any insights into people's real or actual sentiments. The "useful knowledge" problem is further compounded by the nature of individual-respondent data collection. Marxists are looking for major structural and relational dynamics, but it is not possible to derive them from a simple summation of individual responses. From the Marxist perspective, science in general, but neoclassical economics in particular, suffers from this reductionism.

5   *In order for science to be accurate and contribute to the accumulation of real knowledge, it must combine theory and practice.* Scientists must be actively engaged in the matters that they are studying. By itself, detached theorizing will not advance knowledge, as there is no meaningful connection to reality, that is, the material conditions. Therefore, scientists must be a part of the communities that they are studying, not detached observers. And, if these communities are experiencing exploitation and injustice, then it is the scientists' obligation to assist in the process of positive social change. Science, therefore, should be inherently and consciously political. Conventional science strongly disagrees with this stance, as it believes that the objective pursuit of truth requires detachment and non-involvement.

Marx's analysis of capitalism and human societies in general emerges from the world view that is reflected in these assumptions. The dialectical approach in Marx's ontology definitely diverges from the conventional scientific approach, though the materialist part of his ontology shares similar assumptions with conventional empirical science. In fact, Marx called his approach **scientific socialism**. Marx's epistemology starts out in agreement with conventional science, but it soon diverges on account of its emphasis on holism. Marx believed in looking at the whole system (not just parts of it), incorporating history, and looking for the underlying conflicts that tell the real story of what is going on. Without engagement with the real world, science is sterile (Heilbroner, *Marxism*; McMurtry, *The Structure of Marx's World-View*).

Applying these assumptions to human history, Marx reinterpreted all of human experience and created a whole new history that was centered on the ways in which people make their living, rather than empires, wars, and rulers. Friedrich Engels, his long-time collaborator and financial supporter, called Marx's approach **historical materialism.** Marx believed that the fundamental and defining activity of humanity in history was laboring in the production process and that it was always a pre-eminently social experience. It always involved groups of people in relationship with each other and nature. Marx also observed that societies tend to create class hierarchies in which some groups have more power than others, resulting in the weaker groups being exploited. Part of the weaker groups' production is taken from them by the more powerful. This confiscated production Marx called *surplus*. When Marx studied history, he observed a number of qualitatively different societies. These different social formations Marx called **modes of production**. The major examples were primitive communism, ancient civilizations, feudalism, and capitalism. Every dimension of a society, including its reproduction practices, the state, religion, and so on, is incorporated in its mode of production. To Marx, the concept mode of production was all-encompassing and holistic. Marx put production at the center of his analysis because he believed that the material experience and structure of production is the most important dimension of social life for determining all other dimensions.

INTERACTIONS WITHIN THE CLASSICAL MARXIST MODEL

Before discussing further the different historical social formations that Marx identified, it is useful to identify the analytical components of the **mode of production.** Though there is an interactive causal relationship between the components, *the instruments of production*, or the technology utilized in production, play the dominant causal role. The class structure within the relations of production reflects the prevailing instruments of production and establishes the dynamic that generates the form and substance of the other institutions in the society. Though these relations of production establish the range of possibilities, outcomes are not strictly determined. In fact, the prevailing beliefs or ideologies that justify the class structure may significantly influence other changes occurring in the society, even the nature and pace of the underlying technological innovations. Despite the causal uncertainty prevalent in Marx's historical analyses, he did seem to believe that the laws of historical evolution would eventually bring about the communist mode of production. However, before discussing the historical processes, let us first define the active components of the modes of production.

Forces of production

1 *Instruments of production*—the technology that is utilized in the production process. Historically it has ranged from simple tools to major irrigation works to the massive machine-driven factories of more recent times. These are invented and produced by humans. They are the most important part of the material conditions that determine the evolution and qualities of the social formation.

2 *Raw materials*—the basic inputs from nature, from minerals to cultivated crops. Changes in technology determine which natural resources are considered valuable to the production process. Oil pools, for instance, were dangerous traps to be avoided until someone discovered their energy value in the nineteenth century. Together the instruments of production and raw materials make up the **means of production**.

3 *Labor*—the productive activity that people provide. Its effectiveness, or productive efficiency, varies with the skill and knowledge possessed by the workers as well as the type of production instruments available to them. Thus, the productivity of labor depends on these variables.

Relations of production

1 *Structure*—In every social formation or mode of production except communism, there are groups that control the means of production and groups that do not. This asymmetrical relationship produces the fundamental group or **class** antagonism, the dialectical conflict, of the particular mode of production. As Marx and Engels wrote in the *Communist Manifesto*, the history of humankind is the history of *class*

struggles. The nature of the classes and the nature of the struggles vary from one mode of production to another.

2   **Qualities**—Every social formation or mode of production is an "ensemble of social relations" that is shaped by the material conditions. Therefore, how people relate to each other, how they govern themselves, what they believe, what religions they adhere to, what art they create, what cultural practices they follow, and so forth, are primarily influenced by the existing forces of production. Even human nature itself changes with the mode of production.

Historical materialism

Marx's sweeping view of human history compacts all of human history into only five major modes of production: primitive communism, ancient civilizations, feudalism, capitalism, and communism. As noted above, the most important causal factor in the shift from one mode of production to another is a change in the technology of production—the instruments of production. Different technologies of production require different work arrangements. That should be evident to anyone who compares the material working conditions of hunting and gathering societies vs. peasant agricultural societies vs. industrial factory-based societies. At least that is what Marx thought.

Marx believed that humans were unstoppably creative. Consequently, new technologies would inevitably and continually be invented. Eventually, those that were useful would be adopted. What, then, were the technologies that facilitated the emergence of the qualitatively different modes of production in Marx's simple historical schema? In the first historical mode of production, *primitive communism*, "primitive" refers to primitive production technology, the type that we associate with hunting and gathering societies. These societies were made up of small, peripatetic bands that had no elaborate class structure. If we look at the time scale of human history, we see that most of it has been spent in the first mode of production. But the invention of settled agriculture about 6,000 years ago changed everything. Plants and then animals were domesticated. Food production substantially increased and became more reliable. Controlling land and large stores of food provided the motivation for developing the first highly stratified, city-centered social formations. These *ancient civilizations*, such as those in Mesopotamia (current-day Iraq), were the first to have the type of class structure that Marx identified as central to his analysis. He identified the opposing classes in this mode of production as masters and slaves.

According to Marx, with the collapse of the Roman Empire in the fifth century, Europe moved on to the next mode of production, **feudalism**. The centralized authority in Rome was replaced by thousands of small, lord-controlled fiefdoms. Each lord had his manor and surrounding villages where the serfs lived and grew food. The serfs were tied to the land and committed to providing a portion of their crop to the lord, but the lord in turn was committed to protecting the serfs from invaders and ensuring basic subsistence in case of crop failure. This arrangement was supported by a Church-sanctioned reciprocal moral bond that existed between the lords and serfs. Feudalism's decentralization was facilitated by the invention of water- and wind-powered mills that served as local sources of energy. This stood in contrast to the large irrigation systems of ancient civilizations such as Mesopotamia, Egypt, and China that required centralized control. Less than 5 percent of the population in medieval feudal Europe lived in places that could be called cities. During the latter stages of the feudal period, especially starting in the fourteenth century in the Italian city-states, technological developments occurred that would eventually undermine feudalism. They included developments in banking, ship construction, navigation, and military armaments that facilitated the rise of long-distance commerce and mercantile cities. A new class, the merchants, emerged to provide the dialectical tension that challenged the feudal landlords and the continuation of feudalism. From the sixteenth to the eighteenth centuries the merchants promoted a system of international commerce known as mercantilism, which was discussed in the first chapter. Marx saw mercantilism as the transitional stage between the feudal mode of production and the capitalist mode of production.

In China the merchants were up against a strong centralized authority, in contrast to the political fragmentation of medieval Europe. Marx cited the Chinese case as a clear demonstration of the ability of a ruling class to stifle the changes that Chinese-invented technology facilitated elsewhere. The Chinese invented printing, but the emperor did not allow the dissemination of printed materials. The Chinese invented clocks, but the emperor did not allow their public use. The Chinese invented many ship-building improvements and navigation instruments, including the compass, but in the fifteenth century the emperor brought the world's biggest fleet home and redirected the country's resources to land-based activity. Marx recognized that conditions were qualitatively so different in Asia compared to Europe that he gave them their own mode of production designation—the *Asiatic mode of production*. Therefore, the merchant-led transformation that occurred in Europe was not allowed to happen in China, at least not for hundreds of years.

Along with the rise of the political power of the European merchant class, the really revolutionary technological change that doomed feudalism in Europe was the invention of the industrial system of production. Starting in the latter part of the eighteenth century, it created an entirely new set of material conditions: production via machines and factories. This dramatically new production system brought into existence the mode of production with which Marx was most familiar—the *capitalist mode of production*. Even though Marx was very critical of the exploitative conditions created by capitalism, he also saw it as a necessary stage in historical evolution, since it provided the unprecedented increase in output that was necessary for the elimination of poverty. Marx believed that revolutionary action by the working class would assure that capitalism would eventually be succeeded by the *communist mode of production*. In between there would be a transitional period of **socialism** in which the government would own and control the means of production on behalf of the laboring class. The final mode of production envisaged by Marx was communism, when class conflict over the control and ownership of the means of production would be eliminated, as everybody would collectively own and control the means of production. There would be no more class struggle. In fact, there would be no more classes, though minor or quantitative changes would continue. Distributional inequities would not be a problem as there would be enough for everybody: "From each according to his abilities; to each according to his needs" (Marx, quoted in McMurtry, *The Structure of Marx's World-View*, p. 225).

Table 6.1 summarizes the major modes of production throughout history—especially European history—according to Marx, and identifies the classes that are endemic to the material conditions existing within each mode.

Table 6.1 Modes of production through history

				Transitional phases	
				Mercantilism ↓	Socialism ↓
Modes	Primitive communism	Ancient civilizations	Feudalism	Capitalism	Communism
Classes	None	Masters vs. slaves	Lords vs. serfs	Capitalists (bourgeoisie) vs. workers (proletariat)	None

THE CAPITALIST MODE OF PRODUCTION

The mode of production with which Marx was most familiar and about which he wrote the most was the capitalist mode of production. (See Figure 6.1.) This section elaborates on what Marx had to say about it. First, let us take the definitional components of modes of production in general and specify the capitalist content for each component. That will yield a picture of the characteristics of the capitalist social formation. Then we will see how their interaction over time, according to Marx, will bring about the eventual demise of the capitalist system.

Forces of production in capitalism

1 *Instruments of production*—industrial technology. In the first stage of capitalism, production is centralized in factories where machines driven by inanimate energy are organized into assembly lines. Machines now set the pace of production. The speed of technological innovation greatly accelerates, and a process of continuous capital accumulation becomes institutionalized. Productive activity and residency becomes increasingly centralized in cities.

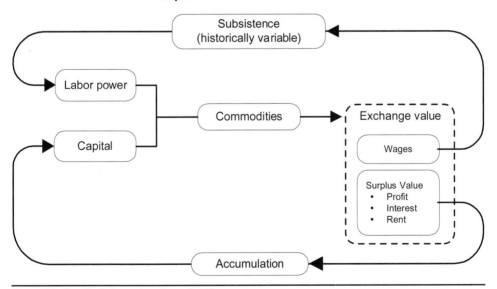

Capitalist Mode of Production

Figure 6.1 Capitalist mode of production.

2 *Raw materials*—shift from largely vegetable and animal substances to largely mineral and eventually artificial (chemically created) materials. In capitalism raw materials are considered commodities, and their exchange value is set by supply and demand in the market.

3 *Labor*—more productive in capitalism because of task division, better education, and capital enhancement. However, labor power is also converted into a commodity and sold in the market. The wages of labor tend to approximate the cost of its reproduction (household food and shelter). In most instances, laborers create more commodity value than it costs to reproduce them. Thus there is usually a difference between the wages that workers receive and the market or exchange value of the products they make. Workers are told that this is the correct valuation because it is determined by the objective process of supply and demand in an impersonal market. Marx believed that capitalists used this market rationalization to hide the exploitive reality of their treatment of labor. Only in the case of the labor commodity is there this discrepancy between the price paid for its labor power (wages) and the commodity production value that it creates. Marx called this difference **surplus value**. Capitalists make most of their profit from the surplus value that they extract from labor. Capitalists use their profits to invest in capital accumulation, the life-blood of capitalism. All dividends, interest, and rent also come from surplus value. In other words, if capitalists were to lose their ability to extract surplus value from workers, the whole capitalist system would collapse.

In order to ascertain the costs of labor reproduction (wages) versus the exchange value of the commodities produced by labor, Marx relied on the **labor theory of value**. From this standpoint, Marx argued that the exchange value of any commodity traded in the market would approximate the "average socially necessary amount of labor time" involved in bringing it to the market. Marx wanted a standard of relative measurement that was drawn from many cases; thus the value comes from an average. He also wanted to make sure that the available knowledge and technology were taken into account, plus he wanted to be sure that laggards were not rewarded for their inefficiency, thus the qualifying phrase "socially necessary." Because the labor time value for any particular commodity was drawn from an average of best-practice cases, the measure has also been called **abstract labor**. Remember that Marx was positing a source of underlying relative values. Actual prices, for a variety of reasons, could diverge from underlying values. In that respect, Marx's theory of value is no different from the market or MCO theories of value as they also recognize the possibility of actual transaction prices diverging from the theoretically predicted value differences. What distinguishes Marx's theory is the insight that he believes it provides into the built-in exploitation of labor that is hidden within the price system of capitalism.

Relations of production in capitalism

1   *Structure*—Private property plays a key role in the class structure of capitalism, because *capitalists* (the ruling or dominant class) legally own as well as control the means of production. *Workers* (the dominated or oppressed class) only control their own labor power. As a consequence of owning the means of production, the capitalists or bourgeoisie own the products that come out of the factories or commercial farms. Therefore, any profit made from the sale of products belongs to the capitalists. Since the discrepancy between what a capitalist has to pay for labor (labor costs) and the revenue that the capitalist earns from selling the products becomes the major source of profit, a fundamental class struggle is embedded in the capitalist system over the extent of that expropriation. In the short run the only way a capitalist can increase his profit is to pay less for labor. And vice versa: The only way that workers or the proletariat can increase their wages is to reduce the capitalist's profit. Though it may be necessary to remain competitive, increasing production efficiency and lowering costs through capital investment does not turn out to be a successful long-term strategy for enhancing the rate of profit. Marx argued that is the case because not only will all other capitalists make the same investment, but also the shift to using more capital and less labor in the production process will reduce the only reliable source of profit, the extraction of surplus value from labor. This paradox will be explained further below.

2   *Qualities*—Money dominates the capitalist mode of production. All economic transactions that count are those priced by the market in monetary terms. All traded commodities receive an **exchange value**, a price, through a supply–demand interaction in the market. As explained above, Marx believed that there was a tendency for the exchange-value price of products to approximate the underlying labor value. Marx further argued that all human relationships are mediated through what Marx called the "**veil of money**," a pervasive system of abstract valuation that hides the profound degree of exploitation built into the capitalist system. Workers are told by the capitalist elite that their market-determined wages reflect their real value, when in fact they are not receiving the true value of their production. The economic ideology of capitalism obscures the underlying human realities. Land, labor, and capital are conceptualized as physical commodities that receive a true market value for their contribution. But in fact it's the landowner that receives the return on land, the capitalist that receives the return on

capital, and the laborer that receives the return on labor. These are all human relationships of unequal power that the price system objectifies and obscures. The capitalistic market transformation of conflictual human relationships into cooperative relationships between things, Marx called *commodity fetishism* (Heilbroner, *Marxism*).

The capitalistic market system creates material conditions that reward behavior driven by greed, aggressive competitiveness, and acquisitiveness. Marx believed that these qualities are not fundamental to human nature, but they are fundamental to being successful in the capitalist system. Consequently, human relations in capitalism are characterized by **alienation**. People are alienated from each other because monetary relationships replace genuine human relationships. Workers are alienated from the true value of their production and from each other as they compete for jobs. Workers and capitalists are alienated from each other in the class struggle. Capitalists are alienated from each other as they compete for profits. Everyone is alienated from nature as it is turned into a commodity for sale in the market. Most people are alienated from understanding the truly exploitative nature of the system by capitalist propaganda that permeates popular culture. This propaganda purposely creates a "**false consciousness**," a misunderstanding of the true nature of the system.

Marx contended that it was difficult for ordinary workers to break through false consciousness and the veil of money, because every structure of power in the society is owned and/or controlled by the capitalist ruling class. The capitalists run the government, no matter how democratic it is claimed to be. Capitalists control the media. Capitalists co-opt organized religion, as it is dependent on funding from the wealthy and political support from the state. The legal system, the art world, education, prevailing ideologies—all are controlled by the capitalists on behalf of their interests. Of course, sometimes the capitalists may allow some dissent and some pseudo-freedom, but only within the limits they consider safe. From Marx's perspective, workers in capitalism are neither economically nor politically free. They are "free" to be "wage slaves" and "political subjects." Marx believed that capitalism was pervaded by high-flying illusions that eventually would all fall down to earth.

Outcomes of the capitalist mode of production

With such a tight network of control, how could one imagine that the capitalist mode of production would eventually be transformed into a qualitatively different mode of production? The answer lies in Marx's dialectical ontology. Remember that it presumes an inevitable evolution from one qualitative state (mode of production) to another, as long as there are driving oppositions. The driving opposition in capitalism is the class struggle. Marx had to discover a necessary sequence of events, one based on scientific laws, that would lead to the downfall of capitalism. And, of course, he did.

Marx believed that he had uncovered the process that would lead to the inevitable *self-destruction of the capitalist mode of production*, based on the two key components of the system: (1) the exploitation of labor and (2) the necessity for capital accumulation. We can understand this process by taking a hypothetical example. If employees work 12 hours a day (not unusual in Marx's day) in a production process that involves only labor, the exchange value of the product made by one worker in a day will tend to be 12 hours' worth (labor theory of value). If providing the subsistence of that worker requires 6 hours of work, then his/her pay will equal 6 hours' worth. The remaining 6 hours of value, the surplus value, would then belong to the capitalist. This 6 hours of surplus value is the basic source of profit. Half of the value (50 percent) of the labor effort expended is, in effect, stolen from the worker. Thus the rate of surplus value, or the rate of exploitation, is 50 percent. And in this case the rate of profit is also 50 percent (percentage of total revenue kept by the capitalist after paying the costs—in this example, only labor).

However, very few products in capitalism are made solely by labor. Some physical capital is almost always involved. In an imagined sequence of events in which the rate of surplus value, as calculated above, is maintained at 50 percent, it can be shown how the increase in the proportion of capital will lower the rate of profit—the most feared outcome for the capitalists, according to Marx. But why do capitalists use more capital? They have no choice if they wish to keep up with technological advances involving the use of capital that lower the per product cost of production. If they do not keep up, they will lose their ability to compete in the market. Table 6.2 shows four hypothetical cases with different proportions of capital and labor. Each increase in the capital proportion increases the productive efficiency of labor and lowers production costs, which leads to lower selling prices in a competitive market. However, what the table demonstrates is the negative consequence for the rate of profit when the proportion of "live" labor in the production mix is lowered. As the proportion of labor comes down, the source of surplus value also comes down. As surplus value—the only source of profit—gets smaller as a proportion of total revenue, the rate of profit has to come down. The table assumes that the rate of exploitation (50 percent) stays the same. This scenario makes sense only if you accept Marx's view that, in a competitive market, labor is the only input from which capitalists can expect a difference between cost and revenue generated. Even though physical capital includes the output of past, or "dead," labor, Marx believed that only "live" labor was exploitable, that is, capitalists could get away with paying it less than the value it created.

Table 6.2 Declining rate of profit from changing labor–capital ratios with constant rate of surplus value (50%)

Case 1	Case 2	Case 3	Case 4
0% capital	20% capital	30% capital	40% capital
100% labor	80% labor	70% labor	60% labor
50% wage	40% wage	35% wage	30% wage
50% surplus value (profit)	40% surplus value (profit)	35% surplus value (profit)	30% surplus value (profit)

The changing proportions of labor and capital associated with a fall in the rate of profit, as shown in Table 6.2, have several dynamic implications. As capitalists use less labor and more capital, unemployment tends to increase. With the increasing supply of labor, the market allows wages to go even lower, increasing the rate of surplus value exploitation. Superficially, that action would seem to compensate for the fall in the profit rates. But the poorly paid and partly unemployed labor force then has less means to buy products, so the capitalists then find themselves with more products than they can sell. Overproduction, or underconsumption, begins to dominate the local economy. An economic crisis ensues. Weaker firms go under, and stronger firms buy up their assets at less than their original value. Surviving companies also look overseas for places to profitably sell their goods and to make investments so that capital accumulation can continue. Eventually, with the emergence of new technologies, new products, and new markets, the remaining bigger and stronger firms begin to make capital investments in the domestic economy. They need to hire additional labor, whose new incomes generate more demand in the economy. The process of expansion begins all over again. This pattern of economic volatility is inherent in the capitalist mode of production. With this analysis, Marx had provided the first comprehensive explanation of the *business cycle* in capitalism.

In Marx's scenario, the business cycle creates ever more severe depressions. In each subsequent economic collapse, more and more small and medium-sized businesses go bankrupt or are absorbed into larger businesses. Consequently, business ownership becomes more and more concentrated. Greater use of capital in the production process leads to more workers becoming permanently unemployed, including many intellectuals. Marx called them "the industrial reserve army." The army of the unemployed serves the interests of capitalists because it enables them to pay lower wages. Each crisis in the system helps workers to penetrate the veil of money and shatter the false consciousness behind which the capitalists have been hiding. Eventually, Marx postulated, the workers would organize against this oppressive system and overthrow the few remaining capitalists. As a paraphrase of his well-known call to the barricades exhorts, "Workers of the world unite, you have nothing to lose but your chains." These revolutionaries would then set up a socialist system run by workers, which would establish the material conditions for moving on to the last mode of production, communism (Marx and Engels, *The Communist Manifesto*).

In summary, the outcomes that Marx anticipated for the capitalist mode of production were:

1   extraordinary increases in production from unprecedented technological innovations and regularized capital accumulation;

2   persistent inequality of income and exploitation of labor;

3   growing concentration of capitalist ownership;

4   pervasive alienation;

5   overseas activities to acquire cheaper resources, additional markets, and capital outlets; and

6   deeper and deeper economic crises until finally the workers revolt and take control away from the few remaining capitalists.

OUTCOMES OF THE CLASSICAL MARXIST MODEL

Capitalism is only one epoch, and a relatively short though necessary one, in the broad picture of human history provided by Marx. To his historical parade of modes of production, Marx does have an end-in-view in which the exploitation that he despises begins to dissipate and eventually disappear. That end-state, of course, is the communist mode of production. Under communism the material conditions will no longer generate opposing classes, so that people will once again cooperate to create a better society.

In order for communism to become the dominant mode of production, the central material condition that must change is the private ownership of the means of production by the small ruling elite of capitalists. Therefore, the first act of the revolutionary workers will be to establish the collective ownership of the means of production. Second, they must eliminate the exchange value system that enables the exploitation of workers. Third, they have to do away with the "mind-numbing" division of labor entrenched in capitalism that stifles workers and privileges unproductive occupations such as those in financial services. However, the division of tasks will continue, as well as the planned coordination of the production process. There will be flexibility and turnover in the tasks that people fulfill, as it is important to prevent some individuals from occupying high-status jobs on a permanent basis. Marx believed that people enjoyed creative and cooperative work, and that communism would enable them to develop their highest potentials.

Communism would be based on fully participatory democracy, as all the people would own and control the means of production. That's why Marx foresaw not only the withering away of classes but also the withering away of the state. Products would trade on their actual use values, not their exchange values, as bank money and capitalist financial systems would be phased out. The competitive alienation of capitalism would be replaced by humans freely associating with one another, leaving behind the commodity fetishism of capitalism. People would not be driven by insatiable greed, as not only would there be plenty for everybody (thanks to the high levels of production made possible by capitalism), but also the cooperative working conditions would bring out a different side of human nature. Humans would also recognize that they have a stewardship responsibility for nature once nature is no longer perceived as just another commodity. Marx did not believe that the fruits of the social production process in communism would be divided equally. As noted earlier, his basic production and distribution principles were "from each according to his ability; to each according to his needs." Even friendly critics see Marx's vision as rather utopian, but Marx maintained that the emergence of this future social formation was based on likely outcomes predicted by the scientific laws of historical materialism (McMurtry, *The Structure of Marx's World-View*).

As mentioned at the beginning of the chapter, Stalin's totalitarian police state was not at all what Marx had in mind. Stalin's justification for imposing a centrally owned and run system was the necessity to prepare economically for the impending invasion from Germany. During the 1930s both the fascist regimes and the Soviet Union were doing much better economically, as they prepared for war, than the capitalist countries, which were still bogged down in the Great Depression. Stalin's system of forced industrialization had a high human cost. The resistance of small farmers to state confiscation of their land and animals (collectivization) resulted in millions of lost lives. Classical Marxists, like Alex Callinicos, argue that Stalin's system was an aberration. It was neither socialist nor communist. Callinicos contends that if you take the defining characteristics of the Stalinist system—(1) a centralized ruling class (Communist Party elite and planners), (2) extraction of surplus value from both workers and farmers, and (3) continuous investment of the surplus value into capital accumulation (industrialization)—you really have a version of capitalism. He called it "bureaucratic state capitalism." Giving the Stalinist Soviet system the name "communism" was a great disservice to Marx (Callinicos, *The Revenge of History*).

No political-economic model encompasses all aspects of human social systems, nor anticipates all the relationships that actual history brings forth.

So far Marx's effort comes closer than most others. As J. K. Galbraith wrote: "No one before, or for that matter since, had taken so many strands of human behavior and woven them together" (*The Affluent Society*, p. 69). Nevertheless, Marx never came close to finishing the agenda he set out for himself. He finished only the first part of a projected six-part treatise on capitalism. *Capital* was to be followed by major works on wage labor, landed property, the state, foreign trade and finance, and the world market and economic crises (O'Hara, in *Encyclopedia of Political Economy*). The next chapter in this book takes a look at how the ideas that he did manage to put in writing have been applied to the contemporary world scene.

REVIEW QUESTIONS

1   What argument could one make that suggests that the works of Karl Marx are still relevant today? What differentiates Marxism from Stalinism?

2   Define what is meant by ontology and epistemology in the context of the basic premises of dialectical materialism.

3   Compare the approach of dialectical materialism to conventional science.

4   What does Marx mean by the mode of production? How did he apply it to human history?

5   What are the forces and relations of production in the capitalist mode of production?

6   What are the meanings of the concepts "labor theory of value" and "surplus value," and how do they inform Marx's analysis of the interactions in the capitalist mode of production?

7   What did Marx mean by "commodity fetishism," and how does it illuminate the difference between Marx's understanding of market capitalism and the free market proponents?

8   Explain how the business cycle works in capitalism, according to Marx.

9   What were the outcomes that Marx anticipated from the development and spread of capitalism around the world?

10 What was the vision that Marx had for communism, the last stage of human history?

▌BIBLIOGRAPHY

Burns, Tony, "Joseph Dietzgen and the history of Marxism," *Science and Society* (Vol. 66, No. 2) Summer 2002, pp. 202–227.

Callinicos, Alex, *The Revenge of History: Marxism and the East European Revolutions* (Pennsylvania State University Press: University Park) 1991.

Galbraith, John Kenneth, "Marxian pall", chapter 4 in *The Affluent Society*, (Riverside Press: Cambridge, Massachusetts) 1958.

Gurley, John G., "Marx and the critique of capitalism," in Randy P. Albeda, Christopher E. Gunn, and William T. Waller (eds.), *Alternatives to Economic Orthodoxy* (M. E. Sharpe: Armonk, New York) 1987, pp. 273–296.

Heilbroner, Robert, *Marxism: For and Against* (W. W. Norton and Company: New York) 1980.

Heilbroner, Robert, *The Worldly Philosophers: The Lives, Times and Ideas of the Great Economic Thinkers*, 6th edn. (Simon and Schuster: New York) 1986.

Hoselitz, Bert, "The dynamics of Marxism," *Modern Review* (No. 3) Summer, 1949, pp. 11–23.

Jalee, Pierre, *How Capitalism Works* (Monthly Review Press: New York) 1977.

Kliman, Andrew, *Reclaiming Marx's Capital: A Refutation of the Myth of Inconsistency* (Lexington Books: New York) 2007.

McMurtry, John, *The Structure of Marx's World-View* (Princeton University Press: Princeton, New Jersey) 1978.

Marx, Karl, *Capital*, vol. 1 (Penguin: London) 1990 (first published in 1867).

Marx, Karl and Friedrich Engels, *The Communist Manifesto* (Appleton-Century-Crofts: New York) 1955 (first published in 1848).

Melkonian, Markar, *Marxism: A Post–Cold War Primer* (Westview Press: Boulder, Colorado) 1996.

O'Hara, Philip Anthony, "Karl Heinrich Marx," in Philip Anthony O'Hara (ed.), *Encyclopedia of Political Economy* (Routledge: London) 1999, pp. 701–704.

Shaikh, Anwar, "The poverty of algebra," in Randy Albelda, Christopher Gunn, and William Waller (eds.), *Alternatives to Economic Orthodoxy* (M. E. Sharpe: Armonk, New York) 1987, pp. 297–322.

Zeitland, Irving, *Marxism: A Re-Examination* (D. Van Nostrand Company: New York) 1967.

CHAPTER 7

Contemporary Applications of Marxist Analysis

The Marxist framework continues to be used by many analysts because it remains one of the most comprehensive and systematic theoretical critiques of capitalism ever created. This chapter covers three topics in which the Marxist approach has continuing relevance: imperialism, regularization theory or the social structures of accumulation, and feminism. The imperialism discussion ranges from the views of Lenin to more contemporary historical materialists who utilize the concepts of neocolonialism and neo-imperialism. Incorporated are short sections on dependency theory and eco-imperialism. Regularization theory comes primarily from French Marxists who are looking at the changes in capitalist strategy over the last hundred years. The different capital accumulation regimes that result range from Taylorism to post-Fordism, or neoliberalism. Finally, we touch upon the relationship between Marxism and feminism.

IMPERIALISM

A sense of Marxism's relevance for today can be gleaned from the following passage in *The Communist Manifesto*, which Marx and Engels wrote in 1848:

The bourgeoisie has through its exploitation of the world market given a cosmopolitan character to production and consumption in every country. To the great chagrin of reactionaries, it has drawn from under the feet of industry the national ground on which it stood. All old-established national industries have been destroyed or are daily being destroyed. They are dislodged by new industries, whose introduction becomes a life and death question for all civilized nations, by industries that no longer work up indigenous raw material, but raw material drawn from the remotest zones; industries whose products are consumed, not only at home, but in every quarter of the globe. In place of the old wants, satisfied by the production of the country, we find new wants, requiring for their satisfaction the products of distant lands and climes. In place of the old local and national seclusion and self-sufficiency, we have intercourse in every direction, universal interdependence of nations. And as in material, so also in intellectual production (p. 13).

Today the "polite" phrase for this historical process is **globalization**, but from a Marxist dialectical perspective, whatever the process is called, it necessarily involves conflict and exploitation. One of Marx's best-known followers, **Vladimir Ilyich Lenin** (1870–1924), called it *imperialism*. In 1916, the year before he returned to Russia to lead the revolution that created the Soviet Union, Lenin published *Imperialism: The Last Stage of Capitalism*. He argued that imperialism, the occupation of foreign lands, was driven by the capitalists' need to find cheaper raw materials for their manufacturing processes, places to invest their excess capital, and customers for their overproduction of commodities. In order for capitalism to avoid economic collapse, it must continue to have capital accumulation. The obvious place to pursue these objectives was the less developed countries of the world. During the nineteenth century European countries imperialistically divided up the territories of Africa and Asia among them. This appropriation went far beyond the colonial trading enclaves and plantations of the prior three centuries. It involved total state territorial control by the imperial countries. The British solidified their hold over India. The Dutch did the same in Indonesia, and the French followed suit in Vietnam. All the European imperial countries—Great Britain, France, Germany, Portugal, Spain, Belgium, and Italy—divided up Africa between them, for which they reached a working agreement in the 1884 Treaty of Berlin. By the outbreak of World War I in 1914, European countries occupied all of the territory of Africa except Ethiopia and Liberia. Lenin believed that the major cause of World War I was the imperial struggle between the capitalist states.

According to Lenin, in the nineteenth and early twentieth centuries capitalists convinced their governments that their overseas economic activities could be more readily pursued if the foreign lands under

VLADIMIR ILYICH LENIN
1870–1924
One of the leaders of the 1917 Bolshevik Revolution that founded the Union of Soviet Socialist Republics. A follower of Marx and updater of his analysis, most famously in his book *Imperialism: The Last Stage of Capitalism* (1916).

their domination were imperial colonies. Territorial control meant that capitalists' investments could be better protected, workers could be more easily controlled, and local competitors could be closed down. Capitalists' strategies focused on extracting wealth, not on local development. For instance, railroads were built in African countries from the mines to the ports that served external trade, but they had little or no connection with local trade and movement of indigenous populations. Railroad construction did absorb excess capital, and cheaper raw materials were made available to the imperial country. As a consequence of British occupation, India went from being one of the foremost textile producers of the world to being the foremost supplier of raw cotton to the British textile industry. Because the imperial colonies were occupied by foreigners, the local populations had no say in these exploitative practices. But the workers in the capitalist countries had little or no say in the process either. The entire imperialist strategy primarily benefited the ruling capitalist class. In fact, several of the early authors on imperialism, both Marxists and non-Marxists, estimated that the imperial governments actually spent more on their imperial adventures in military and administrative expenditures than the tax revenue that they received in return. However, profits were made by the capitalists. They were the only clear winners (Chilcote, *Theories of Comparative Political Economy*).

Imperialism in the nineteenth century was dominated by the British. London was the financial center of the capitalist world order. The British established the rules, such as "free trade," and the financial structure, which was the gold standard. Other Western European countries accepted the global system established by the British and pursued their separate interests within its structure. Non-European countries, including the United States and Japan, also participated in the imperialist "game," seeking their own territorial acquisitions. The United States took over Spanish colonies in the Pacific (the Philippines) and the Caribbean, while the Japanese occupied Formosa (Taiwan), Korea, and Manchuria. But the British, at least until 1914, through both coercion and consensus, controlled the global capitalist structure. During the period of 1850 to 1914 Great Britain was the hegemon. The Italian Marxist Antonio Gramsci (1891–1937) defined the *hegemon* as an entity having not only political and military but also economic and ideological dominance (Cox, in *Gramsci, Historical Materialism and International Relations*).

Marx actually thought that British colonialism in India had played a positive role in at least one respect, namely, by instigating the transformation to capitalism. He observed that India's self-sufficient, caste-controlled villages with no recorded private ownership of land produced a system that was highly resistant to change, in contrast to European feudalism. When the British imposed capitalist attributes such as wage labor and private property law, they jump-started the emergence of the capitalist mode of production, a necessary step in Marx's view toward the eventual evolution to communism. The Japanese have been given credit for providing the most domestically useful capital investment in their colonies (Landes, *The Wealth and Poverty of Nations*).

A group of twentieth-century Latin American Marxist scholars were not optimistic that the Third World victims of colonialism and imperialism would ever be able to experience their own capitalist development. These adherents of **dependency theory** agreed with Raul Prebisch, whose views were presented in Chapter 3, that poor ("peripheral") countries would get stuck exporting agricultural and mineral raw materials while continuing to import manufactured goods from the rich ("core") countries. After all, that was the experience of Latin American countries for over 100 years after achieving independence from the Spanish and Portuguese in the early nineteenth century. Being a member of the MCO school of thought, Prebisch believed that the problem could be alleviated by reforming the structure of world trade and encouraging governments in less developed countries to support the growth of local industry. However, the most pessimistic among the dependency theorists did not believe that the global-capitalist power structure would allow that to happen anywhere. Consequently, they advocated *autarky*—the separation of the less developed countries from the capitalist world system (Blomstrom and Hettne, *Development Theory in Transition*).

Meanwhile capitalism in the more developed countries was characterized by growing concentration of ownership in both the manufacturing and financial sectors. Already by the beginning of the twentieth century many industries were controlled by only a few large corporations. The leaders of these "trusts" had near-monopoly power and extensive political influence. Some of them organized international price-fixing cartels. The major oil corporations are a well-known example. In the United States the most prominent of these was John D. Rockefeller's Standard Oil. But concentration was also happening in railroads, steel, meat packing, tobacco, sugar, copper, rubber, automobiles, and other industries.

Capitalism and its strategy of imperialism were put under great stress in the first half of the twentieth century by two world wars and a great depression, the types of crises that are inevitable in capitalism, from a Marxist perspective. However, although capitalism survived, it changed form, leadership, and strategies. After the end of World War II in 1945 the United States became the global hegemon and the leading imperialist. Looking through their historical-materialist lenses, Marxists observed the continuing shifts in imperialist strategies as the material conditions changed, especially under decolonization. As the colonies in Asia and Africa achieved independence and legal control over their territory, capitalists shifted their control strategies. A set of trading and financial rules and practices were implemented that kept the former colonies subject to dominance from abroad. Since most development aid came from the United States or the U.S.-controlled World Bank, it came with pro-capitalist conditions. As discussed in Chapter 3, for 25 years after World War II the "good-as-gold" American dollar under the Bretton Woods system was the new global currency. During this hegemonic period the United States and its capitalist allies supported a modernization program of capitalist development in less developed countries that opposed the socialist alternative programs supported by the Soviet Union and its allies. For the first several decades after World War II, it looked as if the pessimistic scenarios described by the dependency theorists discussed above were being realized. Marxists and other critics called the situation *neocolonialism*, since the structure of trade discrimination between rich and poor continued under the new framework of domination, the General Agreement on Tariffs and Trade (GATT). As noted in previous chapters, the GATT did not include trade in agricultural products, it restricted textile trade in a side agreement, and it falsely implied that it included tariff preferences for less developed countries (Khor, *The Multilateral Trading System*).

A number of events in the early 1970s made some people think that the hegemonic status of the United States was beginning to falter. The signal events were the severing of the dollar/gold nexus by President Nixon because of the dollar glut and the rising influence of the Organization of Petroleum Exporting Countries (OPEC), due to its success in withholding petroleum from world markets. A counter-hegemonic, or anti-imperialist, movement among less developed (or **Third World**) countries seemed to be gathering momentum. The organization of Third World states known as the Group of 77 proposed the New International Economic Order (NIEO). The NIEO contained a number of demands that were intended to decrease the discrimination against less developed countries and promote their economic development. It called for many of the reforms that are now called for by MCO reformers (see Chapter 5), such as debt relief, controls over transnational corporations, transfer of technology without intellectual property restrictions, substantial increase in foreign assistance, more power for Third World countries in the Bretton Woods organizations, and so on. The movement seemed to have equity and basic fairness on its side. However, the historical materialist Susanne Soederberg argues that the NIEO was really a struggle between the capitalist classes of the industrialized (First World) countries and the

Third World countries for redistributing surplus value among themselves. Its successful implementation would not have been of much help to the working classes in either the First or Third World countries (Soederberg, *Global Governance in Question*).

However, the NIEO was never implemented. The apparent temporary advantage of the Third World in the 1970s quickly evaporated, and the U.S.-led First World capitalist class came back strong in the 1980s. The globally circulated "petrodollars" became the Third World debt of the 1980s (see Chapter 3), and the International Monetary Fund became the major enforcer of the new capitalist regime.

The capitalist ruling elite in Washington—the Washington Consensus— developed a set of conditions that were applied to all loans from the Bretton Woods organizations, the International Monetary Fund and the World Bank. Free market, pro-capitalist conditions were applied to all the loans with which many Third World countries were now saddled. These were the infamous *structural adjustment programs*, or SAPs. These conditions included removing price "distortions" such as fuel and food subsidies, privatizing government enterprises, eliminating government deficits, removing controls over the flow of financial capital in and out of the country, reducing restrictions on foreign investment, and eliminating tariffs. The free market ideology promoted the superiority of market decision-making and denigrated the role of government. Debt leverage was imposed on small countries in Africa, big countries in Latin America, and, later, even on the "transition" economies, that is, those countries that had previously been subject to the Soviet socialist system. Financial leverage was used to the advantage of the capitalist ruling elite, especially the financers. Critics called this new system **neo-imperialism**, because it used financial measures such as conditions on loans to support the interests of the capitalist ruling class (Soederberg, *Global Governance in Question*).

Capitalist strategies in East Asia were different. For geo-strategic reasons related to the Cold War, the United States made significant capital investments in Japan, Taiwan, and South Korea in the 1960s and 1970s. Under tight government control these countries took advantage of these capital resources and pursed economic development programs that were built around exporting strategies. From the perspective of economic growth, their efforts were successful. Taiwan and South Korea were joined by Hong Kong and Singapore and together they became known as the four "Tigers." Their success in the 1980s and 1990s called into question the sweeping generalizations of the most pessimistic of the dependency theorists. Classical Marxists reiterated their view that the conquest of the world by capitalism was inevitable and, in fact, necessary. Only then would the material conditions become ripe for the eventual revolutionary change to socialism/communism.

Marx had argued that in response to different circumstances capitalists follow different strategies in pursuit of their interests. According to the Marxist John Bellamy Foster, starting in the 1960s, capitalists pushed another imperialist strategy known as the **Green Revolution**. It involved exporting the capitalist form of industrial agriculture to less developed countries. The program started with research centers in Mexico and the Philippines financed by the Rockefeller Foundation, whose purpose was the creation of high-yield hybrid seeds for crops such as rice and wheat. The plus side of this development was a short-term increase in crop production that saved some countries, such as India, from severe food shortages. The downside was that the hybrid seeds were foreign-patented commodities requiring chemical fertilizers and pesticides, irrigation water, farm equipment, and larger land holdings. Petroleum provided the energy for the pumps and the tractors as well as the basic ingredient in the artificial fertilizers. Many of these inputs had to be imported. As a result, agriculture was transformed from the self-sufficient, bio-diverse peasant approach to globally connected commercial farming that is unsustainable in the long run. In contrast with the over 3,000 plant species formerly used for food, humans now get about 90 percent of their caloric energy from only 15 species. In some cases it has been necessary to use foreign exchange earned from agricultural exports to pay the service on the debt owed to foreign banks and governments as well as the International Monetary Fund and the World Bank. Some countries, such as Brazil, Côte d'Ivoire, and Indonesia, have resorted to extensive deforestation in order to expand their agricultural output and their export earnings. Unfortunately, these short-term gains, which are encouraged by market signals, result in long-term ecological degradation. For example, the eroded slopes from deforestation greatly magnify the effects of flooding from heavy rains. This impact has been experienced by Honduras, China, Nepal, and many other countries. Foster names the Green Revolution form of capitalist exploitation "**ecological imperialism.**" Global agribusinesses are the big beneficiaries of this form of imperialism (Foster, *The Vulnerable Planet*).

After the Green Revolution and structural adjustment programs generated crises and resistance, the capitalists, as any historical materialist would expect, adjusted their strategies. Green Revolution programs were modified and given names such as "integrated rural projects" and "sustainable agriculture programs." Structural adjustment programs were renamed "poverty reduction programs." Foreign assistance (often loans) was rhetorically connected to the Millennium Development Goals of the United Nations, one of which was the 50 percent reduction of global poverty by 2015. In 2002 at a follow-up conference convened in Monterrey, Mexico, U.S. President George W. Bush pledged a major increase in grant funding to the poorest 79 countries. However, the grants were contingent upon conditions being met, one of which was "economic freedom."

Soederberg claims that "economic freedom" is really a code phrase for the programs that Marxist critics believe to constitute neocolonialism and neo-imperialism. Thus the language changes, but "free market," capitalist-friendly policies continue to be promoted.

According to Soederberg, another example of capitalists trying to mask their true interests is the establishment of the Global Compact in 2000 by the U.N. Secretary-General (*Global Governance in Question*; see also Chapter 5). This replaces the capitalist-aborted Code of Conduct for transnational corporations, which would have had mandatory provisions. The purely voluntary Global Compact has ten principles, which touch on human rights, labor standards, the environment, and corruption. Corporations are asked to sign on and voluntarily comply with the principles to the best of their ability. Not surprisingly, the United Nations has no monitoring or enforcement process. It only has a website where corporations sign up and report their adherence to the principles. The only monitoring is done by non-governmental organizations. The dubious efficacy of the Compact is suggested by the fact that many of the participating corporations have been featured in the *Multinational Monitor's* annual lists of the ten worst corporations in terms of anti-worker, anti-consumer, or anti-environment behavior. The head of the International Chamber of Commerce stated in regard to the Global Compact: "It mobilizes the virtues of private enterprise in fulfillment of the U.N.'s goals." Soederberg responded: "The Compact, as a creation of the U.N., acts to legitimize ideologically the neoliberal norms of the world order, such as self-regulation by powerful corporations, trade liberalization, and the superiority of market rationality over government intervention" (Soederberg, *Global Governance in Question*, p. 89). In other words, it is another strategy of capitalist imperialism.

For Marxists, the inclusion of mandatory pro-capitalist conditions on loans, grants, and debt relief programs for less developed countries, alongside the use of a U.N.-sponsored website for transnational corporations to self-police and self-praise, exemplifies the sophisticated tactics of the new imperialism. However, historical materialists also contend that old-style imperialism has not yet disappeared, as demonstrated by the 2003 U.S. invasion and occupation of Iraq. This act meets all of the Marxist/Leninist criteria for imperialist behavior: territorial occupation, control over a crucial raw material—oil—and an opportunity for excess-capital expenditure. The military–industrial–corporate complex in the United States has benefited from over $1 trillion in government expenditures. Many analysts believe that the Iraq invasion will prove to have been an imperialistic overreach, comparable in many ways to the overreach of extreme neoliberalism in the 1980s and 1990s. But the continuing overreaching crises of capitalism do not surprise Marxists, as they see these episodes as built into the dialectical processes within the capitalist mode of production (Harvey, *A Brief History of Neoliberalism*).

Table 7.1 Colonialism and imperialism

"Ism"	Time period	Method of exploitation	Major agents
Colonialism (mercantilism)	1500–1800	Military domination of trading system	Spain and Portugal; trading companies in the Netherlands, United Kingdom, France
Imperialism (capitalism)	1800–1960	Territorial possessions	United Kingdom, France, Netherlands
Neocolonialism	1945–present	Trade agreements	United States (GATT and WTO)
Neo-imperialism	1975–present	Financial leverage (structural adjustment programs)	United States (IMF and World Bank)

The simple historical typology in Table 7.1 presents the time periods, methods of exploitation, and major agents of colonialism, imperialism, neocolonialism, and neo-imperialism.

Table 7.1 also portrays both the continuities and changes in global domination patterns over the past 500 years from a Marxist perspective. Colonialism and neocolonialism point primarily to the use of trade as a means of exploitation. Imperialism and neo-imperialism, on the other hand, focus on the transfer of wealth by the use of the financial/credit system established under the capitalist mode of production, or, in Marxian terms, by the transfer of surplus value. Surplus value can be transferred from the exploitation of "cheap" labor or by the collection of interest on debt. For example, in the last 20 years of the twentieth century, neo-imperialism facilitated the net transfer of $4.6 trillion from the relatively poor countries to the relatively rich, or the equivalent of over 50 Marshall Plans (the notable U.S. grant program to Western Europe after World War II). The biggest beneficiaries of this transfer have been major financial-services corporations based primarily in London and New York (Stiglitz, *Globalization and Its Discontents*).

Marxists expect this type of crass exploitation in capitalism, but they also expect crises and oppositional movements. Even though capitalism is a system of pervasive contradictions, it has managed to survive so far. The next section will discuss some Marxist insights into how the evolutionary qualities of the contemporary capitalist system have facilitated its survival.

REGULARIZATION THEORY — THE SOCIAL STRUCTURES OF ACCUMULATION

After Marx died the dominant theorists who took their inspiration from his analytical framework emphasized the economic determinants in his system. Consequently, as more countries industrialized, these *economistic Marxists* expected the development of a growing working-class consciousness that transcended national boundaries. Contrary to their expectations, global working-class solidarity did not emerge. In fact, even within countries workers were not developing the strong collective identities that could transform them into effective oppositional forces to capitalism. Ethnic, nationalistic, and even consumeristic appeals were more effective in reaching and mobilizing workers. In an effort to explain why this was happening, other theorists went back to Marx's writings and realized that his analysis was actually much more complex and comprehensive than that of the economistic school of Marxist thought. Marx had argued that the manifestations of capitalism changed with the historical circumstances; and the social, political, and ideological dimensions were often as important as the economic and technological. In other words, a competent Marxist analysis needed to incorporate both the forces and the relations of production as an interactive totality.

Antonio Gramsci (1891–1937) was the first major Marxian theorist to make this more comprehensive argument. His most important work was written in prison, where Benito Mussolini, the fascist dictator of Italy, had placed him for daring to oppose his regime. Gramsci wanted to provide an explanation for why so many workers supported Mussolini. He observed that the workers were primarily influenced by feelings of nationalism and religious identity, not working-class consciousness. Gramsci realized that the ruling class, through its control of all the major institutions including the media, had been able to impose a set of cultural norms that the great majority of people accepted voluntarily as the prevailing "common sense." Coercion was not really necessary. Therefore, he concluded that any explanation of the bases of ruling-class power must include this type of societal **hegemony** that incorporated cultural and ideological controls as well as political and economic controls. Consequently, getting working people to actually recognize the realities of class exploitation required an extensive counter-hegemonic ideological campaign against the prevailing and dominant "common sense" (Gill and Law, in Gramsci, *Historical Materialism and International Relations*).

ANTONIO GRAMSCI
1891–1937
Sardinian-born socialist/Marxist member of the Italian parliament who was imprisoned by the fascists from 1926 until his death. There he wrote his influential work, *The Prison Notebooks* (selections from which were first published in English in 1971). Gramsci countered the economistic drift of Marxist thinking with his emphasis on civil society, cultural hegemony, and ideology.

Gramsci's insights were very influential in the development of *regulation theory* in France in the 1950s and 1960s. Unfortunately for English-speakers, the French and English meanings for the term *regulation* are very different. The French meaning is closer to the English term *regularization*. Regularization occurs when historically specific social and ideological structures are internalized by the population in the way described by Gramsci. Therefore, some of the English-speaking specialists in this school of thought believe that a more appropriate title in English would be **regularization theory** (Jessop and Sum, *Beyond the Regulation Approach*). Regularization theorists were asking some of the same questions as Gramsci. For instance, except for times of profound crisis, how did the capitalist mode of production manage to contain tensions, such as those between capital and labor, and continue to successfully accumulate capital? The theorists identified three periods of profound crisis: the time before the outbreak of World War I in 1914, the Great Depression of the 1930s, and the breakdown of the Bretton Woods system in the 1970s. In between these crises, the ruling capitalist class managed to create workable integrated systems, particular forms of the capitalist mode of production. One could say, therefore, that regularization Marxists are interested in specifying and understanding the attributes of these historically specific subforms of the capitalist mode of production, especially in more developed capitalist countries such as the United States (Hay, in *Routledge Encyclopedia of International Political Economy*).

Regularization theory proposes three main accumulation regimes:

1 Taylorism, or monopoly capital (1914–1930)

2 Fordism (1945–1975)

3 Post-Fordism, or neoliberalism (1980–present)

Taylorism was characterized by the application of scientific engineering to the human part of the production process. Frederick Taylor, the man for whom Taylorism is named, was an efficiency expert who treated workers as if they were machines. He was strongly opposed to unions, but the capitalist-controlled media made cultural heroes of him and his colleagues. One of his fellow time-and-motion consultants, Frank Gilbreth, was the hero of several novels and movies, the most well known being *Cheaper by the Dozen*. As pointed out above, manufacturing fields during this period (1914–1930) were increasingly dominated by a few major corporations. They combined the application of these new work standards with capital investments and generated significant productivity increases. However, the wealth gains, with few exceptions, were not shared with the workers. All efforts by workers to organize into unions were considered illegal by the capitalist-controlled system, which identified them as either subversive or restraints on trade. Workers were distracted from their exploitation by patriotic appeals during World War I and ethnic bigotry and consumerism during the "roaring twenties." The obtaining of more output from workers by providing them with more efficient machinery and work methods without compensating them for the additional output resulted in what Marx called relative surplus value. An inevitable crisis was created by the contradiction of more goods being produced by workers who were not paid enough to buy them. This overproduction crisis culminated in 1929. The capitalists, of course, refused to acknowledge that their behavior had anything to do with the collapse of the economy. They blamed the workers for the Great Depression, accusing them of being responsible for their own unemployment by not accepting lower wages. Henry Ford was an exception in that he did pay his workers enough to buy the cars they made but he remained strongly opposed to unions (Heilbroner, *The Making of Economic Society*).

Coming out of the Great Depression and World War II, a new accumulation regime emerged, labeled somewhat ironically *Fordism* (1945–1975). Most members of the capitalist establishment now reluctantly accepted government as a major player in the economy. Within a decade of the publication of John Maynard Keynes's path-breaking argument that capitalist economies need to use government budgetary intervention in order to alleviate instability, his views were at least partially being incorporated into public policy. As noted in Chapter 3, the United States incorporated Keynesian thinking in the Employment Act of 1946. The welfare state that was set up under President Roosevelt's New Deal flourished as government provided widespread social subsidies and regulated business practices. Unions were legalized and allowed to acquire some political and economic influence. Through the collective bargaining process deals were struck whereby workers realized some of the gains from productivity increases, as long as they did not disrupt the production process through strikes or other means. The arrangement was known as the "invisible handshake." More U.S. corporations became multinational, but there was no doubt about their being primarily American in orientation. Oil, the major global energy source, was controlled by the "Seven Sisters," the U.S.-based Esso, Mobil, Socal (later Chevron), Gulf and Texaco, plus the British-based Anglo-Persian Oil Company (later BP) and the Anglo-Dutch company Royal Dutch Shell. The international economy was anchored to the Bretton Woods U.S. dollar/gold standard from 1946 to 1971. The United States was the hegemon, just as the United Kingdom had been in the latter part of the nineteenth century (Grant, in *Encyclopedia of Political Economy*).

Predictably, at least from the Marxian perspective, the Fordist system—this submode of production—could not last, as its internal contradictions would eventually generate a crisis, and they did in the 1970s. The military-industrial corporations promoted large overseas U.S. dollar expenditures, especially on the Vietnam War in the late 1960s, which created a dollar glut that undermined the dollar/gold standard. The rise of the Organization of the Petroleum Exporting Countries (OPEC) and the ongoing loss of ownership and control of oil and gas reserves by the Seven Sisters to nation-state–based companies in the Third World began a major shift in energy politics. Oligopolistic price-fixing induced double-digit inflation in the United States, but, instead of directing mitigation policies toward the market-power sources of the problem, the free market–thinking central bank (the Federal Reserve, or Fed) imposed very strict monetary policies, as if too much demand was the problem. As a result recessionary conditions of unemployment and weak labor markets were created. These conditions enabled Prime Minister Thatcher and President Reagan to succeed in their all-out attack on labor unions. In the United Kingdom the major target was the mining unions; in the United States it was the air traffic controllers' union. At the same time, financial institutions saw an opportunity to use debt as leverage to restrict the power of labor. The first use of this strategy was in 1975 in New York City. Taking advantage of New York's financial troubles, the major creditor banks used their indispensable lending power to dictate austere budgetary policy to the city government and the municipal unions. It worked so well that the U.S. Treasury encouraged the IMF to use similar tactics against Third World governments when they got into financial difficulties in the early 1980s; there the imposed conditions were part of the structural adjustment programs, discussed earlier in the context of the Third World debt crisis and neo-imperialism. As a consequence of all of these developments, Fordism died and neoliberalism was born (Harvey, *A Brief History of Neoliberalism*).

The period from 1980 to the first decade of the twenty-first century has been labeled *post-Fordism* by regularization theorists. Because this capital-accumulation regime is still in the process of formulation and is changing rapidly, there are different views among the Marxian analysts trying to make sense of it. David Harvey uses his conception of the world view of neoliberalism as the key to understanding what is happening. **Neoliberalism** turns the basic assumptions of the market model into an ideology with special emphasis on private property rights and hostility toward government intervention in the free market economy. The only acceptable government interventions are those programs that support the "free market" interests of capitalist corporations. In the 1980s and early 1990s neoliberalism dominated the political scene in the major capitalist countries, especially in the United States and Great Britain, which controlled the discourse that dominated the world. Keynes was obsolete, and "taxes" became a dirty word. In a re-emergence of the attitudes that prevailed before the Great Depression and the New Deal, unions again became enemies of the free market, but oligopolistic corporations did not.

In order for countries to develop or maintain a competitive business climate, they had to support any move that lowered costs, whether it be restricting labor, downsizing, or eliminating government regulations. Throughout the Third World and the transitional economies, the International Monetary Fund dutifully imposed free market conditions—developed by the Washington Consensus—through the use of their leverage on debt. According to Harvey, the ruling capitalist class orchestrated a clever propaganda program with the help of the media that it controlled. The capitalists transformed an ideology that supported their interests into the "common sense" of the public discourse. "It has been part of the genius of neoliberal theory to provide a benevolent mask full of wonderful-sounding words like freedom, liberty, choice, and rights, to hide the grim realities of the restoration or reconstitution of naked class power, locally as well as transnationally" (Harvey, *A Brief History of Neoliberalism*, p. 119).

One of the major consequences of the success of neoliberalism has been the "financialization of everything" (Harvey, p. 33). In the Fordist era it was stated that American interests were supposedly identical with General Motors ("Whatever is good for General Motors is good for America"). In the post-Fordist era American interests are seen as identical with those of Wall Street; yet Wall Street is run by short-term profit results. Innovations to pursue that objective include more complex financial instruments such as derivatives, the growth of unregulated hedge funds, and the internationalization of finance. Harvey notes that "information technology is the privileged technology of neoliberalism. It is far more useful for speculative activity and for maximizing the number of short-term market contracts than for improving production" (Harvey, p. 159). The financialization pushed by the IMF in the form of uncontrolled short-term capital movements between countries is considered the major cause of the financial crises that affected many countries in the late twentieth century, the most significant being the Asian financial crisis of 1997. Harvey observes that these crises are created by capitalist greed, but the losers are usually not the capitalist ruling class. IMF- and U.S.-backed bailouts of countries experiencing short-term payments crises protected the financial interests of the major lending corporations, but not the small businesses or the general populations in the affected countries. The standard of living in Indonesia, for instance, dropped by one-fourth in 1997, and ten years later it still had not recovered to pre-crisis levels. Overly indebted businesses were forced into accepting foreign acquisition at fire sale prices. This happened even in South Korea, a close ally of the United States (Harvey, chapter 4). The predictable excesses of capitalism continually produce minor crises which somehow capitalism manages to survive.

The Marxists see the growing inequality between the upper-income groups and everybody else in the post-Fordist accumulation regime as reflecting the ongoing class struggle endemic to capitalism. By contrast, free market believers see "reasonable" inequality as part of the necessary dynamic of the market. MCO analysts share with Marxists a critical view of this inequitable outcome. However, Marxists go further; they consider significant inequality not only an inevitable outcome of the structure of capitalism, but also as ultimately not subject to progressive reform. Nevertheless, they do recognize that temporary improvements in income distribution are possible, as occurred during the Fordist regime.

Since the demise of Fordism the capitalist ruling class has used a number of tactics to increase its share of the wealth at the expense of labor. In the United States in 2007 only 10 percent of the workforce in the private sector had union protection. Consequently, non-unionized corporations such as Wal-Mart can keep wages as well as health and pension benefits at a minimum. Corporations that have provided higher wages and benefits in the past are now trying to escape their obligations. One way to do that is to declare bankruptcy, as several of the major airlines have done. Another way is to hire workers on a part-time or temporary basis so that companies can avoid providing benefits. In 2007, 47 million Americans had no health insurance. Even the corporations that still provide pension benefits are shifting from defined benefits (set retirement payment schedules) to defined contributions (retirement payments dependent on the performance of each employee's financial savings account). The defined-contribution approach forces the employees to take the risk that their stock market nest eggs might not retain their value. The proportion of defined-benefit pension plans in the United States declined from 83 percent in 1980 to 39 percent in 2004. In 2007, according to the U.S. Bureau of Labor Statistics, only 20 percent of workers in the private sector had defined-benefit pension plans. President George W. Bush even tried to shift part of the public pension system (Social Security) to private equity accounts. He didn't succeed with this tactic, but he did succeed with substantial tax cuts for the highest-income recipients with the argument that it was good for the economy. Another tactic of the capitalist class to enhance its financial position at the expense of the working class is the use of usury (excess interest and fee payments) associated with credit cards and subprime home mortgage loans. David Harvey calls these tactics of absolute surplus-value extraction "**accumulation by dispossession**" (Harvey, *A Brief History of Neoliberalism*, chapter 6).

One could reasonably inquire how the capitalist ruling class can get away with these dispossession strategies, especially in presumably democratic societies. As noted above, Gramsci's answer was the presence of a program of ideological or cultural hegemony promulgated by the capitalist ruling class. Both the institutionalists (of the MCO school of thought) and the Marxist regularization theorists observe that the ideology of free market individualism and material acquisition is propagated throughout society, beginning with TV commercials directed at small children. Advertising is everywhere. From Internet portals to sports stadiums, the "buy and be fulfilled" message is ubiquitous. Consumption defines the good life. As long as people are absorbed in the latest consumer fad, they are not focusing much on income inequality, even while they sink more and more into debt. In 2006 the net savings rate in the United States was zero. Customers still flock to Wal-Mart, making it the largest retail operation in the United States, even though it is widely known that their employees are poorly compensated and that its cheap Chinese-made goods undoubtedly caused the loss of good manufacturing jobs in the United States. Few Americans even think or care about the working conditions that Chinese workers must endure in order to make products at such low cost. The working-class solidarity that the economistic Marxists expected is almost non-existent.

Some regularization theorists have suggested that "consumerism" is the new religion and that globalization is its missionary vehicle. However, religion is a complex issue for historical materialists as the form of religion changes with the different modes of production, and the modes of production historically overlap as feudalism and capitalism did in the mercantilist transition period. Certain styles of religion were more compatible with feudalism, when most people were neither literate nor scientific in orientation. As societies modernized, religions changed to accommodate the new material circumstances, the Protestant Reformation being an outstanding example. On the other hand, drastic changes in material circumstances can be very unsettling, causing people to turn to religious tradition for solace. For instance, fundamentalism in all major world religions is a twentieth-century dialectical reaction to the disturbances of capitalist modernization. Some people turn to pre-modern absolutist religious traditions as something to hold on to when the social world that their ancestors created is torn apart by modern economic development. Marx famously observed that religion is "the opium of the people." Yet the observation was not really meant as an anti-religious statement, as it has often been interpreted as being, but as a statement of empathy for oppressed peoples undergoing stressful changes. Marx further said, "Religion is the sigh of the oppressed creature, the heart of a heartless world, and the soul of soulless conditions" ("Marx and religion," *Socialist Worker*). Marx's criticisms of religion were directed at organized religion because he saw it as being in collusion with the ruling classes.

Marxists contend that capitalists commonly use divisive social issues in political campaigns to distract populations from their relative economic deprivation. In the United States the pro-capitalist Republican Party has been using the issues of abortion and same-sex marriage to distract voters from their falling real incomes. Another diversionary issue that has worked in many parts of the world is immigration, which often has ethnic and racial dimensions. The issue has become important recently in several

European elections as well as in the United States. The political rhetoric contends that such-and-such immigrant or ethnic groups are threatening the national identity or are responsible for job losses, increased crime, or heavier burdens on the school, medical, and welfare systems, and so on. While the political campaigns focus on the issues surrounding immigration, attention is distracted from corporate downsizing, outsourcing, union-busting, income and benefit reductions, and other issues. Marxist critics argue that the loss of high-paying manufacturing jobs in the United States has more to do with the decisions of corporations to outsource their manufacturing needs to Mexico or China in the pursuit of cheaper labor and higher profits than with immigration, legal or illegal. But voters who have been bombarded with media stories on the "immigrant problem" are more likely to give attention to that issue than to the real sources of the exploitative economic realities that are negatively affecting their own lives. As Gramsci noted, members of the working classes are often successfully manipulated by the purveyors of the "hegemonic common sense" into disregarding their own economic interests. Only in profound crisis situations will there be the prospect of the majority of people seeing through the "smoke and mirrors" (false consciousness, in Marxian terminology), and taking action on behalf of their own interests. So far the capitalist ruling class has managed to successfully adjust its hegemonic strategies to the changing circumstances and retain its staying power (Gill and Law, in *Gramsci, Historical Materialism and International Relations*).

Since the end of World War II the leadership for the global neoliberal campaign has come primarily from the United States, but, as the United States loses its hegemonic power, what will happen to neoliberalism? In other words, does neoliberalism become less potent as the economic, political, and cultural superiority of the United States diminishes? Actually no, says David Harvey (chapter 4). In his view only the leadership changes, as other parts of the world begin to challenge the United States. Different submodes of capitalist production may play more influential roles over time as the leadership shifts. In the early 1980s it was thought that the Japanese capitalist-accumulation regime was going to prevail over the United States. That regime was characterized by more government control and "Toyotism," the Japanese system of production. Toyotism featured just-in-time delivery of components to assembly lines, tighter quality controls, and worker participation in the improvement of the production processes. However, in the 1990s Japan entered into a long period of relative stagnation, from which it has yet to fully recover. Subsequently Europe has emerged as the major contender for global capitalist leadership. In fact, in 2007, according to one data-keeping firm, the market value of European financial assets exceeded that of the United States. Moreover, the European Union's new currency, the euro, has become a credible challenge to the U.S. dollar as the major foreign exchange reserve asset. Unlike the

United States, the EU is not saddled with a huge current account deficit. One of the neoliberal purposes of the EU is to establish a more uniform and market-friendly regulatory system so that corporations can function more effectively across national boundaries. Marxists suggest that the EU's "harmonization" policies are really intended to reduce the power of unions and governments and enhance the power of capitalists. Even Sweden had to cut back on its welfare state and accept the rhetoric of the neoliberal program as the guiding principles for its macroeconomic policies.

Another major change in neoliberal leadership has been occurring in respect to the control of the energy resource that is the life-blood of industrial capitalism—oil. Both the American and European petroleum corporations have had to take a back seat to the "New Seven Sisters." According to the *Financial Times*, these are Saudi Arabia's Aramco, Russia's Gazprom, China's CNPC, Iran's NIOC, Venezuela's PDVSA, Brazil's Petrobras, and Petronas of Malaysia. They control more than one-third of the world's oil and gas reserves, whereas the old Seven Sisters, who have shrunk to four, control only 3 percent ("The New Seven Sisters," in *Financial Times*). From a neoliberal perspective, the New Seven Sisters are not behaving all that differently than the old Seven Sisters.

But the most surprising new capitalist phenomenon is China. According to its GDP, the conventional capitalist measure of performance, China has been growing over 10 percent a year for over two decades. Its leaders have adopted a version of the neoliberal program as their means to economic success. As an authoritarian state, China has demonstrated that capitalism is quite compatible with non-democratic political decision-making. As Clyde Prestowitz notes, "China is the world's greatest promoter of capitalist production. It provides tax-free zones, business-friendly regulation, endless cheap labor, a ban on all but party-run unions, and a stable currency pegged to the dollar" (*Three Billion New Capitalists*, p. 67). In 2007 China's basic manufacturing wages ranged from only 25 cents to $1 per hour for literate and hard-working employees, especially young women from rural areas. Since there are 300 million more potential workers in the countryside, wages are not likely to be going up very fast in the near future. In the first decade of the twenty-first century China has been investing over 40 percent of its GDP, mostly into manufacturing and supporting infrastructure. That's twice the percentage being invested by the United States or the European Union. China is the largest recipient of foreign direct investment. By 2010 or before, China is expected to be the world's largest exporter. China joined the WTO in 2001 and accepted all of its capitalist provisions, though it has a phase-in transition period. In 2007 China even passed a private-property law despite its official status as a "communist state." China has rapidly expanding stock markets, and it is purchasing large blocks of foreign stocks, including U.S. financial services corporations, through its **sovereign wealth funds**. These are state-sponsored "investment funds" that were pioneered by oil-exporting countries such as Dubai. With trade-generated surpluses, states can acquire a variety of financial assets in foreign markets. Harvey observes that, as the business elite becomes integrated with the Communist Party elite, the country is becoming one of the most unequal in the world. He concludes, "China has definitely moved towards neoliberalization and the reconstitution of class power, albeit with distinctly Chinese characteristics" (*A Brief History of Neoliberalism*, p. 151).

The neoliberal agenda is no longer predominantly controlled by the United States, and Harvey believes that the globalization process is best understood as creating a differentiated multi-polar neoliberal, capitalist system. Capitalist structures and ideology are being implemented all over the world, generating diverse capital-accumulation regimes with multiple contradictions, inevitable crises, and different forms of exploitation. The next section addresses one of those forms—the exploitation of women.

MARXISM AND FEMINISM

The relationship between Marxism and feminism is a complex and somewhat discordant one. Both world views focus on exploitation, though Marxists are primarily concerned about the exploitation of the working class, whereas feminists care mostly about the exploitation of women. Although gender does not appear as a major analytical category in Marx's studies of capitalism, both Marxists and feminists share a holistic perspective that transcends conventional disciplinary boundaries. Yet Marxists tend to favor political-economic dimensions, whereas feminists tend to favor social constructivist approaches. Social constructionists see gender as a culturally generated category that varies substantively by time and place. Both points of view see historical conditions as significantly determining, and therefore explaining, differing social outcomes. This shared part of their respective world views puts them both at odds with neoclassical economists, whose basic theoretical model does not include history as a variable. Marxists and feminists also agree that theory and practice are necessarily and appropriately integrated. That position puts them both in conflict with conventional science, which wishes to separate research and application. For instance, scientists discover nuclear energy, but they are not the ones who decide how to use it. Detachment from real human experience, or deliberate distance from active intervention to improve it, is not acceptable to either Marxists or feminists, either analytically or ethically. In contrast, conventional scientists believe that detachment is essential to achieving objectivity. Thus, feminists share several critical perspectives with Marxists. Where they primarily part company is over the issue of patriarchy, that is, the degree of significance given to male domination in the analysis of social conditions (Olson, in *Encyclopedia of Political Economy*).

Another important issue that both feminists and Marxists identify, but on which they differ in relative emphasis, is that of production and reproduction. Marxists tend to consider the production experience as the central determining condition of the social formation. Nevertheless, Marxists have long recognized that the continuous flow of workers for capitalist enterprises depends on the reproduction processes that are based in households. The subsistence wage that workers receive must cover all household reproduction costs. Within households, in most instances, women provide the services required for reproduction, such as child care, cooking, and cleaning, without receiving any wage compensation. Thus, in effect, they provide an unpaid subsidy to the capitalist system. The market value of this uncompensated reproduction service has been estimated to be around 25 to 30 percent of global GDP. Another contribution made by households to the capitalist mode of production is the socialization of compliant workers and consumers (Peterson, *A Critical Rewriting of Global Political Economy*, chapter 4).

In her book *A Critical Rewriting*, the feminist Spike Peterson proposes combining Marxist and feminist perspectives into a world view of political economy that integrates the reproductive, productive, and virtual economies. She argues that in the present post-Fordist accumulation regime capitalists are cutting their labor costs by using more informal, part-time, and flexible working conditions. Since these are the exploitative conditions that women have traditionally been forced to endure, Peterson labels this development the "feminization of the labor force." In more than half of the world's countries a majority of jobs are "non-regular." That means than employment is uncertain, dispersed, not unionized, poorly paid, and even dangerous. Work occurs at home, in small shops, or even on the street. Even when the work involves toxic materials, such as heavy metals or chemical pesticides, basic safety practices are seldom followed. These conditions affect men as well as women, but the greatest impact is on women. At the beginning of the twenty-first century, more than 70 percent of the workers in export industries were women. When men who are displaced from the "regular economy" contribute less to the household budget, women have to pick up the slack. The extraction of surplus value from workers in the formal or regular part of the capitalist economy relies and, in fact, depends on the support provided by the informal or non-regular part (Peterson, chapters 3 and 4).

Peterson argues that limiting the analysis of the global political economy to the productive and reproductive dimensions is no longer realistic. The creation and spread of information technology has meant the emergence of a whole new dimension that she calls the **virtual economy**. The virtual economy has three central components: global financial markets, knowledge and information, and cross-national cultural codes. In capitalism all of these are privatized and monetized. Peterson's discussion of the first component, financial markets or the global casino, parallels that of Susan Strange, the MCO theorist whose contributions were discussed in Chapter 5. Instantaneously connected global financial markets create huge amounts of virtual money and power, at least temporarily. The second component, knowledge and information, the increasingly important "virtual" element in the production process, is largely managed and controlled internationally by the corporate owners of intellectual property. Cross-national cultural codes, the third component, are mostly diffused by the global media. Whether through CNN, the BBC, or Al-Jazeera, the benefits of material consumption, with local variations, are globally disseminated (Peterson, chapter 5).

Peterson makes the interesting argument that, because everything virtual is digitized, the conventional Western binary mind-set continues to dominate the cultural milieu. That mind-set perpetuates the modernist dichotomies of fact/value, primitive/civilized, masculine/feminine, and so on. These are the very ideological dichotomies that both Marxism and feminism have been trying to overcome. She notes that whatever can be digitized can be commodified, and capitalist commodification has been associated with the modernist cultural hegemony that privileges the cultural code of masculinity (competition, instrumental reason, paid work outside of the household, control over nature, hierarchical authority, etc.) and devalues the cultural code of femininity (cooperation, moral obligations, unpaid work in the household, harmony with nature, shared authority, etc.) (Peterson, chapters 5 and 6).

As can be ascertained from the above discussion, scholars using insights from Marxist analysis have much to say about the contemporary capitalist situation. Their commentaries differ substantially from those who are making observations from the perspective of the "free market" world view. Although MCO adherents share with Marxists many of the same criticisms of capitalism, their explanations of how the political-economic system works and their proposals for change do diverge. The last chapter summarizes the differences between the three world views on several major IPE issues.

REVIEW QUESTIONS

1 What did Lenin mean by imperialism? Why did he believe that it was the last stage of capitalism?

2 How did Antonio Gramsci use the concept of "hegemon" in his disagreement with the economistic Marxists?

3   Define and distinguish between neocolonialism and no-imperialism according to Marxists.

4   What are neoliberalism and the Washington Consensus? What do Soederberg and Harvey think about them? What informs their opinions?

5   What is the Green Revolution? Why does J. B. Foster think that it is part of neo-imperialism?

6   How do Marxists see the world changing as the United States loses its hegemonic status?

7   What is regularization theory? How is it related to classical Marxism?

8   Identify and discuss the attributes of the three accumulation regimes into which the regularization theorists divide the twentieth century.

9   In what ways are Marxism and feminism similar, and in what ways are they different? How does Peterson bring them together in her version of global political economy?

BIBLIOGRAPHY

Blomstrom, Magnus and Bjorn Hettne, *Development Theory in Transition: The Dependency Debate and Beyond: Third World Responses* (Zed Books: London) 1984.

Chilcote, Ronald, *Theories of Comparative Political Economy* (Westview Press: Boulder, Colorado) 2000.

Cox, Robert, "Gramsci, hegemony and international relations: A essay in method," in Stephen Gill (ed.), *Gramsci, Historical Materialism and International Relations* (Cambridge University Press: Cambridge, United Kingdom) 1993.

Fairris, David, "Social structures of accumulation," in Phillip Anthony O'Hara (ed.), *Encyclopedia of Political Economy* (Routledge: London 1999.

Figart, Deborah and Ellen Mutari, "Feminist political economy: Paradigms," in Phillip Anthony O'Hara (ed.), *Encyclopedia of Political Economy* (Routledge: London) 1999.

Foster, John Bellamy, *The Vulnerable Planet: A Short Economic History of the Environment* (Monthly Review Press: New York) 1994.

Gill, Stephen and David Law, "Global hegemony and the structural power of capital," in Stephen Gill (ed.), *Gramsci, Historical Materialism and International Relations* (Cambridge University Press: Cambridge, United Kingdom) 1993.

Gramsci, Antonio, *Selections from the Prison Notebooks*, edited and translated by Q. Hoare and G. Nowell-Smith (International Publishers: New York) 1971 (written in 1926–1936).

Grant, Hugh, "Social structure of accumulation: Capital–labor accord," *Encyclopedia of Political Economy* (Routledge: London) 1999, pp. 1054–1056.

Guttmann, Robert, "Social structure of accumulation: Financial," in Phillip Anthony O'Hara (ed.), *Encyclopedia of Political Economy* (Routledge: London) 1999.

Harvey, David, *A Brief History of Neoliberalism* (Oxford University Press: Oxford) 2005.

Hay, Colin, "Regulation theory," in R. J. Barry Jones (ed.), *Routledge Encyclopedia of International Political Economy* (Routledge: London) 2001.

Heilbroner, Robert, *The Making of Economic Society* (Prentice-Hall: Englewood Cliffs, New Jersey) 1986 (first published in 1962).

Heilbroner, Robert, *The Worldly Philosophers: The Lives, Times and Ideas of the Great Economic Thinkers*, 6th edn. (Simon and Schuster: New York) 1986.

Hopkins, Barbara, "Feminist political economy: Major contemporary themes," in Phillip Anthony O'Hara (ed.), *Encyclopedia of Political Economy* (Routledge: London) 1999.

Jessop, Bob and Ngai-Ling Sum, *Beyond the Regulation Approach: Putting Capitalist Economies in their Place* (Edward Elgar: Cheltenham, United Kingdom) 2006.

Khor, Martin, *The Multilateral Trading System: A Development Perspective* (United Nations Development Programme: New York) 2001.

Landes, David S., *The Wealth and Poverty of Nations: Why Some Are So Rich and Some Are So Poor* (W.W. Norton: New York) 1998.

Lenin, V. I. *Imperialism: The Highest Stage of Capitalism* (International Publishers: New York) 1939 (first published in 1917).

Marx, Karl and Friedrich Engels, *The Communist Manifesto* (Appleton-Century-Crofts: New York) 1955 (first published in 1848).

"Marx and religion," *Socialist Worker*, March 4, 2006. Available at www.socialistworker.co.uk.

"The New Seven Sisters: Oil and gas giants that dwarf the West's top producers," *Financial Times*, March 12, 2007, p. 11.

Olson, Paulette, "Feminist political economy: History and nature," in Phillip Anthony O'Hara (ed.), *Encyclopedia of Political Economy* (Routledge: London) 1999, pp. 327–337.

Peterson, V. Spike, *A Critical Rewriting of Global Political Economy: Integrating Reproductive, Productive and Virtual Economies* (Routledge: London) 2003.

Prestowitz, Clyde, *Three Billion New Capitalists: The Great Shift of Wealth and Power to the East* (Basic Books: New York) 2005.

Soederberg, Susanne, *Global Governance in Question: Empire, Class and the New Common Sense in Managing North–South Relations* (Pluto Press: London) 2006.

Stiglitz, Joseph, *Globalization and Its Discontents* (W. W. Norton: New York) 2002.

CHAPTER 8

Summation and Review

The previous chapters have presented the three dominant world views in the field of International Political Economy (IPE). This concluding chapter will compare and contrast the main features of the three schools of thought and discuss the likely approach of each to four major IPE issues: trade, transnational corporations, development, and the environment. The discussion of development will also cover the changes in dominance of world views in development policy during the post–World War II period. The analysis and preferred policies on all of these issues differ rather predictably among the three perspectives.

THREE WORLD VIEWS COMPARED

Table 8.1 summarizes much of the discussion in the previous chapters of the three different world views, highlighting their different beliefs about central actors, decision-making, and value creation, and listing their intellectual ancestors and major scholars.

Central actors

So far as central actors are concerned, the free market world view focuses on individuals; the multi-centric organizational (MCO) world view focuses on organizations; and the classical Marxist world view focuses on classes. The market perspective sees individuals as the basic building blocks in any economy because individuals are the only real entities. To free market

Table 8.1 Three world views in IPE—a summary

School of thought	Central actors	Decision-making	Value theory	Ancestors (18th–19th centuries)	Major scholars (20th century)
Free market (neoclassical economics)	Individuals	Markets	Subjective preference	Adam Smith	Friedrich von Hayek Milton Friedman
Multi-centric organizational (neo-Ricardians & institutionalists)	Organizations (especially corporations & nation-states)	Power negotiations	Cost of production	David Ricardo	Thorstein Veblen Piero Sraffa John Kenneth Galbraith
Classical Marxism	Classes (capitalists & workers)	Capitalist mode of production	Abstract labor	Karl Marx	V. I. Lenin Antonio Gramsci Baran & Sweezy

adherents, organizations and classes are simply collections of individuals. Individual preferences, especially individual consumer preferences, are the basic determining force in the economy. In contrast, adherents to the MCO school of thought argue that major roles in the political economy are played by organizations such as businesses, governments, unions, and non-profit associations—not individuals. They believe that people organize themselves into complicated relational networks that have long-lasting hierarchical and structural forms. Therefore, they consider the focus on individuals as key players unrealistic. Classical Marxists agree with this MCO critique of the free market world view, but for the Marxists the pre-eminent analytical grouping is class. Classes are conglomerates of people who share a similar relationship to the production system. In fact, the members of a class may not have a formal organization or even be aware that they share a similar situation. That's why developing class consciousness is an important part of the process that drives change.

Decision-making

Consistent with these different positions on the central actors are three different decision-making conceptions. For those who adopt the free market world view, the impersonal mechanism of the competitive market facilitates the making of all the production and distribution decisions without any arbitrary intervention from governments. The aggregation of individual choices through the demand–supply processes makes societal decisions in a free and open way. "Not realistic," say the MCO adherents, for political-economic decisions are mostly made by the organizational exercise of power. Prominent MCO scholars, including J. K. Galbraith, have expressed amazement that the academic branch of the free market world view—neoclassical economics—essentially ignores the role of power. Galbraith believed that only a decision-making model that takes into account the overwhelming influence of powerful organizations, especially big corporations and big governments, can come close to providing realistic insight into how the economy actually works. Members of the MCO school of thought argue that only by understanding the process of strategic negotiation between major centers of organizational power can anyone hope to achieve useful knowledge about modern political economies, national and global.

Marxists are even more disdainful of the ability of free market economics, or what Marx called "vulgar economics," to represent reality. From the Marxist perspective the market is simply an exchange mechanism through which the ruling capitalist class imposes its will on the working class. The capitalists also use the political and ideological processes of the society to exercise their dominance. Therefore, decision-making can only be fully understood by analyzing the full scope of the capitalist mode of production. Government is merely the capitalists' "handmaiden." Except for unusual circumstances, the working classes have little role in societal decision-making. Even democracy is a sham. The only decision-making negotiations that really count are between different segments of the capitalist class.

The societal analysis of these three decision-making models ranges from the relatively narrow coverage of the free market to the comprehensive coverage of the Marxist approach; that is, the market model limits itself to the economic sphere, whereas the capitalist mode of production model encompasses the whole of society. The MCO model has a more focused political-economic lens, broader than the market model but not as holistic as the capitalist mode of production model.

Value theories

In the realm of *value theory* the three world views have distinct approaches. Value theories attempt to ascertain the derivation of the relative worth of things produced and used in an economy. That is, they address the question of what ultimately determines how much something is worth in comparison to something else. All three world views recognize that the particular prices prevailing on a day-to-day basis may not exactly coincide with underlying relative values. There is a tendency for prices to reflect underlying values, but divergences for a variety of reasons are to be expected.

As was pointed out in Chapter 2, the market-oriented value theory is called *subjective preference* because the determining drive comes from the expressed individual preferences of consumers. However, in the market model the actual determinant of value is the relationship between demand and supply. The price of any product or resource is established at the equilibrium point where these two variables come together. However, for these prices to be "efficiently," that is, accurately, set, consistent with subjective preference value theory, the premises of the market model must hold. Rationality, competition, and mobility must fully prevail.

Neither the MCO'ers nor the Marxists find the market value theory credible. They question both that the rationality it assumes is realistic and the likelihood of pure competition prevailing among the actors. As explained in Chapter 4, the MCO model's *cost of production value theory* contends that underlying comparative values are determined by the structure of production, which includes three components: (1) level of aggregate income and activity, (2) technical conditions of production (input–output relationships), and (3) distribution of social product between business and labor. The most variable component is the distribution between business and labor, because it is determined by historically changing positions of relative power. Thus, the changing outcomes of this struggle will determine how much goes to profits and how much to wages. That, in turn, will not only determine the immediate cost structure, but also affect the future because a part of current production is capital products that will be utilized in the generation of subsequent commodity production. Therefore, the ratios of value will be determined within the production process.

As an institutionalist Galbraith described this process somewhat differently. He focused on market power and the corporations that have most of it. Through their control over technology, the supply chain, and even consumer preferences (the revised sequence), corporations have the most influence on "market" prices and market decisions. How much influence corporations have on prices depends on the degree of independent power that governments and labor unions are able to exercise. As mentioned in Chapter 4, when Galbraith wrote in the 1950s and 1960s, governments and labor unions did seem to have some substantial countervailing power over and against corporations. In the ensuing decades corporations significantly increased their market power, much to Galbraith's dismay.

Marxists have an even bleaker view of the value-determining process in capitalism, because they believe that the workers will almost never get the full value of their contribution to production. As presented in Chapter 6, the underlying values of commodities are derived by calculating the average socially necessary amount of labor time involved in making them. This *labor theory of value* is not a simple time calculation, because the quality of the labor input varies according to the workers' level of skill and the capital applied in the production process. Furthermore, *abstract labor* time involves averaging over a large number of cases in which the best available levels of productivity are assumed. However, because of the predictable gap in capitalism between the values that workers create and the "subsistence" wages that businesses are able to get away with paying, workers will almost never receive their true worth. Capitalists are able to engage in this exploitation because the exchange values set in the market justify this gap between wages and product values. Since subsistence levels are historically variable, none of these calculations are simple. Market proponents argue, therefore, that making these calculations in any reliable way is impossible. The Marxists and the MCO adherents respond that the free market claim that values are determined at supply–demand market margins, such as marginal productivity, is the really absurd contention (Edwards, *The Fragmented World*).

It's useful to keep in mind that all of these value theories are just that—theories, invented to provide explanatory insight. The more complex the systematic relationships that the theories are trying to explain, however, the greater the possibilities of mismatches between the theories and observed events. In that respect, some theories do a better job than others. The advocates of each of the value theories presented here argue that their theory is more in touch with reality than the other theories and therefore does a better job of explaining it. Because these theories are embedded in broader world views, even the sense of what reality is varies between them. That is why the choice of *which* world view to use *when* is to some extent a matter of personal resonance. What resonates tends to be a function of a person's own pre-existing world view and the perspectives contained within it. For instance, some students in my IPE courses have discovered, to their surprise, that at the end of the semester they have actually found the Marxist world view the most persuasive. But, they often admit, they would probably never tell their parents. On the other hand, there have been students who come into class committed to one or another of the IPE world views and proclaim proudly at the end of the semester that they haven't changed their minds one bit. That type of rigidity suggests that a particular world view has become for that person an ideological commitment. A more flexible approach would involve the recognition that all of the world views have both strengths and weaknesses; and that one does not have to accept one entire world view over all others, but could instead use parts of the analytical frameworks in changing combinations depending on the particular problem that is being addressed. However, it should be observed that taking this eclectic approach presents the intellectual challenge of achieving coherence among the chosen elements.

Ancestors and major scholars

The last columns of Table 8.1 identify important figures in the development of the three world views. As noted in Chapter 1, the Scottish moral philosopher *Adam Smith* (1723–1790) is identified as the founder of the free market school of thought. After him *Friedrich von Hayek* (1898–1992) and *Milton Friedman* (1912–2006) both made important intellectual as well as public discourse contributions. Hayek was associated with the Austrian branch of economics, and Friedman was attached to the University of Chicago, the academic center of neoclassical economics in the United States. They were openly acknowledged as key mentors by the political leaders who were central to the resurgence of the free market world view in the 1980s. U.K. prime minister Margaret Thatcher gave credit to Hayek, and U.S. president Ronald Reagan cited Friedman (Yergin and Stanislaw, *The Commanding Heights*).

As discussed in Chapter 4, the multi-centric organizational (MCO) world view is an amalgamation, specific to this text, of at least two schools of thought: the neo-Ricardian and the institutionalist. Obviously, the ancestor of the neo-Ricardians is *David Ricardo* (1772–1823), an English financier of the early nineteenth century, who disagreed with Adam Smith on some issues. As noted in Chapter 1, their most important disagreement was on the distributional consequences of a free market society. Smith was the optimist, believing that workers would eventually receive increasing benefits from their contributions, whereas Ricardo was a pessimist about that eventuality. The generally recognized founder of neo-Ricardianism is *Piero Sraffa* (1898–1983), a twentieth-century Italian economist. Thanks to the initiative of John Maynard Keynes, Sraffa was invited to Cambridge University, where he became editor of the collected works of Ricardo. That multi-year project undoubtedly led to the germination of the ideas in Sraffa's 1960 publication that presented a major challenge to neoclassical economics: *The Production of Commodities by Means of Commodities*. The institutionalist school of thought started with *Thorstein Veblen* (1857–1929), a Norwegian-American academic, who wrote in the late nineteenth and early twentieth centuries. Veblen was well versed in the writings of all the great classical political economists as well as the newly emerging school of neoclassical economics. Veblen took a critical stance toward them all, but especially the neoclassicists. *John Kenneth Galbraith* (1908–2006) picked up where Veblen left off and became the most prolific and influential of the twentieth century's institutionalists. A professor at Harvard for most of his career, Galbraith studied under both Keynes and Sraffa at Cambridge. Besides being a widely published scholar, Galbraith also held important posts in the presidential administrations of Franklin Delano Roosevelt (as director of the Office of Price Administration during World War II) and

John Kennedy (as ambassador to India) (Parker, *John Kenneth Galbraith*). Galbraith's effectiveness as a critic of neoclassical economics and as a builder of an alternative model is demonstrated in a back-handed way by a remark made by P. J. O'Rourke, an economic journalist and a follower of Milton Friedman's free market approach. In his 1998 book *Eat The Rich: A Treatise on Economics*, O'Rourke advises his readers to read everything by Milton Friedman, but "There are also certain books you should avoid . . . everything ever written by John Kenneth Galbraith" (p. xvi). On the other side of the ideological divide, the president of Venezuela, Hugo Chàvez, who has characterized himself as a "democratic socialist," said exactly the opposite while addressing the U.N. General Assembly in 2007 (Grandin, in *The Nation*, October 15, 2007, p. 5).

It seems redundant to note that Karl Marx (1818–1883) is the founder of classical Marxism, though he did have lots of help from his collaborator Friedrich Engels (1820–1895). The second and third volumes of *Capital* were actually compiled by Engels from manuscripts left by Marx when he died. Among twentieth-century Marxists two of the most prominent are *Vladimir Ilyich Lenin* (1870–1924) and *Antonio Gramsci* (1891–1937), a Russian and an Italian, respectively. Lenin stands out because he made both intellectual and political contributions. The Soviet Republic, of which he was one of the founders in 1918, might have developed differently had he not died in 1924 at the relatively young age of 54, leaving an opening for Joseph Stalin. Actually Gramsci died even younger (at 46), probably from the conditions he endured in the Italian dictator Mussolini's prison. As discussed in Chapter 7, Lenin described the role of imperialism as the last stage of capitalism, whereas Gramsci rescued Marxism from excessive economistic interpretations by revisiting the importance of cultural and political dimensions to Marxist analysis. *Paul Baran* (1910–1964) and *Paul Sweezy* (1910–2004) were probably the most prominent American Marxists in the twentieth century. Separately they wrote important books and articles, but together in 1966 they published the seminal Marxist essay on America, *Monopoly Capital*. Sweezy was a founder and long-time editor of the foremost Marxist periodical in the United States, *Monthly Review*.

The next section compares the positions of the three world views on important issues in International Political Economy. The issues are trade, transnational corporations, development, and the environment. The intent is to demonstrate salient differences between the three schools of thought, not all the variations of opinion within the schools, which certainly exist. For each issue there is a comparison table in which the central problem and preferred solution identified by each school of thought is highlighted.

THREE VIEWS ON TRADE

In the realm of international trade the free market world view sees protectionism as the big problem because it interferes with the ability of the market to allocate resources efficiently. *Protectionism* is defined as tariffs and non-tariff practices such as regulations and subsidies that inhibit and distort trade. The free market solution for dealing with these problems is clear and unequivocal: free trade. Eliminating protectionist measures and implementing free trade is presumed to improve market efficiency, promote economic growth, and lower costs. Free trade encourages the development of a competitive export sector that enhances local production capacity and quality. Furthermore, for less developed countries export revenues can be used to import more technologically advanced capital goods that may not be available in the domestic economy.

Proponents of the MCO school of thought are not against trade, but they are opposed to the unfettered application of comparative-advantage free trade in the international arena. They are especially critical of free trade between countries that are at very different levels of economic development. As discussed in Chapter 5, they believe that this free trade approach almost always results in the poorer countries' remaining as suppliers (exporters) of raw materials and importers of expensive manufactured goods. Thus not only are the resulting trade relationships unequal and discriminatory, but they also inhibit economic development. Because markets tend to favor the already more economically advanced countries, MCO analysts advocate government intervention, such as infant-industry protection, in order for trade to become economically helpful rather than detrimental. Historically, in fact, all highly developed countries have utilized protectionist policies during their developmental phase, so MCO proponents believe that it is hypocritical for them to try to impose a free trade regime on the currently less developed countries. Furthermore, even when countries are at similar levels of development, the conditions that Ricardo stipulated must be satisfied in order for trade to be mutually beneficial, such as capital immobility, almost never exist. Therefore, free trade in practice may not be all that mutually beneficial, especially between countries at different stages of economic development (Khor, *The Multilateral Trading System*).

Marxists contend that trade is just another vehicle for capitalists to maximize their profits, especially through labor exploitation in both rich and poor countries. One of the ironies of the current world situation is that self-proclaimed communist countries, such as China and Vietnam, are engaging in capitalist-style exploitation of their own workers in order to promote cheap exports. In the short run, the major beneficiaries of this transfer of surplus value through cheap exports based on cheap labor are primarily capitalists and secondarily consumers in the already industrialized

Table 8.2 Three IPE world views on trade

School of thought	Trade problem	Trade solution
Free market	Protectionism	Free trade
Multi-centric organizational (MCO)	Unequal and discriminatory exchanges	Fair trade through government intervention
Marxism	Labor exploitation from putting profit first	Global worker solidarity

economies. This global exploitation of workers will continue, according to classical Marxists, until there is a successful global uprising of organized labor against the international capitalist class. Therefore, the classical Marxists see exploitation through trade as yet another way to build class solidarity among workers. On the other hand, the neo-Marxist dependency theorists have argued for drastic reductions in trade between the rich and poor countries so that the poor countries can develop on their own. The dependency theorists argue that the rich capitalists will never let the poor countries develop as long as they can gain from exploiting them. The classical Marxists believe that their prediction that capitalist development will occur everywhere is vindicated by the rapid economic development occurring in Asia, especially now in China and India, the two most populous countries in the world. In response, the dependency theorists point to the dismal development situation in Africa and elsewhere as confirmation of their point of view. Thus, Marxists agree that trade is a vehicle of capitalist exploitation. They disagree on the best strategic response.

A summary of these viewpoints on trade is given in Table 8.2.

THREE VIEWS ON TRANSNATIONAL CORPORATIONS

Only the MCO school of thought explicitly includes large corporations as central actors in its basic model. Although the free market model has individuals as central actors, it does presume that there are production organizations. But corporate production organizations are conceptualized as benign individuals, simply reacting to the price signals sent their way by the competitive market. Though neoclassical economists are aware of oligopolistic market structures, free market advocates worry more about government intervention in the economy than about corporate manipulation. A demonstration of this perspective is provided by the Index of Economic Freedom, a joint undertaking of the Heritage Foundation and *The Wall Street Journal*. For over a decade they have published an annual comparison of countries' performances on this index in terms of ten areas, ranging from trade freedom to labor freedom. Higher scores are attained in each component when there is a minimal "level of government interference." None of the ten components address corporate market power in any way. The 2007 Index grades 157 countries; only seven of them have very high freedom scores (of 80 percent or more). The top seven include the United States (no. 4) and the United Kingdom (no. 6). Hong Kong and Singapore are no. 1 and no. 2, respectively, while China is no. 19 (Kane et al., *2007 Index of Economic Freedom*).

Consequently, for free market proponents *transnational corporations* (TNCs), no matter how large and powerful, are not a problem. On the contrary, they are praised for bringing jobs, advanced technology, and competitive business drive to all parts of the world. As noted above, the problem is excessive regulation by governments, which interferes with the ability of TNCs to operate efficiently. However, from the MCO perspective TNCs are not so benevolent. Rather they are powerful, publicly unaccountable organizations that are prepared to impose their profit-oriented will anywhere they can get away with it, regardless of the adverse consequences. Small, poor countries are especially vulnerable. As noted in Chapter 5, David Korten has labeled TNC behavior "corporate colonialism." An enforceable global corporate code of conduct that includes democratic governance controls is seen as an essential reform by MCO advocates. By contrast, free market adherents see corporations as good global citizens that can effectively govern themselves. Following Adam Smith, they believe that the market is the disciplining mechanism. They believe that no matter how well meaning they are, government regulatory interventions are bound to undermine economic prosperity. Not surprisingly, those seeing the world from the MCO perspective regard this position as naïve or self-serving. MCO adherents believe that effectively enforced government regulations are necessary to prevent excessive corporate behavior such as driving competitors out of business, undermining efforts to improve labor conditions, and destroying the environment.

Marx warned of the danger of growing ownership concentration as capitalism developed, or what other Marxists call "monopoly capitalism." Baran and Sweezy made monopoly capital the centerpiece of their Marxist analysis of post–World War II American capitalism. By monopoly capital they actually meant oligopolistic market structures. From a strictly structural perspective, monopoly capital shares some similarities with the MCO model. However, from the Marxist point of view the MCO model incorporates neither the systematic analysis of worker exploitation by the capitalist ruling class, nor the surplus value circulation that is inherent to the Marxian model. Furthermore, the government regulation reforms preferred by MCO'ers are not seen as politically feasible because governments are controlled by the capitalists, not by the general public. Therefore, the power of TNCs will not be broken until the workers'

Table 8.3 Three IPE world views on transnational corporations (TNCs)

School of thought	TNC problem	TNC solution
Free market	Excessive government regulation	Business-friendly governments
Multi-centric organizational (MCO)	Excessive corporate power and lack of democratic accountability	Global corporate regulation People-controlled governance systems
Marxism	Monopoly and capital exploitation	Shift ownership and control to workers

revolution topples capitalism. Interim strategies involve the support of programs and policies that strengthen anti-capitalist consciousness and the organizational capability of global labor. Marxists believe that the implementation of responsive MCO reform strategies could delay the inevitable worker-led revolution.

A summary of these three points of view on transnational corporations is found in Table 8.3.

THREE VIEWS ON DEVELOPMENT

As noted in Chapter 1, major attention by political economists to the issue of *economic development* goes back at least to Adam Smith, as the full title of his treatise, *An Inquiry into the Nature and Causes of the Wealth of Nations,* makes clear. The first major part of his work is devoted to the "causes of improvement in the productive power of labour," while another chapter discusses the "accumulation of capital." Almost 100 years later Karl Marx continued Smith's line of investigation, focusing on capital accumulation as a central process of capitalism. Chronologically in between Smith and Marx, in addition to David Ricardo, there was an interesting author by the name of *Friedrich List* (1789–1846). List, who lived in both Prussia and the United States, founded the school of thought known as *economic nationalism*. He focused on the analysis of policies that promoted the attainment of national "prosperity, civilization and power," in other words, national development. He is probably most famous for advocating infant-industry protection for less industrialized agricultural countries, but he also understood that Great Britain's free trade policy in the nineteenth century was a nationalist strategy for enhancing its manufacturing dominance of the global economy (Helleiner, in *International Studies Quarterly*). Because of his use of culture, national identity, history, and politics as key components in his analysis, List is most compatible with our second school of thought—the multi-centric organizational world view. The same is true for *Joseph Schumpeter* (1883–1950), an early member of the institutionalist school of thought, who also dedicated significant scholarly attention to the development issue. Schumpeter's 1912 book *The Theory of Economic Development* is a recognized classic that focused on the role of innovation and the entrepreneur in the development process (Ebner, in *Routledge Encyclopedia of International Political Economy*).

However, as a program of action, a concern of public policy, and a recognized academic field of study, "**development**" is a post–World War II phenomenon. The geo-political reality of the period after the war that shone a spotlight on the need for development was the liberation of previously colonized countries that were not industrialized and were consequently relatively poor. The two historical events that shaped development strategy in the immediate postwar era were the success of the Soviet central planning system at promoting industrialization in the 1930s and the persuasive argument made by the English economist John Maynard Keynes, also in the 1930s, that government could play a useful role in achieving economic prosperity. Consequently, after the war development programs were launched all over the world that relied on planned government intervention. Virtually every less developed country, starting with India, had to have a five-year plan. Foreign aid programs were put in place by the wealthy countries in support of these plans. The rationale for these assistance programs was a combination of a perceived moral obligation to help the poor and the Cold War rivalry between the United States and the Soviet Union, which led them to compete to show which of their systems was the most effective at facilitating economic development. In Western universities a whole raft of modernization theories was created in order to explain past development in the already industrialized countries and to make recommendations based on that experience for the most effective development programs in the less developed countries. One of the best-known modernization manifestos was published in 1960 by the American economic historian W. W. Rostow. Titled *The Stages of Economic Growth: A Non-Communist Manifesto*, it postulated five universal stages of economic development: (1) traditional society, (2) pre-conditions for take-off, (3) take-off, (4) drive to maturity, and (5) age of high mass consumption. The key trigger for achieving take-off is the continuous dedication of at least 10–20 percent of the national income to saving/capital investment (Rapley, *Understanding Development*).

The five-year plans set economic growth goals and capital investment targets for both private and public sectors, focusing on leading sectors such as heavy industry and energy. Public enterprises were established in areas such as telecommunications, in which it was presumed private-sector investment would not be immediately forthcoming. Governments pursued their development objectives with the use of interventionist tools such as taxes, subsidies, and price controls; one price that was typically set by the government was the foreign exchange rate. Local industry was protected with tariffs. Mobilizing the required saving for the capital investment program sometimes involved coercive measures. Broad-scale democracy, therefore, had to be a long-term objective, not an immediate part of modernization strategy because excessive populism, such as that which took root in Argentina, could stifle the saving/investment discipline required for sustained economic growth. From an economic growth perspective, the five-year plan development strategy worked reasonably well in the 1950s and 1960s. However, in the 1970s the government-led, MCO-compatible strategy ran into trouble, and it came under increasing criticism from free market advocates (Rapley, *Understanding Development*).

From the free market point of view the government-led development strategies had predictable problems: resources were misallocated; inefficiency was pervasive; inflation was endemic; agriculture was oppressed; corruption was everywhere. The agricultural sector had borne the brunt of the strategies pursued, for on the one hand it was the most heavily taxed, and on the other hand its prices were controlled in order to keep food prices down for urban consumers. Consequently, there was no incentive for farmers to invest and increase agricultural yields. Tariff-protected industries also had limited incentive to increase their efficiency. Artificially overvalued foreign exchange rates meant that cheap imports had to be rationed, a built-in platform for corruption. Government bureaucracies were bloated with employees that could be supported only by government deficits that created inflation. From the free market perspective the solution to all of the problems that they identified was patently obvious: significantly cut back on the role of government and impose market decision-making (Rapley, *Understanding Development*).

In the 1980s, armed with their own development theories and their strong preference for market-led rather than government-led decision-making, free market advocates took advantage of the political opening provided them by the election of free market–oriented leaders in many of the world's leading economies, especially, as mentioned earlier, President Reagan in the United States and Prime Minister Thatcher in the United Kingdom. Thus it is hardly surprising that the development policies pursued by the U.S. government, World Bank, and International Monetary Fund in the 1980s and 1990s emphasized privatization, free markets, and deregulation. As noted earlier, this policy package was known as the "Washington Consensus." The reduction of government involvement in the economy included the selling-off of public enterprises, elimination of budgetary deficits by reducing government expenditures, rescinding of price supports for food and fuel, tariff reductions, devaluation of currency, and removal of controls on cross-border flows of financial capital. Many countries adopted these policies, sometimes involuntarily as part of structural adjustment programs imposed by the IMF and the World Bank.

Unfortunately, many of the results from the adoption of the Washington Consensus policies were not as positive as the free market promoters had expected. Several less developed countries experienced extensive rioting when they implemented the IMF program removing price subsidies for food and fuel. In many instances, private enterprises did not turn out to be any more efficient or less corrupt than public enterprises. The "shock-therapy" imposition of market prices in the former Soviet bloc (transitional) countries resulted in severe downturns in their economies. The reduction of government expenditures in both the transitional and less developed countries usually targeted social programs that served mostly women and children. The easy mobility of financial capital ("hot money") across borders triggered and then exacerbated financial crises all over the world. The worst of these, discussed earlier, was the financial crisis of the late 1990s that engulfed most of Asia, including countries as developed as South Korea. The free market approach did not turn out to be the panacea that was promised. Market fundamentalism seemed to create as many problems as government fundamentalism did (Rapley, *Understanding Development*).

None of these troublesome results surprised Marxists. Because of capitalism's internal oppositions, periodic crises were inevitable. Samir Amin, an Egyptian neo-Marxist, rejects both the market and government-led development strategies, calling them "liberalism and statism." He strongly objects to the World Bank mantra, "Get your prices right," because he believes that the market prices the World Bank wishes to impose are capitalist-engineered prices. They include all the built-in distortions that favor the interests of the capitalists over the workers and the general public. Amin contends that the capitalist class in the developed countries has an extension in the less developed countries, which he calls the "comprador class." The *compradors* represent the interests of global capital, not their own people. Though Amin writes mostly about Africa and the Middle East, the term "comprador" actually originated in China. Amin contends that three-quarters of the scarce resources in the less developed countries go to support the consumption of the better-off, mostly in the developed countries. This represents a massive surplus transfer from the poor to the rich. In his view the World Bank's market-based policy prescriptions that support these exploitative relationships are based on nothing but ideology. In contrast, he considers his Marxist analysis both scientific and secular. Therefore, he opposes religious fundamentalism as much as he does consumerism (Amin, *Maldevelopment*).

Since all three schools of International Political Economy are products of the modern era, they all support science as an integral part of the development process. They all consider religious fundamentalism as pre-modern. But each school of thought considers itself more scientific than the others. MCO proponents believe that their model is based on empirical observations and inductive generalizations ("real science"), whereas the market model is based on a non-empirical deductive system. The Marxists claim that they are the only true scientists because of their holistic and dialectical methodology. The free market advocates remind their adversaries that they were the ones historically who first supported scientific endeavors in opposition to religious absolutism, especially as they related to improvements in the technology of production.

Amin's vision for a post-capitalist world includes socialism, democracy, and locally controlled decisions. He believes that the rule of profitability needs to be replaced with shared responsibility and egalitarianism. However, as noted earlier, Amin is a neo-Marxist and a member of the dependency school, which believes that less developed countries can have their own popular, socialist revolutions without going through all the stages of capitalist development. He advocates "delinking" less developed countries from the rich capitalist countries, enabling them to establish their own internal value systems (Amin, *Maldevelopment*). Classical Marxists are sympathetic to Amin's position, but they believe that he misunderstands the laws of historical materialism, which stipulate that all parts of the world must be in the state of advanced capitalism before conditions are ripe for successful, permanent worker-led revolutions.

In the first decade of the twenty-first century none of the three schools of thought can claim that their approaches to development have demonstrated clear superiority. All can point to some positive accomplishments, but all have run into difficulties. Assessing the Marxist approach is the most problematic because from the classical perspective the communist way of running developed societies has not been tried yet. Its adversaries reply to this that at least state-planning socialism was tried in many countries, pre-eminently the Soviet Union, and even though it facilitated impressive industrialization, eventually it collapsed on account of its internal inconsistencies and destructive wastefulness. The MCC government-led modernization approach worked fairly well for several decades, but it ran into the problems mentioned above. The free market approach of the 1980s and 1990s cleared up some problems created by government mistakes, but created many others of its own making, also mentioned above. In 2005 the World Bank published a study, titled *Economic Growth in the 1990s: Learning from a Decade of Reform*, which reviewed the track record of the different development strategies and concluded that strategies work or don't work depending on the country context (Rodrik in *Journal of Economic Literature*). For example, even the lack of private-property institutions, which free market proponents consider the number-one necessity for successful development, does not seem to have prevented rapid economic growth in China. However, the publication of one balanced study by the World Bank calling for eclecticism in the application of development strategies has not prevented committed advocates within all three schools of thought from continuing to push for exclusive use of their own world view's approach. See a summary of these views in Table 8.4. Even the World Bank itself is still using an amended version of the Washington Consensus at the operational level, despite advice to the contrary in its own publications (Rodrik, in *Journal of Economic Literature*).

In recent years the World Bank has at least rhetorically been advocating the importance of "good governance," recognizing that development requires more than free markets. But free trade remains one of its foremost recommendations for the less developed countries. Martin Khor of the Third World Network agrees with David Korten that the push by the rich countries in the WTO for less developed countries to lower their tariffs while the rich retain their agricultural subsidies is "corporate colonialism" and "anti-development" (Khor, in *Third World Resurgence*). On the other hand, Jeffrey Sachs, an American economist associated with the Millennium Project of the United Nations, believes that the end of global poverty in the next few decades is possible. However, trade is not the solution for the poorest countries. What is required is a doubling of official development assistance. For the United States that would mean $38 billion more per year (in 2003 dollars). That does not seem like much in light of the $10 billion a month the United States has been spending in support of its military and economic activity in Iraq (Sachs, *The End of Poverty*). Unfortunately, despite the well-publicized pleas of Sachs and the rock star Bono, neither the President nor the Congress seems inclined to more than double the foreign assistance budget, even though the percentage of GDP involved would still then be less than the commitment of 0.7 percent that was made by the United States and other developed countries in the 1970s and reaffirmed in the 2003 Monterrey Consensus. Furthermore, although Sachs's estimate includes funding for the poverty mitigations of adequate food, fuel, and clean water, no funds are included to deal with the costs of the anticipated environmental devastation in many less developed countries from global warming. All strategies of development pursued so far have generated serious environmental costs. The next section addresses the different approaches to the environmental issue taken by the three IPE world views.

Table 8.4 Three IPE world views on development

School of thought	Development problem	Development solutions
Free market	Excessive government role in economy, thus inefficiency and corruption	Reduce government role and rely more on markets
Multi-centric organizational (MCO)	Poverty and institutional barriers	Developmental states
Marxism	Exploitation of workers and peasants	Global revolution or delinking and establishing workers' social democracy

THREE VIEWS ON THE ENVIRONMENT

While all three schools of thought recognize the existence of environmental problems such as pollution and resource degradation, they differ with respect to causes and solutions (see Table 8.5).

The free market school identifies three major causes of environmental problems: poverty, government mismanagement, and market externalities. *Poverty* is a cause because people who are poor are more interested in staying alive than in preserving the environment. Because of high infant mortality, poor people also have more kids, so the population pressure on fragile environments becomes even greater. Marginal lands are cultivated and grazed, resulting in soil degradation, and forests are decimated by the need for fuel. Not surprisingly, the free market remedy for the poverty/population cause of environmental degradation is economic growth. Greater economic and health security leads to smaller families and reduced population pressures. More affluent countries can afford the environmental protection programs that their citizens demand. *Government mismanagement* is responsible for the continuation of obsolete programs that subsidize water, grazing, fishing, and timber cutting, resulting in the serious misuse and overuse of scarce resources. Consistently, the solution is to eliminate the subsidies and use market pricing, which would force people to behave more responsibly. Furthermore, when governments impose environmental regulations they are often unrealistically strict, sometimes forcing companies to reduce output, lay off workers, maybe even move overseas. Intrusive government environmental regulations are usually unnecessary and self-defeating. Obviously, the market-oriented solution is deregulation. Finally, the free marketers do concede that some environmentally destructive behavior is not priced correctly by the market. They recognize the existence of *market externalities*. For instance, as discussed in Chapter 5, dumping pollution into the air, water, or land during the production process is not counted as a cost to the producer by the market. Therefore, it is external to market pricing, which results in the

Table 8.5 Three IPE world views on the environment

School of thought	Environment problems (sources of environmental degradation)	Environment solutions
Free market	Poverty Government mismanagement Externalities	Economic growth Corporate responsibility Market-oriented incentive systems
Multi-centric organizational (MCO)	Corporate irresponsibility Market failures	Government intervention: • internalize externalities • ecological regulations and taxes
Marxism	Capitalist exploitation of nature	Socialist revolution Return to use value

underpricing of the products arising from that polluting process. The lower prices will lead to more sales; more sales require more production; and more production means more environmental damage. This market failure allows the manufacturers to externalize their environmental costs onto society. The most fervent free market advocates, such as Milton Friedman, have not favored government intervention to correct this obvious market failure because they believe that government intervention usually makes the situation worse. However, there are some free market believers who think that some government involvement might be appropriate in dealing with this externalities-created problem. But they believe government should intervene with market-oriented incentive systems, not regulations or taxes. Examples of this approach are the acid rain and greenhouse gas *emissions permit–trading programs* that already exist in the United States and the European Union. The government establishes the emissions caps for participants, and then the private market establishes the value of, say, one ton of carbon emissions. Firms can then decide whether to install pollution controls so that they come in under their caps and can sell their leftover "rights to pollute" in the market, or they can pollute more than their caps and buy pollution permits in the market up to the amount by which they exceed their caps. Total pollution is limited to a certain maximum amount, but firms make market-type decisions on how to manage their emissions (Beckerman, *Through Green-Colored Glasses*). Another approach discussed in Chapter 5 is using market-based cost–benefit analysis to determine which expenditures are the best investments. An interesting example of this approach is the so-called "Copenhagen Consensus," a gathering of eight well-known neoclassical economists, three of whom are Nobel laureates, convened by the "sceptical environmentalist" Bjorn Lomborg. Utilizing studies of ten major problems facing the world—climate change, disease, education, conflict, hunger, migration, clean water, armed conflicts, financial instability, and trade barriers—they ranked them by their benefit–cost ratios. Programs dealing with climate change came in last (Lomborg, *Global Crises, Global Solutions*).

Multi-centric organizational proponents are unhappy with the positions of free market advocates on the environment. That's because the MCO'ers believe that the market system itself is a primary cause of environmental problems. Therefore, relying on the market or market-oriented behavior to alleviate environmental problems is like relying on the fox to protect the chickens. As discussed in Chapter 5, the externality problem is a major failure of the market. Furthermore, the market system actually encourages businesses and consumers to overuse resources and overlook pollution and environmental degradation. Short-term profit rules, not environmental sustainability. Therefore, MCO proponents believe that without effective government intervention that counters market-driven behavior, environmental degradation will continue until the earth is no longer capable of sustaining even a third of the number of people now alive, if that. All the historical evidence of prior behavior that was based on market incentives supports this contention. Businesses with only market prices as their guide are incapable of dealing with environmental problems on their own. That's because businesses cannot ignore market-determined bottom lines, yet the market ignores the environmental consequences. Examples of government interventions advocated by MCO adherents include imposing ecological taxes such as a carbon tax, putting controls on emissions, charging polluters, valuing nature as irreplaceable capital, reducing or even eliminating lengthy global supply chains, making countries responsible for their ecological debts, and replacing the misleading GDP measure with the Genuine Progress Indicator, or GPI (Daly and Cobb, *For the Common Good*).

Marxists argue that the environmental crisis is not caused by the market alone; it is created by the entire capitalist mode of production. Capitalism inherently exploits all the commodities it feeds on, both labor and nature. In fact, to classical Marxists capitalism is the most environmentally destructive system ever devised by human beings. The institution of private property gives people the right to exploit their property in any way they see fit. If short-term maximum profit can be gained by environmentally destructive behaviors, capitalists will behave accordingly. The advanced technologies of capitalism give players in the economy an extraordinary ability to cause havoc, from global warming to species destruction. In response to this argument, free market and MCO proponents pose this challenging question: "If capitalism is the major culprit, why do countries that claim loyalty to the principles of Marx (the former Soviet Union, its allies, and now China) have the worst records of environmental pollution and destruction?" The classical Marxist answer to this challenge is that these countries were never truly communist. In fact, as discussed in Chapter 6, classical Marxists claim that their systems were really examples of bureaucratic state capitalism (Foster, *The Vulnerable Planet*).

Classical Marxists argue that the threat to the natural environment upon which human survival depends will not end until capitalism itself is destroyed. Free market capitalism is the ultimate destroyer of nature, and believing that capitalist-controlled governments will act responsibly is totally naïve. The only solution is the overthrow of capitalism. Marx thought that the working class would be the first to rebel against the oppressive qualities of capitalism and create the revolution that would eventually bring about the next mode of production. However, today many Marxists are suggesting that the environmental contradiction of capitalism may very well create the first rebellion—the rebellion of nature. If capitalism is overthrown before it is ecologically too late, the communist mode of production will usher in the social ownership of natural resources that will replace private greed with social responsibility. Market exchange values will be replaced by a system of use values that recognizes and facilitates the long-term sustainability of both nature and human communities (Foster).

Environmental degradation provides a fitting last example of contrasting world views in International Political Economy. Not only is it an exceptionally important issue, but it also demonstrates the significant differences among the three world views on causes and remedies. It reminds us again that how we see the world depends on what lens we are looking through. Any one person's policy preferences will be affected by the world view(s) that informs her or his understanding of how the world does work and should work. The field of International Political Economy recognizes the implications of this insight and provides alternative perspectives for its students, but it is ultimately up to each student to find the perspective or combination of perspectives that helps him or her to best understand the world in which we live.

REVIEW QUESTIONS

1 Compare the central actors, decision-making loci, and value theories of the three world views of IPE.

2 Discuss the differences among the three schools of thought on the problems related to international trade and transnational corporations and their solutions.

3 Present the different theories of development put forth by the three world views and how they have historically played out since the end of World War II.

4 Juxtapose the positions of the three world views on the environmental issue. Which position is most persuasive to you, and why?

5 If you had to identify one of the world views that makes most sense to you, which would it be, and why? Would your preferred IPE analytical stance be based primarily in one of the world views or would you prefer some combination? Give the reasons for your choice(s).

BIBLIOGRAPHY

Amin, Samir, *Maldevelopment: Anatomy of a Global Failure* (United Nations University Press: Tokyo) 1990.

Baran, Paul A. and Paul M. Sweezy, *Monopoly Capital: An Essay on the American Economic and Social Order* (Monthly Review Press: New York) 1966.

Beckerman, W., *Through Green-Colored Glasses: Environmentalism Reconsidered* (Cato Institute: Washington, D.C.) 1996.

Blomstrom, Magnus and Bjorn Hettne, *Development Theory in Transition: The Dependency Debate and Beyond: Third World Responses* (Zed Books: London) 1984.

Boaz, David and Edward H. Crane (eds.), *Market Liberalism: A Paradigm for the 21st Century* (Cato Institute: Washington, D.C.) 1993.

Daly, Herman E. and John B. Cobb, Jr., *For the Common Good: Redirecting the Economy toward Community, the Environment, and a Sustainable Future* (Beacon Press: Boston) 1989.

Ebner, Alexander, "Joseph Alois Schumpeter," in R. J. Barry Jones (ed.), *Routledge Encyclopedia of International Political Economy* (Routledge: London) 2001.

Edwards, Chris, *The Fragmented World: Competing Perspectives on Trade, Money and Crisis* (Methuen: London) 1985.

Foster, John Bellamy, *The Vulnerable Planet: A Short Economic History of the Environment* (Monthly Review Press: New York) 1994.

Grandin, Greg, "Chavez: 'Galbraithiano'," *The Nation* (Vol. 285, No. 11), October 15, 2007, pp. 5–8.

Helleiner, Eric, "Economic nationalism as a challenge to economic liberalism? Lessons from the nineteenth century," *International Studies Quarterly* (Vol. 46) 2002, pp. 307–329.

Kane, Tim, Kim Holmes and Mary Anastasia O'Grady, *2007 Index of Economic Freedom* (The Heritage Foundation and Dow Jones and Company: Washington, D.C.) 2007.

Khor, Martin, "Clash of paradigms behind latest WTO failure," *Third World Resurgence* (No. 202), June, 2007, pp. 5–6.

Khor, Martin, *The Multilateral Trading System: A Development Perspective* (United Nations Development Programme: New York) 2001.

Lomborg, Bjorn (ed.), *Global Crises, Global Solutions* (Cambridge University Press: Cambridge, United Kingdom:) 2004.

O'Rourke, P. J., *Eat the Rich: A Treatise on Economics* (Atlantic Monthly Press: New York) 1998.

Parker, Richard, *John Kenneth Galbraith: His Life, His Politics, His Economics* (Farrar, Straus and Giroux: New York) 2005.

Rapley, John, *Understanding Development: Theory and Practice in the Third World*, 2nd edn. (Lynne Rienner: Boulder, Colorado) 2002.

Rodrik, Dani, " 'Goodbye Washington consensus, hello Washington confusion?' A review of The World Bank, *Economic Growth in the 1990s: Learning from a Decade of Reform*," *Journal of Economic Literature* (Vol. 44, No. 4), December, 2006, pp. 973–987.

Rostow, W. W., *The Stages of Economic Growth: A Non-Communist Manifesto* (Cambridge University Press: London) 1960.

Sachs, Jeffrey, *The End of Poverty: Economic Possibilities for Our Time* (Penguin Press: New York) 2005.

Smith, Adam, *The Wealth of Nations* (Prometheus Books: Amherst, NY) 1991 (first published in 1776).

Sraffa, Piero, *The Production of Commodities by Means of Commodities: Prelude to a Critique of Economic Theory* (Cambridge University Press: Cambridge, United Kingdom) 1960.

Yergin, Daniel and Joseph Stanislaw, *The Commanding Heights: The Battle for the World Economy*, revised edition (Simon and Schuster: New York) 2002.

GLOSSARY OF CONCEPTS

absolute advantage: Having the ability to sell a product at a lower price than any competitor while covering all costs. A viable basis for trade between countries exists when participating countries have absolute advantages in different products.

abstract labor: Refers to Marx's theory of labor value. Relative values of commodities tend to approximate the *average* socially necessary amount of labor time expended in producing them.

accumulation by dispossession: Phrase used by the Marxist David Harvey to describe the exploitation of the weaker classes for the purpose of mobilizing capital for investment (capital accumulation). Current strategies of dispossession include privatizing public goods, predatory financial practices, engineering economic crises, and state redistributions (tax and subsidy programs) that favor capitalists.

alienation: Marx's characterization of the nature of conflictual class relationships in capitalism. All parties are in conflict with one another over the allocation of material rewards, creating separation and distrust. Money, as the all-pervasive intermediate medium, obscures and replaces person-to-person relationships.

artificial persons: Status of corporations under U.S. law. That is, the law in the United States treats corporations as individuals, giving them similar rights and responsibilities.

balance of payments: Accounting system recording the financial flows in and out of countries. It includes the monetary flows associated with the cross-border movements of goods, services, and capital. It presumes that the amount-in will equal the amount-out.

balance of trade: Net figure of the financial worth of goods flowing in (imports) and out (exports) of countries. In the short run the flows may not be equal, such that countries can run deficits (the value of imports is greater than the value of exports) or surpluses (export value is more than import value).

balanced budget: When the tax revenues coming in to a governmental unit equal the expenditures going out, the budget is considered balanced. Free market advocates believe that the natural state of any governmental budget should be balance, whereas Keynesians believe that under certain economic circumstances the national budget should be unbalanced, in deficit when the economy is weak and in surplus when the economy is too strong. (See also **compensatory fiscal policy**.)

banks: Financial organizations that collect deposits and then lend most of them out for interest returns. In modern economies they are also called *intermediaries*, as they bring together savers (depositors) on the one hand and investors (borrowers) on the other hand. This definition is consistent with the market world view. In the MCO world view banks are credit-creating institutions that primarily serve the financial elites. In the Marxist world view banks are mobilizers of the surplus value extracted from workers.

bills of exchange: Promises to pay between parties, usually based on some underlying store of wealth. They have potential for use as a broader medium of exchange.

bonds: Long-term credit instruments, usually transferable in bond markets. They are issued by corporations and governments to pay for expenditures not covered by current revenues. Effective interest rates vary inversely with the market price of the bond.

Bretton Woods: The location of a resort in New Hampshire where a 1944 conference was held that proposed the establishment of the International Monetary Fund (IMF) and the International Bank for Reconstruction and Development (or World Bank). Consequently, both of these organizations are frequently called the *Bretton Woods institutions*. The fixed dollar/gold standard that prevailed in the international financial system from 1945 to 1971 was also designed at Bretton Woods, so it was called the Bretton Woods Monetary System. Even though the General Agreement on Tariffs and Trade (GATT) is often identified as a Bretton Woods institution, it was not a product of the Bretton Woods Conference.

capital: In neoclassical economics *capital* has at least two meanings: physical and financial. In the physical sense, capital refers to those human-made productive means that are used to make other things such as consumption goods and services. The making of physical capital is called **capital investment**. The ability to engage in capital investment is dependent on the availability of savings. Since savings in a market economy are monetized, stores of saved money available for capital investment are also called capital. This latter use represents the financial meaning of capital. Economists tend to favor the first use of the term because physical capital investment is the vehicle for achieving economic growth. For clarity and consistency, this text uses these definitions of capital throughout. However, the term capital has been given many other meanings and applications. Marx, for instance, referred to all monetized inputs in the capitalist production process as capital, including labor, which he called "variable capital."

capital account: One of the two major components of the balance of payments between the economies of different countries. It includes both short-term (financial) and long-term (physical) forms of capital. A country with a deficit in its current account will compensate for the deficit by importing capital from other countries.

capitalist mode of production: The phrase used by Marx to describe the structure and process of the capitalist system. It encompasses all facets of society, from the technology of production to the nature of the class system.

cash crops: Crops grown for overseas cash sales. Crops such as tobacco, sugar, and cotton were the basis of the first global trading system, which relied heavily on slave labor. Today many Third World countries still depend economically on the export of cash crops, such as bananas, peanuts, sugar, coffee, beans for chocolate, timber, palm oil, and cotton.

class: From Marx's perspective, classes are the major social grouping in society. Membership in a class is a function of one's relationship to the means of production. Those who control and/or own the means of production are the dominant class and those who do not are the subordinate class.

climate change: The warming of the earth's climate that is now occurring, primarily due to the burning of fossil fuels associated with industrialization. Most climate scientists believe that unless the warming trend is controlled, the earth will experience severe environmental consequences.

communism: The last stage of human history, as envisaged by Karl Marx. In this mode of production, since the means of production are collectively owned and controlled, there is no more class struggle, nor the need for a repressive government.

comparative advantage: The theoretical basis for mutually beneficial trade between countries, even when one country has an absolute price advantage in all tradable products of interest. David Ricardo argued that if trading countries had different internal cost ratios in the production of the same commodities, they could still increase their economic welfare by each country specializing in producing and exporting those products in which it had a comparative cost advantage and importing those products in which it had a comparative cost disadvantage. Positive mutual results for the countries following this approach depend on a set of strict conditions being satisfied, the most important one being capital immobility.

compensatory fiscal policy: The best policy for a national government to follow in order to maintain full employment and price stability over time, according to John Maynard Keynes. When the economy is below full employment, the budget should run a deficit in order to stimulate demand; when the economy is overheated, the budget should run a surplus. The size of the deficit or surplus should be appropriate to the economic need. Implementing this policy is politically very difficult.

compensatory tariffs: A policy, proposed by Ravi Batra, that would involve developed countries putting substantial tariffs on imports from less developed countries in order to offset their low prices, which are presumably made low by the use of below-standard environmental and labor practices. The purpose is to discourage these practices and to support local production that meets the higher standards.

consumer sovereignty: Refers to the controlling role of consumers' preferences assumed by the market model in determining answers to the basic decisions on production and distribution.

consumers: One of the three major roles in the market model. Consumers are expected to maximize their consumption satisfaction by rational spending and saving decisions.

controllers of resources: Those actors in the market model who control the resources of land, labor, and capital. They offer them in the resources market, where supply and demand will determine their value, that is, the incomes that the controllers will receive.

corporate colonialism: Phrase of David Korten that refers to the exploitation of labor and the environment in foreign countries by transnational corporations in the same manner practiced by colonial governments in the past.

corporation: The modern form of business organization that has a variety of special attributes: is state-chartered, has an indefinite lifetime, shares ownership with limited liability, and enjoys unlimited fundraising capacity and operational size. John Kenneth Galbraith considered the corporation the key organization of modern society, potentially eclipsing governments in their power.

cost of production theory: The value theory proposed by neo-Ricardians. Instead of subjective preference or abstract labor determining relative values, neo-Ricardians believe that relative values are determined by dynamic components in the production process: the level of technology, minimum labor-cost requirements, and the power negotiations between labor and business.

current account: The most significant item in balance of payments accounting. It measures the net flows resulting from the imports and exports of goods and services between countries. In a healthy global economy current account balances should not manifest long-term deficits or surpluses.

debt: The total amount of past borrowing that a governmental entity, business, or person owes to its creditors. Debt used to be owed mostly within national boundaries, but with expanding financial globalization debt is increasingly owed to institutions and individuals all over the world. For instance, financial institutions in China, Japan, and Saudi Arabia have large holdings of U.S. Treasury securities.

debt relief: Since the 1970s Third World countries have been advocating for relief from the burden of heavy debt payments. Some progress has been made, but many countries, especially in Africa, are still handicapped with heavy debt payments in hard currencies to external creditors.

deficit: When expenditures exceed revenues, usually on an annual basis. Deficits can occur in government budgets or in international payments, such as trade and the current account.

deindustrialization: When an economy allows its manufacturing capacity to be significantly reduced while satisfying its need for manufactured goods through imports.

demand-side economics: The macroeconomic theory that identifies inadequate demand as the central cause of unemployed resources. By contrast supply-side economics identifies disincentives for suppliers, such as high taxes, as the major cause.

democracy: The form of governance that is responsive to the wishes of the broader public with reliance on the rule of law, minority rights, elections, and checks and balances of power.

dependency theory: A school of thought that was especially influential in the 1960s and 1970s. It contended that the structure of the world economy discriminated against poor countries by forcing them to keep exporting their natural resources at relatively cheap prices while being forced to import manufactured goods at relatively expensive prices. In other words, the state of underdevelopment was imposed on poor countries by rich countries.

depression: A state of the economy characterized by significant declines in income, production, investment, and employment. Historically the most salient example of this phenomenon was the Great Depression of the 1930s.

derivatives: Financial instruments whose value is derived from underlying assets. Initially derivatives were based on well-understood financial instruments such as stocks, bonds, foreign exchange, and interest contracts. However, the twenty-first century witnessed an explosion of derivative types that became more and more complex. They were so complex that most buyers and sellers were not really aware of what the underlying assets were or what they were really worth. The most infamous were those that combined many different types of debt, including low-quality debt such as subprime mortgages. Yet these questionable derivatives were sold in large quantities all over the world, so that when the "bubble burst," a global credit crisis ensued in 2007–2008.

development: In Political Economy, this term usually refers to the economic development of a society, coming primarily from successful industrialization. Since World War II the pace of development has been measured by increases in GDP, though the theory of development has encompassed more variables than the purely economic, such as cultural and political dimensions.

dialectical materialism: The phrase that refers to the basic philosophical approach of Karl Marx. The term "dialectical" refers to the process of continuous change driven by oppositions, and "materialism" refers to the view that reality is fundamentally physical in nature. In Marx's view the physical reality that really counts is the production process.

discount rate: Interest rate charged by the U.S. central bank (the Fed) to depository institutions, such as commercial banks, when they borrow from the Fed. During the 2007–2008 credit crisis the Fed aggressively used the **discount window**, through which it made loans available at the discount rate, for the first time in years. A new group of beneficiaries from the discount window are investment banks, even though they are not currently regulated by the Fed.

ecological footprint: Human resource use converted into the spatial measure of acres of land and water surface required to support the economic activity under consideration. There are great footprint disparities between countries, and the world's annual footprint now exceeds the available biological capacity. That excess is made possible by the mining of non-renewable resources accumulated over millennia.

ecological imperialism: Phrase used by John Bellamy Foster to describe environmental exploitation activities by rich and powerful countries in poor and vulnerable countries. Examples include toxic waste dumping, unregulated mining, and debt-motivated deforestation.

economic growth: Increase in total production as measured by the GDP from one year to the next. Growth in modern economies is generated primarily by technological innovation and capital investment. It's the key measure of success in the free market world view. MCO advocates see economic growth as a mixed blessing: positive when it alleviates poverty, negative when it is done in an environmentally unsustainable way. Marxists see continuous economic growth (capital accumulation) as a defining characteristic of capitalism. The positive aspect is that it raises the standard of living. The negative aspect is that it leads to the exploitation of workers and the inevitable economic crises. According to Marx, these positive and negative outcomes are both dialectically necessary for humanity to move on to the next mode of production—communism.

epistemology: Branch of philosophy that deals with the theory of knowledge—that is, how we know what we think we know.

exchange value: The price at which a product or resource is exchanged in the market, ostensibly set by the relationship between supply and demand. This concept is recognized by all three schools of thought, but each school has a different theory about the underlying dynamic that determines the relative values prevailing in the economy.

externalities: Social and environmental benefits and costs of economic activity that are not incorporated in market prices. When externalities exist, the market is considered to have failed to provide socially appropriate exchange values. Compensating for this market oversight requires government intervention, especially according to the MCO perspective.

fair trade: Trade relationships that are structured to provide fair returns to the small producers at the bottom of the production chain. They are mostly implemented where small-scale farming is involved, such as in coffee production.

false consciousness: A Marxian phrase used to describe the failure of people to see through the veil of deceptions perpetrated by the ruling class to cover up their exploitative behavior. In capitalism, for instance, workers do not perceive that the whole system is structured to their disadvantage.

federal funds rate: The interest rate that U.S. commercial banks charge each other for overnight loans. It is the rate that the Fed targets in its efforts to influence the prevailing interest rates.

Federal Reserve System (Fed): The central bank of the United States. The Fed has the major responsibility for implementing monetary policy.

feudalism: The social formation that prevailed in Europe during the Middle Ages. It is an agriculture-based system in which largely self-sufficient manors make up most of the economy. There is very little geographical mobility for either the lords of the manor or the peasants who work there. They have mutual obligations that are defined by custom, not market pricing.

fictional commodities: A phrase used by Karl Polanyi to describe the market transformation of labor, nature, and gold-backed money into commodities that can be bought and sold. They are fictional because their commodity status is an invention of the human imagination, an invention that he believed has negative consequences for the social fabric.

fiscal policy: Use of governmental budgets as instruments to achieve social objectives such as reducing poverty or maintaining full employment.

foreign exchange: Currencies issued by other governments. *Hard currencies* are those issued by governments with stable and dependable economies. They are readily accepted in international transactions, and governments hold them in reserve. Examples include the U.S. dollar, the euro, the Japanese yen, the British pound, and the Swiss franc. The ratios between currencies are sometimes fixed by government fiat, but the ratios between the hard currencies are determined in the foreign exchange markets. Therefore, they are examples of what are called flexible or floating currencies.

fractional reserve banking system: A system in which only a small percentage of depositors' funds are kept on reserve while the rest are lent out. This enables the banking system to create additional bank money or credit in multiples of the original deposits. It's an important component of capitalist economies.

free trade: The open-market exchange of goods and services between countries without any government interventions of a protectionist nature, such as tariffs or non-tariff barriers. Central principle of the free market world view. MCO and Marxist adherents argue that free trade is used as an ideological cover for capitalist exploitation through means such as intellectual property rules and financial leverage.

full utilization: One of the outcomes of the market model whereby any product or resource that is offered in the market is sold at some price. That is, the market always clears.

globalization: A term widely used in the last few decades to describe the evolution of capitalism from the national level to the transnational. The original emphasis was more economic, focusing on dimensions such as trade and investment, but cultural and political practices are now often included. Furthermore, reactions to the spread of capitalism are also becoming globalized, such as terrorist resistance.

gold standard: A monetary system in which both domestic and external prices are related to the amount of gold held by the world's governments. Most extensively utilized in the latter half of the nineteenth and the early twentieth centuries. An external or international gold standard, sometimes called the dollar/gold, or Bretton Woods, system, was in place from 1945 to 1971.

Green Revolution: A significant increase in crop yields in Third World countries due to the development of new hybrid seeds and the application of industrial agricultural methods. Probably saved some countries, such as India in the 1960s and 1970s, from widespread famine. However, it may not be permanently sustainable as some of the key ingredients (mined water, chemical fertilizers, and fossil fuels) are becoming more scarce and expensive, and they cause environmental damage. Clearly, the use of "green" in this concept does not refer to the "green" of environmentally friendly practices.

Gross Domestic Product (GDP): The total monetary value of all final goods and services produced in a national economy in one year. The most important performance measure used by the free market or neoclassical economic approach.

hegemony: A situation in which one country or group of countries has domination over all others. Sometimes limited to military, political, and economic power. The Marxist

Antonio Gramsci added cultural domination to the means by which hegemonic power is exercised.

historical materialism: The Marxist approach to human history, which explains the evolution from one mode of production to another based on the class struggle that emerges as the technology of production changes.

households: A central component of the market model. As households face the product market they engage in consumption and saving. As households face the resources market they provide the factors of production: land, labor, and capital.

Index of Sustainable Economic Welfare (ISEW): An alternative measure to the GDP proposed by John Cobb and Herman Daly. It incorporates quantitative measurements of unpriced activities, both positive and negative. Therefore, it includes the positive benefits of voluntary labor, such as child-rearing, and the negative effects, such as pollution, resource degradation, and sickness. The Index is also known as the Genuine Progress Indicator, or GPI.

Industrial Revolution: Economic transformation that began in the eighteenth century in Great Britain based on machine technology and mineral energy. The key invention was the steam engine. Industrialization generated tremendous increases in the efficiency of production.

inflation: Increase in the overall level of prices. Measured by weighted averages of consumer or producer goods and services. It is a major concern for capitalist economies because of its destabilizing potential. Therefore, keeping inflation under control is the primary objective of central banks.

institutionalism: School of thought that studies the evolving historical forms of organized social groupings. It is a major alternative to the free market school of thought, whose model institutionalists criticize as atomistic, ahistorical, and divorced from reality. The institutionalist school in the United States is associated with the contributions of Thorstein Veblen and John Kenneth Galbraith. (See also the **multi-centric organizational (MCO) model and world view.**)

instruments of production: Marxist term for the physical-capital embodiment of the available technology in the production process. Considered by Karl Marx to be the key causal variable in social change.

interest/interest payment/interest rate: In the market interest is the payment received by savers for making their funds available. It is usually stated as a rate or percentage. Interest payments to savers come from those wishing to make capital investments. It is the special cost that capital investors have to pay in order to get access to the saved funds and the claims on productive capacity that they represent. The prevailing rate of interest, which is determined by supply and demand according to the market model, telegraphs the cost of the future in reference to the present. The higher the prevailing interest rate, then the higher the value the society places on the present. Since so many economic decisions are based on the interest rate, it is the central variable that monetary authorities try to influence or control. MCO analysts believe that setting interest rates is an act of power manipulation, not just supply and demand. Marxists see it as another tool of capitalist exploitation.

International Political Economy (IPE): The interdisciplinary social science field of study that investigates, analyzes, and proposes changes in the processes of economic flows and political governance that cross over or transcend national boundaries. The field contains several schools of thought that offer different perspectives on these issues.

labor theory of value: This theory claims that the underlying determinant of the relative values of items exchanged in an economy is the amount of labor involved in making them. Over time prices will tend to reflect these underlying values. Different versions of the labor theory of value prevailed among the classical political economists, culminating in its use by Karl Marx. (See also **abstract labor.**)

labor-intensive production: Production using more labor relative to other resources, especially capital.

laissez-faire: Philosophy originating in France and adopted by Adam Smith that advocates limited government intervention in the economy and major reliance on the market. Polanyi argues that *laissez-faire* was used as an ideological cover for government imposition of a market structure favorable to business.

least-cost combination: The market model principle that guides production managers in their decisions about what mix of resources (land, labor, and capital) to use in their production processes.

liberalism: A phrase widely used in nineteenth-century Britain that referred to a free market philosophy in which individual choice is maximized. Some groups, such as libertarians, still use it that way. However, semantic confusion occurred when anti–big government Republicans in the United States began labeling those favoring the New Deal government social programs, created in response to the Great Depression, as "liberals." (See also **neoliberalism.**)

low-level equilibrium trap: A phrase used by John Maynard Keynes to describe a state of the economy in which consumption, saving, and investment decisions produce a stable equilibrium far below full employment. If none of these major macro variables change, the economy is trapped there, unless external intervention occurs, such as government deficit spending.

macroeconomics: A major branch of economics, essentially invented by John Maynard Keynes. It focuses on the national or macro-level variables, such as production, income, employment, investment, and price level. In contrast, **microeconomics** focuses on the market decision-making process at the consumer, worker, and firm level. The market model is essentially a microeconomic analytical device.

managers of productive organizations: One of the three major roles in the market model. The job of managers, for which the market determines their compensation, is to maximize profits. Therefore, they try to maximize revenues by responding to consumer preferences while minimizing their resource costs through least-cost-combination production strategies.

marginal analysis: Central idea of neoclassical economics. Prices are determined at the margins, that is, where the offered price of the last supplied item equals the last purchasing price that the demanders are willing to pay. That is the point of equilibrium. MCO adherents find the application of marginal analysis to the resource market particularly unrealistic because of the uneven power held between businesses and workers, especially if the workers are not well organized.

market: This term has many meanings. In pre-modern times the market was a physical location where trading occurred. In modern times "market" refers to the way in which an entire society is organized around the buying and selling of just about everything.

market model: The basic model used by those committed to the free market world view. It's a circular set of relationships in which households and productive organizations meet in both the product and resource markets for exchanges at the prices determined by supply and demand.

market power: A phrase used mostly by MCO analysts that points to market situations in which large corporations or governments have the power to administer prices rather than prices being determined by supply and demand in a competitive free market.

means of production: The physical structures and equipment that are used in the making of goods and services. In capitalism they are mostly owned by private companies.

measure of relative value: One of the three functions of money. Money serves as a unit of account so that all items that are exchanged can have a differential value on one accepted scale. The MCO school of thought believes that this is the most important function of money.

medium of exchange: One of the three functions of money. Since money represents value, it can be used for purchases, payment of obligations, and general facilitation of commerce. What serves as the recognized medium can vary from sea shells to checking accounts. The market school of thought focuses on this function of money because of its central role in the supply/demand exchange process.

mercantilism: The international economic system that prevailed among the dominant European countries from the fifteenth to the nineteenth centuries. It was characterized by state-franchised monopoly trading companies utilizing colonial methods on behalf of private and state interests. Marx considered it the transitional system between feudalism and capitalism, with the merchant class acting as the cutting-edge change agent.

mode of production: The Marxian concept that structures the components of a particular social formation such as feudalism or capitalism. It is composed of the forces of production and the relations of production. Production permeates all these concepts because Marx believed that the technological and physical conditions of the production experience (forces) interactively determined the class relationships and all other aspects of society (relations). Marx identified the forces of production as the basic material conditions.

model: One of the central organizing concepts used in this text. A simplified and logically consistent representation of how some aspects of human societies work. The three political-economic thought models presented in the text are structured around their premises (assumptions), their internal interactions, and their outcomes. Since models are simplified abstractions, they are used for heuristic and not descriptive purposes.

monetarism: The philosophy associated with Milton Friedman that emphasizes the use of monetary policy to maintain stability and prosperity in the economy, rather than fiscal policy.

monetary policy: The use of the regulatory powers of the central bank to achieve stability in the economy, especially price stability. The Fed, the Bank of England, the Bank of Japan, the European Central Bank, and others use similar means to achieve their objectives. Their most important instrument is the influence they have over the prevailing interest rates.

monetization: The process by which more and more of the economic transactions of a society are made through the medium of money. Full monetization is necessary for the market model to be fully operational.

moneyness: A term used by MCO analysts to indicate that money is essentially a publicly established unit of account, not a commodity.

multi-centric organizational (MCO) model and world view: One of three major schools of thought presented in this text. The MCO world view criticizes the free market approach for being unrealistic. According to the MCO view, modern economies are dominated by large corporations that exercise immense power. The model presented in the text comes primarily from the writings of John Kenneth Galbraith. His model focuses on power negotiations between major organizational players in the economy, not individuals in a competitive market. Governments are another major organizational player, but Galbraith agreed with Susan Strange that power is distributed among several major players.

multilateral environmental agreements (MEAs): International agreements (sometimes treaties) that commit signatories to specific actions to protect or preserve the environment. One of most successful is the 1987 Montreal Protocol, which limits the emissions of gases that destroy the ozone in the atmosphere. Probably the most prominent in the news is the United Nations Framework Convention on Climate Change.

multiplier effect: A term used mostly in Keynesian economics. It refers to the multiple progression of income expansion from the injection of new expenditures into the economy. If income recipients spend 90 percent of the income received, the potential expansion multiplier is 10, as income passes from one recipient to the next. A similar progression occurs in the fractional reserve banking system.

national income and product accounts: The accounting method by which the GDP is determined. It is conceptually based on the two equal sides of the market model, the market for products and the market for resources.

natural capital: A concept that counts natural resources as capital rather than as consumption commodities. Consequently, the degradation of the environment would be included as a depreciation cost for producers, which currently does not occur in conventional market-based accounting. A proposal associated with ecological economist Herman Daly.

neoclassical economics: The dominant school of thought in the discipline of Economics for over 100 years. Its underlying thought model is the purely competitive, self-regulating market. Its value theory is based on the expression of individual preferences through the mechanism of supply and demand. Resources or factors of production include land and capital as well as labor.

neocolonialism: Exploitation of the poor, especially in the Third World, through the use of discriminatory trade or trade-related practices, usually with the assistance of world, regional, and bilateral trade agreements.

neo-imperialism: Exploitation of relatively poor and vulnerable countries by rich and powerful countries and corporations through the exercise of financial power, sometimes with the assistance of the International Monetary Fund and the World Bank. One of the strategies is debt leverage, exercised through structural adjustment programs that were implemented in the 1980s and 1990s.

neoliberalism: The phrase applied to the practices of neocolonialism and neo-imperialism, usually in a pejorative manner. It implies an excess of free market, free trade, free capital movements, and privatization to the detriment of the poor populations in the Third World.

neomercantilism: Use of state intervention to acquire national advantage in the international economy despite the post–World War II commitments to free trade in the General Agreement on Tariffs and Trade (GATT) and the World Trade Organization (WTO). Tactics include quotas, subsidies, controlled exchange rates, and health and safety regulations, among other policies. Also known as economic nationalism, though its focus is broader than economic, as it also incorporates the promotion of national identity and other non-economic objectives.

neo-Ricardianism: The school of thought based on the works of David Ricardo but enhanced by the additional contributions of Piero Sraffa. This school focuses on the historical process of distribution between labor and capital as being more institutionally determined by relative power than by the impersonal and harmonious processes of the market.

oligopolistic market: A market in which a few sellers dominate so that power rivalries, and not market competition, determine the outcomes. MCO adherents believe that more than half of the economies in highly industrialized, capitalistic countries are controlled by corporations in oligopolistic markets.

ontology: The branch of philosophy that deals with the nature of reality.

open market operations: Refers to an instrument of monetary policy by which central bankers try to influence the price of money by intervening in markets with large purchases or sales. The most likely market for central bank intervention is the market for short-term interest rates. Also some central banks frequently intervene in the foreign exchange markets.

open-system error: The belief that a system is open and therefore has no limits when in fact the system is closed. MCO advocates accuse free market advocates of making this error when they promote unending economic growth, when in fact the natural resource base is limited. As ecological footprint analysts point out, if everybody on earth lived like U.S. residents, we would need five planets.

optimum allocation of resources: One of the major outcomes of the market model, in which every resource (land, labor, and capital) is dedicated to the use for which it receives the highest price, meaning that the total creation of value in the economy will be the greatest possible from the available resources.

per capita product: The average amount of product value available per person. Calculated by dividing the total population of a country into the GDP.

polluter-pays principle: The person or organization responsible for polluting the environment should pay the full cost that is incurred by the society because of the pollution. Despite the moral force of this principle, it is seldom implemented.

precautionary principle: The conservative principle that advises against going ahead with any activity that has the possibility of catastrophic consequences. Waiting for absolute certainty that some activity is extremely harmful before restricting that activity may not allow enough time to counteract the impending devastation. Global warming is the salient case in which this principle could be applied, but there are others such as placing nuclear weapons in space. If individuals had followed this principle in recent years, no one would have started smoking tobacco.

productive organizations: One of the key locations in the market model where factors of production are acquired and mobilized in order to make consumption and capital products, with the primary motivation being the maximization of profit.

protectionism: The use of various techniques, such as tariffs, quotas, subsidies, and health and safety regulations, for the purpose of protecting local producers from foreign competition.

purchasing power parity (PPP): A comparative standard-of-living measurement involving the use of similar living expenses across countries rather than foreign exchange ratios. This method attempts to overcome the distortions that are built in to foreign exchange ratios such as government fixed rates. However, the PPP method has also come under scrutiny because of various inadequacies in its calculation.

real interest rates: The rate that remains after the rate of inflation is deducted from the actual or nominal rate of interest. Comparing interest rates across countries can usefully be done only via real interest rates. It's possible for real interest rates to be negative, the situation which actually prevailed in international financial markets during the late 1970s.

reductionism: The breaking up of large entities into small, discrete parts for purposes of analysis, but where doing so obscures the relevant relationships between the parts and the organic functioning of a whole system. A criticism made of both conventional science and the free market model.

regularization theory: "Regularization" is an English-language translation of the French term "regulation." Regularization (or regulation) theory is a modern French Marxist theory that looks at various strategies that capitalists have used to prevent the inevitable crises of capitalism from leading to its demise. These organized systemic strategies are identified as accumulation regimes, such as Fordism and post-Fordism.

reserve ratio: The percentage that depository institutions, such as commercial banks, must keep on reserve. The ratio is usually set by the central bank. The higher the reserve ratio, the smaller the multiple of bank money that the fractional reserve system can create.

revised sequence: Term invented by John Kenneth Galbraith to describe consumer sovereignty being replaced by producer sovereignty. Producers manipulate consumer preferences through advertising so that demand is generated for the goods and services that they want to produce. It's the opposite of the presumption in the market model that consumers with their own preferences establish the demands for products.

saving: An important part of the economic process because saving makes capital investment possible. The three schools of thought differ on how saving is generated, but they all recognize its necessary role in capital accumulation. The market model sees saving as voluntarily coming from households whose occupants are rewarded with interest payments for abstaining from immediate consumption. The MCO model sees saving as generated primarily from the market power of the corporate/financial sector whereas the Marxian model sees saving as involuntary extraction from workers through the generation of surplus value. Saving plays the central role in the global interrelationships among macroeconomic variables (see Figure 3.4, p. 82).

scientific socialism: A phrase that Marxists use to claim that their analysis is based on scientific method and that the ultimate outcome of human history will be socialism, a more humane system.

self-regulating market: An intellectual invention generally attributed to Adam Smith in which the competitive market will not only make most of the production and distribution decisions, but also make them in a just and morally defensible fashion. By being self-regulating the market runs the economy without government interference while providing consumers with the products they want at the cheapest possible prices. In one passage Adam Smith used the phrase "the invisible hand," and that is the short-hand moniker that many of Smith's admirers now use to refer to the self-regulating market.

socialism: An economic system in which the means of production are owned by the public rather than private individuals or corporations. Socialism may or may not be associated with a democratic polity. Social-democratic political parties combine their belief in democratic decision-making with their belief in some degree of socialism. Definitional and policy confusion occur when people confuse the welfare state, such as the one in Sweden, with socialism. Socialism can also be compatible with market or non-market systems of decision-making. Marx differentiated between socialism and communism because he imagined communism as an eventual mode of production without market decision-making.

sovereign wealth funds (SWFs): State-run "investment funds." Countries with large surpluses in their balance of payments place some of their foreign exchange accumulations in funds that buy financial assets around the world. Oil-exporting countries such as Saudi Arabia, Norway, and Dubai are major players along with such major exporters as China. In 2007 the amounts committed to sovereign wealth funds were estimated in the 3 to 5 trillion dollar range. Initially these funds were very conservative in their purchases, buying assets such as U.S. Treasury bonds, but recently they have shifted to equities and buying shares in major transnational corporations. If the funds follow market criteria in their acquisitions, then their "capital" infusions are welcome. However, if they begin to be used as foreign policy instruments of their home states, as the MCO analysts would expect, then political concerns are inevitable. Marxists have no doubt that SWFs are simply another means of capitalists globally circulating monetary capital (surplus value) in order to keep the system viably profitable as long as possible.

Special Drawing Rights (SDRs): A foreign exchange asset created by the International Monetary Fund (IMF) for its members. Countries are issued a certain number of SDRs, based on their deposits with the IMF, that can be used to settle obligations to other countries.

Stalinism: The totalitarian, central-planning form of socialism imposed upon the Soviet Union by Joseph Stalin in 1928. Because Stalin used Marxism/Leninism as his ideological cover, the Soviet system became associated with Marx, even though Marx never imagined, and therefore never advocated, such a system. He certainly would not have called Stalin's system communism.

stocks: Equity shares in a corporation upon which dividends may be earned and which usually can be bought and sold in stock markets. When first issued, they are one of several means by which corporations get access to saving that can be used for capital investment.

store of value: One of the three functions of money. By keeping its value over time, money facilitates dependable future transactions by individuals, businesses, and governments. Excessive inflation is a major threat to this function as it disrupts all future planning.

subjective preference theory: The basic value theory of the market model. The determination of value begins with the expression of individual consumer preferences through the demand schedules in the market. When an effective demand matches a willingness to supply in the competitive market, a correct exchange value is forthcoming.

surplus value: A central concept in the capitalist mode of production. Karl Marx argued that the cost of bringing labor to the workplace was usually less than the exchange value that the worker created during the production process. Because the means of production are privately owned in capitalism, the capitalists own this difference between the cost of labor and the value created. Marx called it surplus value, which is the measure of worker exploitation and the major source of profit for capitalists from which they acquire the ability to continue the necessary capital accumulation.

sustainable development: Development that does not drain nature of its ability to replenish itself so that future generations will have the same support from the natural resource base as the current generation. Unfortunately for future generations, the current rates of consumption and toxic pollution significantly exceed the sustainability of natural processes, thereby incurring a substantial ecological debt.

technology: Ideas about new products and new ways of producing that when adopted enhance economic activity. Technology is a key variable in Karl Marx's theory of social change, and it is a major contributor to economic development in all three schools of thought. However, technology has the capacity to either improve (modern medicine) or worsen (nuclear weapons) the human condition.

technostructure: A term invented by John Kenneth Galbraith that describes the highly technical cadre of professionals that he believed would be actually making corporate decisions rather than top executives. This component of his original model has yet to be realized to the extent that he expected.

teleological system: An evolving system that has an end-in-view or a predictable outcome. The simpler versions of historical materialism are teleological.

terms of trade: The ratio of the value of imports to the value of exports. In most of the nineteenth and twentieth centuries, countries exporting primary products and importing manufactured goods experienced negative terms of trade, that is, it took more and more primary products to buy the same amount of manufactured products. The terms of trade could move in a different direction in the twenty-first century as primary products become scarcer and more expensive.

Third World: A term that began to be used in the 1950s to identify the relatively poor, less powerful, often formerly colonized countries of the world. The First World was the capitalist West; the Second World was the communist East. Because of all the changes in the last 50 years, all three of these terms are now of dubious definitional usefulness, but as a symbol of identity the term "Third World" seems to have staying power.

Third World debt crisis: A major financial crisis in the 1980s in which many Third World countries, especially in Latin America and Africa, required assistance in meeting their debt obligations. The assistance from the International Monetary Fund and the World Bank came with conditions known as structural adjustment programs, promoting the neoliberal, or Washington Consensus, agenda.

Tobin tax: A very small tax on foreign exchange transactions proposed by the economist James Tobin with the purpose of discouraging excessive speculation.

transnational corporations (TNCs): Corporations whose activities in countries outside their home country exceed those in their home country. Because of global ownership, management, and operations these corporations are presumed to have limited loyalty to their home countries. However, if necessary, they are quite prepared to enlist the assistance of their home governments in order to pursue their business interests more effectively.

triangular trade: Usually refers to the trading arrangements in the sixteenth to nineteenth centuries between Western Europe, Africa, and the Americas in which slave-based plantation cropping was the central economic activity. Ships plied from Europe to Africa to the Americas and back to Europe. Europe provided manufactured goods, slaves were extracted from Africa, and the Americas provided cash crops such as cotton, sugar, and tobacco.

value theory: Theories that attempt to explain the underlying bases of the relative worth of items exchanged in an economy. The three schools of thought presented in this text have different value theories. The market model relies on the subjective preference, or supply–demand, theory. The MCO model uses the cost of production, or negotiated outcomes, theory. Classical Marxism uses the labor theory of value.

veil of money: A Marxist phrase that refers to the way in which market pricing hides the structure of exploitation that permeates the capitalist system.

virtual economy: A phrase used by the feminist political economist Spike Peterson to identify those electronic and symbolic realms that increasingly influence the functioning of the global political economy.

Washington Consensus: A phrase coined to encapsulate the neoliberal or free market agenda of the 1980s that was emanating from the U.S. Treasury Department, the International Monetary Fund, and the World Bank.

world view: A central organizing concept of this text. World views provide coherent perspectives that include assumptions about how elements of human societies work and how they should work. World views have cognitive, affective, and moral dimensions.

SUGGESTED FURTHER READING

PERIODICALS

Keeping up with the rapidly changing events in International Political Economy can be challenging, especially if you care about getting different perspectives on the same events. Most sources are available in print or on the web. Here are my suggestions.

Daily

The Financial Times—moderate business bias

Weekly

The Economist—moderate free market bias

Monthly to quarterly

The CATO Journal—strong free market bias
Challenge: The Magazine of Economic Affairs—moderate institutionalist bias
Dollars and Sense: The Magazine of Economic Justice—moderate socialist bias
New Political Economy—academic journal; moderate heterodox (non-conventional) bias.

BOOKS

Selections for in-depth reading from authors and books referenced throughout this text (listed in order of discussion):

Robert Heilbroner, *The Worldly Philosophers*—the most readable synopsis of the lives and thoughts of the major political economists, from Adam Smith to John Maynard Keynes.

Milton Friedman, *Free to Choose*—the most straightforward argument on behalf of the free market approach, available in paperback and on video (TV series).

John Kenneth Galbraith, *Age of Uncertainty*—the most widely read institutionalist response to Friedman. Friedman's above TV series was a response to Galbraith's own TV series with this title, also available in book and video form.

John Kenneth Galbraith, *The Affluent Society*—the author's basic approach, most effectively presented (originally published in 1958 but reissued by Penguin Books in 1999 with a new introduction by Galbraith).

David Korten, *When Corporations Rule the World*—a more recent institutionalist work that continues Galbraith's concerns with the dangers of excessive free market economics, corporate power, and environmental degradation.

Karl Marx, *The Communist Manifesto*—if you want a flavor of his style and critique of capitalism, there is nothing like the original.

David Harvey, *A Brief History of Neoliberalism*—a recent and readable Marxist critique of free market capitalism.

Daniel Yergin and Joseph Stanislaw, *The Commanding Heights: The Battle for the World Economy*—an interesting rendition of the post–World War II struggle between market capitalism and "Keynesianism," also both a book and a TV series. The hero of market capitalism and of the authors' tale is Friedrich von Hayek.

Herman Daly and John Cobb, *For the Common Good*—probably the most powerful critique of neoclassical economics from an environmental perspective.

John Rapley, *Understanding Development*—a useful and well-written history of development policy since World War II, now in its third edition.

Chris Edwards, *The Fragmented World: Competing Perspectives on Trade, Money and Crisis*—if you have a scholarly interest in reading the intellectual inspiration for the structure of this text, this would be the book, currently out of print, but available through libraries and used book dealers.

INDEX

Page references followed by *f* and *t* refer to figures and tables respectively.